THE MORALIST INTERNATIONAL

ORTHODOX CHRISTIANITY AND CONTEMPORARY THOUGHT

SERIES EDITORS
Aristotle Papanikolaou and Ashley M. Purpura

This series consists of books that seek to bring Orthodox Christianity into an engagement with contemporary forms of thought. Its goal is to promote (1) historical studies in Orthodox Christianity that are interdisciplinary, employ a variety of methods, and speak to contemporary issues; and (2) constructive theological arguments in conversation with patristic sources that focus on contemporary questions ranging from the traditional theological and philosophical themes of God and human identity to cultural, political, economic, and ethical concerns. The books in the series explore both the relevancy of Orthodox Christianity to contemporary challenges and the impact of contemporary modes of thought on Orthodox self-understandings.

THE MORALIST INTERNATIONAL

Russia in the Global Culture Wars

KRISTINA STOECKL AND DMITRY UZLANER

FORDHAM UNIVERSITY PRESS
New York • 2022

This publication has received funding from the European Research Council (ERC) under the European Union's Horizon 2020 research and innovation programme (POSEC, grant agreement no. ERC-STG-2015-676804).

European Research Council
Established by the European Commission

Fordham University Press has no responsibility for the persistence or accuracy of URLs for external or third-party Internet websites referred to in this publication and does not guarantee that any content on such websites is, or will remain, accurate or appropriate.

Fordham University Press also publishes its books in a variety of electronic formats. Some content that appears in print may not be available in electronic books.

Visit us online at www.fordhampress.com.

Library of Congress Cataloging-in-Publication Data

Names: Stoeckl, Kristina, author. | Uzlaner, Dmitry, author.
Title: The moralist international : Russia in the global culture wars /
    Kristina Stoeckl and Dmitry Uzlaner.
Description: First edition. | New York : Fordham University Press, 2022. |
    Series: Orthodox christianity and contemporary thought | Includes
    bibliographical references and index.
Identifiers: LCCN 2022013133 | ISBN 9781531502157 (paperback) | ISBN
    9781531502133 (hardback) | ISBN 9781531502140 (epub)
Subjects: LCSH: Human rights—Russia. | Conservatism—Russia.
Classification: LCC JC599.R8 S76 2022 | DDC 323.0947—dc23/eng/20220810
LC record available at https://lccn.loc.gov/2022013133

Printed in the United States of America

24 23 22   5 4 3 2 1

First edition

CONTENTS

PREFACE

On March 6, 2022, Forgiveness-Sunday in the Orthodox tradition, the Patriarch of Moscow preached that the world is divided between two forces, one good and divine, the other evil and sinful. Powerful forces were threatening Russia and its religious believers to stray from the path of righteousness by imposing on them a regime of liberties, the final and most terrible of which was the holding of gay parades. Gay parades, the patriarch explained under the gilded vaults of Moscow's Christ Savior Cathedral, were the ultimate test of loyalty imposed by the reign of evil on the Orthodox flock, which for the sake of its very salvation was called to fight back (Patriarchia 2022). March 6, 2022, was the eleventh day of Russia's brutal aggression launched against Ukraine. The patriarch's sermon used the language of the global culture wars for a justification of the war.

The culture wars denote a division between progressive and conservative values and between the individuals, groups, and countries that identify with one or the other. Unlike the "clash of civilizations" and interreligious strife imagined by Samuel Huntington (1993), the culture wars led to ideological alliances between religions and to sharper divisions inside them. In Huntington's civilizational scheme, a war between two Orthodox nations was improbable; in the world of the global culture wars, the Russian Orthodox patriarch justifies the war against Orthodox believers in Ukraine with a sermon about gay parades.

This book is about how the Russian Orthodox Church got to this point. It shows how Russian actors first learned and adopted the language and codes of the global culture wars and then started to use them. We researched and wrote this book before the events of 2022, but what we found out speaks to the processes that precede and underlie current events. The transnational perspective on Russian conservatism offered in this book takes the analysis of Russia's illiberal and autocratic turn beyond the narrow focus on nationalism and highlights the ideological and personal connections between Russia and the political and Christian Right in the United States and Europe. The Russian culture-war story from the 1990s until today is about global ideological dynamics and the refashioning of Russian Orthodox social teaching in the language of transnational moral conservatism. It covers Russian clerics, activists, politicians, and oligarchs pitching Russia as a stronghold of traditional values to the world and Western actors falling for a traditionalist Russia of their own making. With this book, we want to lay open the mechanisms of polarization and dissect the role of Russia and the Russian Orthodox Church on the frontlines of the global culture wars.

The Moralist International

Introduction

November 23, 2019, was a cold day in Moscow's Sokolniki Park, but the freezing temperatures notwithstanding, roughly 200 people assembled to listen to Vsevolod Chaplin,[1] archpriest of the Russian Orthodox Church, speak against the proposed federal bill for the prevention of domestic violence.[2] "Do our people need this law?" he cried out to the crowd. "No!" they shouted back. "Don't touch the family," Vladimir Khomyakov, leader of the right-wing "People's Council," exhorted the audience. Those who asked for stricter legislation on domestic violence were "just the vanguard of a foreign threat that's trying to destroy the country from within" (Meduza 2019b). The protesters in Sokolniki Park were not alone in this opinion. A few days later, the Moscow Patriarchate's Commission for Family, Defense of Motherhood and Childhood published a statement sharply condemning the proposed bill, calling it "unacceptable" and pointing out that it was "actively supported by organizations associated with radical anti-family ideologies ('LGBT' ideology, feminism), as well as a significant number of organizations officially

1. Father Vsevolod Chaplin (1968–2020) was an influential priest of the Russian Orthodox Church. From 2009 to 2015, he was chairman of the Synodal Department for the Cooperation of Church and Society of the Moscow Patriarchate. He was known for his ultra-conservative positions and very provocative comments to the media.

2. "This law" is the reform bill on the Federal Act "On the Prevention of Domestic Violence in the Russian Federation." Domestic violence in Russia is currently only an administrative offense, and the contested reform bill was aimed at changing this.

receiving foreign funding" (Patriarchal Commission for Family Affairs 2019b).

The opponents of the reform bill decry its supporters as representatives of international foreign powers and bearers of radical alien ideologies, positioning themselves as staunch patriots, defenders of Russia's traditional family and its spiritual and moral values. However, they themselves draw on ideas that originate in the international context. The Patriarchal Commission's statement includes a reference to an expert report entitled, "Legal Analysis of the Draft Federal Law 'On the Prevention of Domestic Violence in the Russian Federation'" (FamilyPolicy.ru 2019), which has been prepared by the Russian Center for Family Policy in close collaboration with the World Congress of Families—plainly an internationally run and funded body. The authority of the source is explained on the very first page of the report: "[The World Congress of Families is] the most representative international association of supporters of family values, including hundreds of organizations from 80 countries" (FamilyPolicy.ru 2019). The patriotic protest rally in Sokolniki Park took place one month after the publication of an article entitled, "Stop the Law on Domestic Violence!" in the Russian section of the website of CitizenGO, an international Christian conservative organization based in Madrid (CitizenGo 2019). The paradox, if not the irony, is transparent: the Russian Orthodox faction opposed to the law on domestic violence accused its opponents of being backed by transnational foreign organizations, while it relied in the same way on its own set of transnational organizations.

This spotlight on the national and transnational dimension of controversy over domestic violence legislation in Russia brings us to the heart of the two topics that we explore in this book:

First, *The Moralist International* is a book about the transnational dimension of conflicts over public morality. By conflicts over public morality, we mean controversies over the legal regulation of areas such as sexuality and gender, family, bioethics, education, and religious freedom. Today, domestic conflicts between socially progressive and socially conservative actors on issues of public morality, described as "culture wars" in the United States by James Davison Hunter (1991), increasingly reflect transnational dynamics and influences, as the previous example shows. We are not the first to notice that the culture wars have moved beyond America's borders to become a global phenomenon (cf. Bob 2002, 2019; Buss and Herman 2003; Butler 2006; Kaoma 2014; McCrudden 2015). But this book is the first to offer a comprehensive account of the relevancy of Russia and Russian Orthodoxy to the contemporary global culture wars.

Second, *The Moralist International* explores the impact of the global culture wars on Russian Orthodoxy. The struggle between social conservatism and social progressivism has often been depicted as a conflict between religious traditionalism and secular liberal modernity. This position is adopted by many, including Hunter himself, who in his famous book described the culture wars as conflict between two moral visions—one rooted in some sort of transcendent order and the other rooted in autonomous individual choices. A similar approach is that of Jürgen Habermas, who frames this conflict as the difference between faith and reason (Habermas and Ratzinger 2006). Likewise, Ronald Inglehart considers traditional religions as naturally connected to "pro-fertility" norms and analyzes secularization and cultural conflicts of our time as rooted in the rejection of these norms—together with religions themselves—by new generations for the sake of "individual-choice" norms (Inglehart 2021). Rather than seeing the culture wars as the result of a confrontation between tradition and modernity or between religion and secularism, we take the perspective that it is the culture wars themselves that bring forth a specific kind of religious traditionalism (and arguably also its counterpart, moral progressivism). The Russian Orthodox Church's "No!" to a law on domestic violence cannot be comprehended without taking into account the transnational culture wars waged over the definition of the family, the role of the state, and the meaning of human rights. Modes of framing and politicizing moral conflicts that originate in the culture wars in the West have an impact on the self-understanding of Russian Orthodoxy and reshape not only contemporary Russian Orthodox traditionalism, but also Russian domestic and foreign politics.

The book, in short, analyzes how the Russian Orthodox Church in the last thirty years first acquired knowledge about the dynamics, issues, and strategies of the global culture wars; how the Moscow Patriarchate has shaped its traditionalist agenda accordingly; and how, since it has learned the rules of the game, it has become a norm entrepreneur for international moral conservatism in its own right.[3] As we examine this process and

---

3. "Norm entrepreneurship" is a term developed in international relations to refer to actors who frame claims in a human rights language in order to "exit" the domestic political arena and pursue their goals on the international level. See more on this later.

identify its key factors, causes, and results, we make three theoretical and empirical claims:

First, with regard to debates about religion and modernity, we develop the concept of *conservative aggiornamento* to describe Russian traditionalism as the result of conservative religious modernization and the globalization of Christian social conservatism.[4]

Second, with regard to debates on international norm-entrepreneurship, we continue a line of research on the globalization of the culture wars that challenges the widespread perception that it is only progressive actors who use the international human rights regime in order to achieve their goals. We show that transnational conservative actors do the same.

Third, with regard to debates about the religion and politics in Russia, we offer a new, transnational perspective that firmly embeds the conservative turn of post-Soviet Russia under President Putin in the transnational dynamics of the global culture wars.

Culture Wars as Conflicts over the Identity of Society

Our analysis of contemporary morality conflicts starts from the assumption that the culture wars do not originate from a conflict between religion and secularism, but from unresolved (and ultimately unresolvable) tensions in the modern condition itself. Drawing on Peter Wagner (1994, 2012), we define the modern condition as one in which individuals autonomously and collectively determine the rules by which their societies organize: autonomously, because no single, overarching worldview provides the overall frame of reference for all; and collectively, because the rules by which people live together need to be shared. Seen in this way, the modern condition is never stable, but oscillates dynamically between individual and collective self-determination, between the liberty of setting rules autonomously and the discipline of being part of a community. The duality and tension between these two positions is constitutive of the modern condition itself.

The culture wars over public morality, as first described by Hunter in 1991, are one articulation of modernity's constitutive tension between individual

---

4. *Aggiornamento* is an Italian word that means "bringing up to date." After the Second Vatican Council of the Catholic Church, it is often used in the religious context to describe the process of modernization of religious traditions. See more on this later.

self-determination and autonomy, on the one side, and collective self-determination and discipline, on the other. The culture wars originate from what Wagner (2012) describes as "the crisis of organized modernity" in Western societies in the 1960s. During this time, the civil rights movement and the peace movement, workers' and students' protests, and the radical youth counterculture articulated an overall and radical objection to the conservative social, economic, and political mainstream of the time. Progressive NGOs and civil rights groups that emerged in this period advocated more individualism, autonomy, equality, and liberty; in contrast, conservative party platforms and Christian Right groups held on to community, rules, hierarchy, and tradition (Hartman 2015). Fifty years have passed since the initial confrontation between social progressivism and social conservatism, but if anything, the resulting conflict has become even more acute and accentuated, with the global expansion of progressivist causes like SOGI-rights (sexual orientation and gender identity-rights) and climate action on the one side and the new urgency ascribed to the preservation of traditional social structures on the other. Social progressivism and social conservatism are two *modern* reactions to the crisis of organized modernity; both have universalist aspirations, and both have become—by the twenty-first century—global ideologies.

The central conflicts in these global culture wars are over questions pertaining to sexuality and gender (homosexuality, gender-rights, feminism), family (definition of family, family law, domestic violence), bioethics (abortion, surrogacy, euthanasia), education (religious subjects at school, sexual education, theory of evolution, homeschooling), and religious freedom (religious symbols in the public space, conscientious objection). But these were not always at the top of the agenda. Older conflicts over morality policies concerned issues like tobacco-control, gambling, foxhunting, bullfighting, and alcohol prohibition. So if moral controversies appear not to originate in the nature of the particular "thing" itself—that is, that the thing need not be something "fundamental" to human identity like sex or childrearing—then what makes an issue morally controversial? We follow the definition by Julia Mourão Permoser, who writes:

> Morality issues are those that speak to deep-seated unresolved conflicts over the role of religion, tradition, morality, and values in the identity of the polity. [They] hinge upon issues of symbolic importance in the public image of the nation, in its self-definition as a community

of values, united not only by chance and territory but by the fact that its citizens share certain core principles. It is this perception that an issue goes to the essence of "who we are" that has given many morality issues a prominent position in today's value conflicts. (Mourão Permoser 2019, 311)

Morality conflicts, in other words, are conflicts over the identity of society. Under conditions of modernity, the question of "who we are" can only be answered through a process of individual and collective autonomous self-determination—a process that necessarily entails tension between individual liberty and the need for some substantive grounding of the collectivity. What precisely becomes the crystallization point of a conflict in a given time and place (whether it be same-sex marriage, abortion, or school education) is ultimately contingent on circumstances, but the question underneath the controversy is that of the identity of society as a whole. By stating this, we are not suggesting that the questions raised in morality conflicts are not also deeply personal, but we want to stress that whatever the items on the agenda, they stand for a deeper-seated conflict over individual and collective self-determination, of which these controversies are an expression.

In the context of societies with historical Christian roots, for example, value conflicts are essentially a dispute over whether these societies are still Christian or have definitively moved to post-Christian foundations (Anderson 2015). In this situation, every position on family values is a position in a symbolic dispute. The legal definition of the family as a "union of man and woman" is a symbol of the fact that society is still Christian, that this society has a Christian identity, and that Christians are still a group with special privileged status. Broadening the understanding of the family to include same-sex unions or single-parent households, in contrast, symbolizes the rejection of a public Christian identity. In our analysis of the Russian context, we strive to unpack arguments about national, religious-historical, and spiritual identity. These arguments always make a claim to a specific definition of "who Russians are" and what Russia stands for. It is not as such remarkable that different groups in Russia make such claims, but what is remarkable and worthy of inquiry is how and why these claims are made in the language and with the topics, strategies, and institutional arrangements of the global culture wars.

Conservative *Aggiornamento*, Norm-Entrepreneurship, and Russia's "Traditionalist Turn"

Though religions are not at the root of the culture-war dynamic, they have nevertheless become increasingly involved in this conflict. However, it is not predetermined which side they will find themselves on. Back in the 1960s, Christian groups stood on both sides of the divide, with some Christians supporting the cause of social justice and equality while others opposed it. The same is true today. Religious traditions are substantially shaped by the culture-wars confrontation: they frame their foes and allies, their credo, their agenda, and their strategies along the lines of the confrontation between social progressivism and social conservatism. They also internally divide along these conflict-lines: some representatives of one and the same confessional tradition may end up on the side of social conservatism, others on the side of social progressivism. Both options involve intense theological debates. The culture wars lead to cleavages inside religious traditions, but they also lead to unexpected alliances between different denominations and new realignments of the religious-secular landscape.[5]

The Moralist International analyzes how Russian Orthodoxy positions itself in the culture wars context following a delay of almost fifty years. For the Russian Orthodox Church after communism, this was a completely new challenge. Communism had kept the church on a tight leash for most of the twentieth century, impeding the development of any form of coherent social teaching. Traditional Russian Orthodox anti-modernism and anti-Westernism did not map well onto the religious landscape of the culture wars; it had no place for questions like same-sex marriage, homeschooling, or other modern life challenges. Not even abortion was high on the agenda of the Moscow Patriarchate during communism or immediately after. And as for Christian groups from the West eager to preach traditional values to Russians, the Moscow Patriarchate viewed these with suspicion. Yet thirty years after the end of communism, the picture has completely changed. As the scene from the beginning of this introduction shows, Russian Orthodox actors today denounce the existence of a foreign "LGBT-ideology," organize protest rallies for the traditional family, and

---

5. The same, by the way, is true for the secularist camp, as the shift from left to right of the neoconservative movement and the rise of the New Left demonstrates (Vaïsse 2011; Hartman 2015).

link up with transnational networks like CitizenGo and the World Congress of Families. How can we explain why Russia, a relative newcomer to the global culture wars, has risen in the last three decades to become "the last protector of traditional Christian values" and a "new powerful ally for the American Christian Right" (Michel 2017)? Who are the actors and what are the theological, ideological, and institutional processes that have placed Russian Orthodoxy solidly on the side of social conservatism in the global culture wars?

In the Roman Catholic tradition, there is a word for the transformative interaction between religion and secular modernity: *aggiornamento*. It was used by Pope John XXIII in 1959 during his announcement of the Second Vatican Council and signified the future Council's desire to make Catholicism catch up with the spirit of the age. This historical context has determined the meaning of *aggiornamento* until today: the religious-secular interaction encapsulated in the term is interpreted as one of modernizing and opening up to the secular, liberal, and democratic order. The analysis in this book shows that there is also a second option: *aggiornamento* in the direction of conservatism. This second option is often dismissed in the literature as fundamentalism, but the concept of fundamentalism functions like blinders: it dismisses religious conservative positions as reactive, anti-modernist, and obscurantist resistance to the progressive march of liberal modernity. In the case of Russian Orthodoxy, such a perspective blinds the observer to the novelty of Russian social conservatism.

Following José Casanova's program of a global sociology of religion (2019), we shift the analysis of contemporary Russian Orthodoxy from the frame of the national political and cultural context to the frame of the transnational context. *The Moralist International* offers a meticulous genealogy of Russia's pathway into the global culture wars, mapping the entry points of Russian Orthodox actors into transnational conservative networks and tracing their transition from conservative apprentices to rising leaders. We argue that the social conservative *aggiornamento* has substantially changed the Russian Orthodox Church: today, the Moscow Patriarchate finds its allies among the Western Christian Right, includes abortion, same-sex marriage, and homeschooling in its agenda, and restructures its policy initiatives along the line of the culture wars' dynamics. As a result, many liberal voices inside the church have been silenced, many alternatives have been forgotten, and the church has allied with the state.

Religions in the context of the global culture wars are mobile, networked, and hyper-conversant among denominations. Hunter pointed out in his book on the culture wars in America that value conflicts over public morality and the dynamic of the culture wars have a divisive effect on religious traditions. They divide them into conservative wings, which reject progress in modern society, and liberal wings, which adapt to changes in modern society and (to an extent) embrace them. Hunter observes that, as a consequence, these liberal and conservative camps drift apart from one another and instead find common ground with ideologically aligned groups from other confessional traditions. We see this phenomenon clearly in the Orthodox-Protestant-Evangelical-Catholic alliances documented in *The Moralist International*.

The Russian case also illustrates the changing role of the language of human rights in politicizing value conflicts, both domestically and internationally. The tacit assumption in the literature has been that this strategy—norm entrepreneurship—has been employed mostly by progressive actors. The classic work *Activists beyond Borders* (Keck and Sikkink 1998; but see also Risse and Sikkink 1999; Nash 2009) gives examples of progressive human rights groups that move beyond the nation state to achieve their goals through the mechanisms of the international human rights regime. The diffusion of sexual orientation and gender identity rights in particular has been explained as the result of such strategies (cf. Ayoub 2013; Waaldijk 2000).

However, not only progressive actors use the international human rights regime to achieve the implementation of what they consider human rights. Conservative actors do the same: they successfully promote their conservative reading of human rights in the international arena and in the domestic practices of nation states. The American, Russian, and European organizations and actors that we discuss are evidence for a burgeoning conservative norm entrepreneurship that is turning the culture wars into a global phenomenon. Previously discussed by American scholars (Bob 2012; Butler 2006; Buss and Herman 2003), this book adds the case of Russia and the Russian Orthodox Church as transnational moral conservative norm-entrepreneur.

Since the 1990s, the position of the Russian Orthodox Church vis-à-vis the Russian state has changed from a position of relative independence and mutual suspicion to close cooperation and interdependence (Knox 2003). Russian Orthodox actors play an ever-more-central role in agenda-setting and political decisionmaking. Since around 2012, when President Vladimir Putin entered office for a third time, moral conservatism in support of "traditional values" has become the dominant social, cultural, and political model. Since 2012, laws have been passed in Russia that conjure up a culture-war dynamic while allowing the state to manage and curtail political protest: new laws targeting "immoralism" have been implemented (against blasphemy, against public display and information on "nontraditional" sexual relations). At the same time, panic about "foreign funded agents" promoting liberal values has given currency to the vision of Russia as a religiopolitical entity with a global mission to defend these traditional values against the liberal West. The development culminated in the constitutional reform of 2020, which enshrines faith in God, the defense of traditional family values, and marriage as a union between man and woman as core Russian political principles.

The Russian conservative turn is usually studied "in a box," as a phenomenon that can be explained exclusively through Russia's particularistic history and cultural trajectory (see Sharafutdinova 2014; Stepanova 2015; Agadjanian 2017; Østbø 2017; Robinson 2017). Our global perspective, on the contrary, sees the conservative turn under President Putin as firmly embedded in the transnational dynamics of the global culture wars. One of the main ideas that runs through this book is that today's Russian moral conservatism is not a uniquely Russian ideology, the expression of a particular national identity, of a notorious Russian *Sonderweg*, or the result of the country's imperial history or of Orthodox religion. Instead, we will consistently show how Russian moral conservatism is a hybrid of national factors and reflections of the global culture wars. Our analytical and methodological focus lies on actors and organizations—in particular, on Western Christian NGOs that became active in Russia after the fall of the USSR and on Russian Orthodox NGOs that were created under their influence. We argue that Christian Right activism in Russia and interconfessional relations between the Moscow Patriarchate and Western churches throughout the 1990s have laid a discursive and institutional groundwork on which the Russian Orthodox Church and Orthodox lay activists have selectively built their moral conservative agenda both domestically and internationally.

Since around 2010, Russia has positioned itself as the defender of traditional religious values against secularism, liberalism, and individual human rights as espoused by international institutions like the United Nations or the Council of Europe. Russian foreign policy, having internalized the rules of the game, uses the opportunity structures of the liberal international order to promote its social conservative agenda. The inclusion of Russia and Russian Orthodoxy into international ideological controversies hitherto dominated by the Islamic states, the Vatican, and American Christian Right NGOs reconfigures the coordinates of international human rights politics.

The Structure of This Book

The Moralist International offers a comprehensive account of the impact of the global culture wars on Russian Orthodoxy, and it explores the relevance of Russia and the Russian Orthodox Church to the contemporary challenge of conflicts between social progressivism and conservatism. The book is divided into two parts. Part I is dedicated to Russian Orthodoxy "learning the culture wars" by exploring the impact of the global culture wars, with their topics, strategies, and networks, on Russian Orthodoxy. Part II analyzes how Russia and the Russian Orthodox Church are "doing the culture wars" by looking at the connections, activities, and policies of church and state as international moral norm entrepreneurs.

In Part I, Chapter 1 develops in detail the argument—presented in a nutshell in this introduction—of *conservative aggiornamento*. It argues that not only reformist, but also traditionalist religious positions are the result of change, modernization, and a learning process that works across confessional borders.

Chapter 2 presents original research on the origins of contemporary Russian conservatism and the influence of American Christian Right groups on Russian actors between the late 1980s and 1997. Contemporary Russian conservatism is the product of multiple ideological sources: Russian Orthodoxy, conservative societal attitudes of the late Soviet period, and foreign influence, especially from the American Christian Right. The process of "learning the culture wars" takes place against the backdrop of Russia's own crisis of organized modernity—namely, the collapse of the socialist social order and the uncertain transition to a new social and political regime.

One source of Russian conservatism that merits detailed attention is the legacy of Pitirim Sorokin, explored in Chapter 3. Sorokin is a key intellectual for moral conservatism in the United States and Russia. Four aspects are especially relevant here: his emphasis on values, his notion of the "sensate culture," his ideas about the family, and his vision for moral revival. Through a firsthand analysis of moral conservative discourse and documents, as well as qualitative interviews, we show how Sorokin can be seen as a nodal point that binds together individual actors and ideas across national, cultural, and linguistic barriers.

Chapter 4 discusses the rise of traditional-values conservatism in Russia and elaborates the domestic context of Russia's rise to prominence inside the transnational moral conservative movement. We show how the Russian state was gradually converted to a culture-war type of social conservatism, with the Russian Orthodox Church serving as the key actor in this process. The chapter adds context and complexity to our analysis by showing that traditional-values conservatism is contested inside Russia and stands in contrast to low levels of religious practice.

Part II explores how Russian Orthodoxy and the Russian state act as moral-conservative norm entrepreneurs domestically and in international politics. Chapter 5 provides an analytical timeline of the Russian Orthodox Church's engagement in the culture wars. We argue that the church led the way in formulating a clear transnational moral conservative agenda. It was also the church that constructed the narrative according to which Russia, as a country that has experienced communist "militant atheism," is predestined to play a leading role in the fight against cultural liberalism globally. However, in two case studies—the relations of the Moscow Patriarchate with the Vatican and its cooperation with the Billy Graham Evangelistic Association—we show that, ultimately, the Patriarchate has not been very successful in positioning itself as an independent moral conservative player. It is weighed down by internal tensions—in particular, by fundamentalist Orthodox groups that do not support the transnational conservative engagement of the church leadership. As a result, the Russian role as a champion of conservative values passes from the church leadership to the Kremlin and to religious grassroots movements.

Chapter 6 shifts its focus of analysis from the leadership of the Russian Orthodox Church to religious civil society. This chapter offers an in-depth study of the Russian partners inside the World Congress of Families, a transnational pro-family NGO, and their strategies of joining transnational moral conservative networks. Here we argue that on the level of civil society, conservative-norm entrepreneurs started to take over the church's traditional values discourse and promote it to Christian Right groups abroad. "Russia as defender of traditional values" has become a trademark for these actors, who promote their own ideological and business interests through their partnerships with conservative networks abroad.

In Chapter 7, we look in detail at the one issue that has defined the American and global culture wars more than anything else: abortion. The history of the Russian pro-life movements is a showpiece for how Orthodox actors have first learned about and then joined the culture wars, working out their own strategies vis-à-vis Russian politics, society, and the global pro-life networks.

Chapter 8, finally, analyzes the agenda of Russian state diplomacy at the level of the United Nations and the Council of Europe. We show that items on the conservative agenda—traditional values, family, freedom of religion, and juvenile justice—are promoted on the level of Russian state diplomacy. The chapter shows how Russia is "taking over" the conservative agenda from previous important players like the Vatican or the Organization of Islamic States. The Russian-led moral-conservative strategy inside these institutions puts moderate religious actors in a dilemma because they end up simultaneously supporting a cause they consider important, such as traditional family values, as well as a political regime they actually find problematic—that is, autocratic Russia.

In the Epilogue we look at the tensions that may potentially arise inside transnational moral-conservative networks as a result of Russia's active role. A culture war between conservatism and progressivism is one possible response to the deep pluralism of our societies. As we come back to Russia's war against Ukraine and reflect on the impact that the weaponizing of the global culture wars may have on the Moralist International, we conclude that the search for alternatives to polarization has never been more urgent.

PART I

LEARNING THE CULTURE WARS

In the novel *Secondhand Time* (2016), Nobel Prize winner Svetlana Alexievich tells the story of a young man who finds out that the father of his future spouse worked for the Soviet secret police during the time of the Stalinist terror and has executed declared "enemies of the people." He talks about his deeds without signs of remorse, and the young man, appalled, flees the house and never returns to his prospective bride. In *The Whisperers* (Figes 2008), the historian Orlando Figes digs into the oral history archives of the Memorial Foundation for a grim portrait of the silence that befell Soviet society for decades after Stalinism. The book ends with the story of an elderly woman, Antonina, who, encouraged by the greater freedom during *perestroika*,[1] decides to reveal to her daughter that she has hidden her real identity from the entire family throughout her entire life, never daring to tell anybody that her parents had perished in the Gulag. She learns that her ex-husband also comes from a family of "enemies of the people" and that he, just like her, changed his name to be admitted to the university. Her broken marriage, she realizes, had been one of silence.

The list of collective grievances that afflicted Russian society at the end of communist rule was long; the sense of a pervasive social and moral crisis

---

1. *Perestroika* is a Russian word that means "restructuring." This concept refers to a series of political and economic reforms of the Soviet Union. It was started in 1985 by Soviet leader Mikhail Gorbachev. Rethinking Soviet past with its crimes was an important aspect of these reforms.

was acute. How do people, how does a society, how does a church find the language to address these grievances? What do they say *first*? What structures their narrative? What bits and pieces of information do they search for to fill in the blanks in their story?

Three decades after the end of the Soviet Union, the Russian state and the Russian Orthodox Church have settled on the language and the story: What Russia really needs is a return to traditional values and to faith in God and the Fatherland. Some things under communism may have been bad, but the Soviet period instilled a strong sense of collectivity that is now put at risk by liberalism, individualism, and secularism. And, the story goes on, as long as marriage is constitutionally defined as a union between man and woman, the Russian family is safe.

We call the first part of this book "Learning the Culture Wars" because in the chapters that follow we analyze how a certain way of addressing the social and moral crisis of post-Soviet society, a specific way of prioritizing some arguments over others, and a certain narrative about who is to blame and what is to be done became dominant in the official discourse of the Russian Orthodox Church, the Russian government, and the state administration. The narrative is that of the culture wars; it views society as the battleground for two social forces, one progressive and one conservative, that are in a bitter contest over the future and destiny of the people. It sees the conservative camp as rooted in Christian religion, a traditional way of life, and a strong sense of patriarchy and hierarchy and the progressive camp as secular, liberal, egalitarian, democratic, and cosmopolitan. This culture-war narrative originates in the West, more precisely in the mid-twentieth century in the United States, where it unfolded around topics such as traditional values, family, gender, abortion, and education.

In post-Soviet Russia, the influence of Western actors was instrumental in the process of "learning" this culture-war narrative. Soviet communism had been bad, but liberalism—such was the message of the Western right to their Russian interlocutors—was no alternative. We show in the next chapters how traditional values, family, gender, abortion, and education became, for powerful actors inside the Russian state and Orthodox Church, central to addressing the grievances and moral crisis of post-Soviet society.

1

RELIGION

CONSERVATIVE *AGGIORNAMENTO* AND
THE GLOBALIZATION OF THE CULTURE WARS

Much of the literature about the culture wars has theorized the role of religion in morality conflicts somewhat superficially, seeing religion (or its absence, secularism) as the main factor that explains the interests and motivation of actors. The topics over which culture wars are fought—abortion, same-sex marriage, religious symbols, education—have been seen as rooted in a conflict between religion and secularism, between faith and reason. But those approaches that recognize that religions may also stand on both sides of the culture-wars divide usually distinguish between reformist and traditionalist currents, implicitly assuming that the reformist currents stand for change, adaptation, and moderniza-tion, whereas the traditionalist currents stand for immutability, incom-patibility, and fundamentalism. An alternative empirical and theoretical perspective reveals that the role of religion in the culture wars is more com-plex, however. It is not the case that only reformist religious approaches change, adapt, and modernize; traditionalist positions too are the result of change, adaptation, and—in Jürgen Habermas's words—a learning process.

Especially in parts of the world where the culture wars are a new phenom-enon, the topics over which they are fought first must be *turned into* religious topics. As religious ideas, actors, and institutions are made to fit the culture-war confrontation, the culture wars in turn shape the public role of religion. This paradoxical role of religion as the source of culture wars and at the same time the product of the culture wars is particularly evident in the Russian case.

The term we use for our examination of this phenomenon is *aggiornamento*. Coined in the context of the Second Vatican Council of the Roman Catholic

Church, *aggiornamento* means the transformative interaction between religion and secular modernity. The historical context of the reforms undertaken inside Catholicism in the second half of the twentieth century (liturgy in vernacular, recognition of religious freedom, ecumenism) has determined the meaning of *aggiornamento* until today: the religious-secular interaction encapsulated in the term is interpreted as one of modernization and reform and as the opening-up of a traditional religion to a secular, liberal, and democratic order.

Jürgen Habermas models his three-step "modernization of religious consciousness" on this Catholic experience and comparable developments in Protestantism (see Stoeckl 2017). He identifies three modern challenges that religious traditions have to overcome to achieve greater compatibility with secular, modern society:

> (1) Religious citizens must develop an epistemic attitude toward other religions and world views that they encounter within a universe of discourse hitherto occupied only by their own religion. . . . (2) Moreover, religious citizens must develop an epistemic stance toward the independence of secular from sacred knowledge and the institutionalized monopoly of modern scientific experts. . . . (3) Finally, religious citizens must develop an epistemic stance toward the priority that secular reasons enjoy in the political arena. (Habermas 2006, 14).

Habermas quotes the German Roman Catholic theologian Thomas M. Schmidt and the German Protestant theologian Friedrich Schleiermacher in support of his claim that the work of "religious self-enlightenment" is in the hands of "the non-agnostic philosopher of religion" (Habermas 2005, 144n46). A successful process of modernization of religious consciousness is for Habermas the prerequisite for the inclusion of religion in the secular, democratic public sphere. With Habermas, we concede that religions cannot escape the challenges of modernity, but against Habermas, we argue that it cannot be taken for granted that they confront them in a reformist way that renders them more compatible with a secular, liberal democratic order.

It is simply not the case that religious reformists embrace change whereas religious traditionalists remain the way they have always been. Instead, both currents inside a religious tradition undergo a process of change, adaptation, and learning, except that one aims at compatibility with the secular, liberal democratic order, while the other aims at distinction. *Aggiornamento*, in other words, does not take place in the direction of progressivism alone, but also of conservatism. A good example is given by Andrew Lewis in *The Rights Turn in Conservative Christian Politics* (2017), which analyzes how conservative Christian groups in the United States updated and changed their anti-abortion strategies to make them more compatible with a legal and public debate about human rights. A comparable process, we argue, has taken place inside the Russian Orthodox Church in the last thirty years.

Russian Orthodoxy and the Absence of Social Ethics

Until the very end of the twentieth century, Russian Orthodoxy had no tradition of systematic reflection on social issues. No developed branch of theological argument under the label of social ethics or social teaching existed inside Russian Orthodox theological academies. Theological discourse and pious teaching did not foreground social problems or the task of the church to give its answers to the challenges that modern society posed. Much to the contrary of the Catholic and Protestant churches, the Russian Orthodox Church did not have a coherent social doctrine; it even lacked a developed theological language in which social ethics could be discussed.

The reasons for this state of affairs are related to the peculiarities of both the Orthodox tradition in general and Russian Orthodoxy in particular. Vasilios Makrides highlights the following general features of Orthodox theology, which did not allow the Orthodox tradition of social ethics to develop. First, unlike the Catholic Church, for most of their history the Orthodox churches did not exist separately from the state. Under the regime of close church-state relations, "social issues were never considered as adhering to the immediate responsibilities of the church, but to those of the state" (Makrides 2013, 288). Second, the general otherworldly orientation of Orthodoxy, different from the more secular involvement of Catholicism and Protestantism, contributed "to a neglect of history and society, not to an active involvement in the world" (Makrides 2013, 293). Attempts by individual Orthodox clerics or theologians to respond to the challenges of the time and to be actively involved in world affairs often provoked a negative reaction from the church mainstream, which considered such tendencies as the result of "Western influence and a deviation from traditional Orthodox monasticism" (Makrides 2013, 296). Third, for many Orthodox, the nonformalization and lack of systematization inside the Orthodox theological tradition represented a virtue, a beneficial distinction from other Christian traditions. In addition, Western branches of Christianity were confronted with the "social question" much earlier than the Orthodox churches (Makrides 2013, 299–302).

All these general reasons pointed out by Makrides also apply to Russian Orthodoxy and the Russian Orthodox Church. In Tsarist Russia, an expansion of the church's influence beyond its spiritual competence was undesired, and internally strong monastic currents stood for a "principled lack of interest in the world" (Kostyuk 2013, 387). The situation in Russia was further aggravated by the fact that the Communist revolution of 1917 cut short the first attempts at developing a social doctrine. The three-volume work by archpriest Nicholas Stelletsky entitled *The Experience of Moral Orthodox Theology in Apologetic Lighting* illustrates this fateful interruption very clearly. Two volumes of his work, published between 1914 and 1916, were devoted to general ethical questions. The third volume, which was supposed to tackle questions of public morality, never reached the reader. In the contemporary re-edition of this work, the publisher's comment at the place where the manuscript interrupts—a paragraph on the Christian state—is revealing: "On this unfinished phrase the printing of the book by Archbishop Nikolai Stelletskyi ended due to the revolution that was gaining momentum" (Stelletskii 2011). For the decades that followed the church was largely silenced, and Stelletsky himself was arrested by Chekists in 1919 and killed.

The Russian Orthodox Church gained a little more freedom after 1943 during Stalin's efforts to secure religious support for the war effort. But the Moscow Patriarchate remained under tight control of the Soviet state and had no opportunity, at least not officially, to develop its own social doctrine. At most, it moved along the lines of the ideological agenda of the Soviet Union, dealing with nuclear disarmament, world peace, and the struggle of workers.

It was only after the collapse of the Soviet Union that the church finally gained freedom and independence from the state. After 1991, the road was opened to developing a theological doctrine on social ethics—but it was a road through uncharted territory. For the reasons pointed out earlier, the Russian Orthodox Church had no Orthodox role models to draw on. Consequently, it turned—at least in part—to Western Christian models instead, or it reiterated Soviet public morality in a religious key.

This paradoxical move is particularly evident in the church's teaching on family. Family is one of the key items on the agenda of moral conservatives, but with the exception of the pro-family theology formulated by the priest Gleb Kaleda (Kaleda 1998), Orthodox theology is above all an ascetic tradition in which marriage is a choice for those who cannot do more, who cannot become monks and devote themselves entirely to God ("The man who marries does well, but the one who doesn't marry does even better"; 1 Corinthians 7:38). Orthodox asceticism can be traced, for example, in the administrative structure of the church (only monks can occupy the highest administrative positions), in the lives of saints (family life is not the path of holiness), and in the general underdevelopment of this theme in Orthodox theological reflection. Brandon Gallaher expresses the view that "even if it is an over-statement to claim that Orthodoxy is anti-family, at best it is often suspicious and even patronizing towards family life" (Gallaher 2018, 61). For him, the contemporary Orthodox pro-family agenda is essentially a modern creation. Also, John McGuckin in the introductory essay to the collection *Love, Marriage and Family in Eastern Orthodox Perspective*, with all his desire to elevate the family and marriage from an Orthodox position, cannot help but notice that

> the church has had very few theologians who have really celebrated the glory of the married condition rhapsodically, and from the lived inner experience of it. Being predominantly approached from the perspective of celibates, and often denigrated as something defective, or at least much less elevated than the celibate ascetical life, it has not yet been sung about in a full range of necessary theological keys. (McGuckin 2016, xiii)

Orthodoxy, in short, is much less well-equipped to embrace theologically the unconditional support for family than, for example, Protestantism, where there is no monastic tradition and the family is one of the key divine mandates in which a Christian must realize himself (along with work, church, and state). But this difference in doctrine and tradition notwithstanding, contemporary Russian Orthodox conservativism revolves around the theme of family.

The reason for the centrality of family in contemporary Russian conservatism and Russian Orthodox social teaching is—we argue in this book—not only to be found inside the Orthodox tradition, but outside, in the global context in which the post-Soviet Russian Orthodox Church finds itself. This is the global context of the culture wars.

Global Culture Wars

Before moving on in our analysis, it is helpful to sketch the context in which the conservative *aggiornamento* of the Russian Orthodox Church has taken place—namely, that of the culture wars and their globalization. James Davison Hunter's classical study *Culture Wars: The Struggle to Define America* (1991) has given the name to an entire research field (see Hunter and Wolfe 2006). With this concept, Hunter sought to understand the confrontation in American society over topics such as family, abortion, education, art, and law. He identified two opposing positions in this confrontation: "the impulse toward orthodoxy" and "the impulse toward progressivism" (Hunter 1991, 43). By "orthodoxy," Hunter did not mean Christian Orthodoxy (in fact, Orthodox Christianity does not figure in his book at all), but a traditionalist position, based on the firm belief in the transcendent origins of human laws and institutions, which are therefore not subject to reform at the will of particular groups or individuals (Hunter 1991, 108–13). Elsewhere in the book he also describes this position as "fundamentalist." "Progressive," in contrast, implies a different moral vision of the principles on which human society in general and American society in particular should be based. The progressive position regards these rules and institutions as human-made and therefore subject to reform in the light of new cultural and social realities (Hunter 1991, 113–16). The culture wars are conflicts over the identity of society, with one side holding on to tradition and discipline and the other side emphasizing individuality and liberty.

Hunter drew attention to a number of processes that the confrontation between the orthodox and progressive vision set in motion inside religious communities. First, these conflicts led to a radical realignment of the religious and public space: instead of the usual categorization of the religious landscape by confessions (Protestants, Catholics, Jews, Mormons), new interconfessional and even interreligious alliances formed. Coalitions between conservative Protestants, Catholics, Jews, and Mormons, united by their common rejection of the progressive agenda and concern about its successful advancement, were formed (Hunter 1991, 96). Their foes were liberals, leftists, and religious reformists. Indeed, from the 1970s onward, social progressivism that had started out in the 1950s–60s as a radical youth counterculture promoted by a few marginal rebels was rapidly becoming the new mainstream. And the forces that opposed this counterculture very quickly turned from being the moral majority to being dissidents surrounded by an environment hostile to their views (Himmelfarb 2006, 81). The 1973 Supreme Court decision in the *Roe v. Wade* case, which liberalized the right to abortion throughout the United States, as well as discussions about the Equal Rights Amendment, became the symbols of profound cultural changes that radically reshaped the American public (see, in particular, Jenkins 2006).

Second, the realignment along orthodox and progressive lines led to divisions inside religious communities, dividing these formerly solid groups into conservative and progressive parts. Conservative Protestants felt less and less connected to their progressive coreligionists. Consequently, the proximity between conservative Protestants and conservative Catholics (as well as Orthodox Jews and Mormons) increased. Different religious communities were no longer divided or united based on their position on dogmatic issues, but rather on which side they took in the culture wars (Wuthnow 1990). As Hunter has noted, "The politically relevant divisions in the American context are no longer defined according to where one stands vis-a-vis Jesus, Luther, or Calvin, but where one stands vis-a-vis Rousseau, Voltaire, Diderot, and Condorcet, and especially their philosophical heirs (including Nietzsche and Rorty)" (Hunter 1991, 132). What Hunter described was a truly epochal transformation that is as relevant today as it was when he wrote his book: we are dealing with the revision of the traditional divisions between religious communities along denominational lines and their replacement by new fault lines, this time based on a political and ideological agenda and running right through the individual religious communities. Especially for Russian Orthodoxy, this transformation constitutes, as we show later, a great novelty.

Third, the dramatic term "cultural *warfare*" was deliberately chosen by Hunter, who insisted on the uncompromising nature of this confrontation. In these wars, the parties do not hesitate to represent their disagreement with their opponents as a struggle between good and evil in the literal sense of the word, as a battle in which the fate of not only America, but humanity as a whole, is at stake. Each side discredits its opponent by portraying it as extremist (Hunter 1991, 144), and each struggles to monopolize symbols of legitimacy, like the American Constitution (Hunter 1991, 147) or—as we show later—the Universal Declaration of Human Rights. Each side portrays the other as dangerous and totalitarian (Hunter 1991, 150). The trope of totalitarianism is, as we will see, frequently used in the Russian context, where Russian actors present themselves as the—victorious—survivors of leftist totalitarianism, who have a special legitimacy to lead the conservative side in the culture wars. American conservatives, in turn, have taken to describe themselves as dissidents against liberal totalitarianism, and they look to Orthodoxy for refuge. One example for this trend is the influential American writer Rod Dreher, who converted to Orthodox Christianity and sees his own society as on the brink of civil war and totalitarianism (Dreher 2020b).

The culture wars in America have given rise to a social and political movement that occupies a key role in the narrative of this book: the Christian Right. The American Christian Right can be defined as a "social movement that attempts to mobilize evangelical Protestants and other orthodox Christians into conservative political action" (Wilcox and Robinson 2011, 6). It emerged in the second half of the 1970s as a response to the cultural revolution of previous decades, as an attempt to counteract what conservatives perceived as harmful tendencies for society and with the intention to bring "spiritual and moral renewal" to American society (see the history of this movement: Williams 2010; Dowland 2015).

For our understanding of the American Christian Right as a social and political movement, Wilcox and Robinson's definition is good starting point:

> The Christian Right has no single agenda, but rather a collection of overlapping agendas. Some Christian Right activists focus almost entirely on ending abortions in America; others are concerned primarily with issues surrounding homeschooling. Some are motivated to fight what they call the "radical homosexual agenda," whereas others focus on banning same-sex marriage. Others seek to reduce the amount of sexually explicit material in television, movies, and popular music. Some seek to promote a role for religion in public life: prayer in public schools, nativity scenes on city property, and a public acknowledgment that the United States is a Christian (or sometimes Judeo-Christian) nation. (Wilcox and Robinson 2011, 10)

The Christian Right is a movement that consists of a multitude of organizations, some extremely large and influential, others quite small. Among the most prominent of these are the *Catholic Family and Human Rights Institute* (C- Fam), the *Family Research Council* (FRC), *Concerned Women for America* (CWA), *The Howard Center for Family, Religion, and Society*, *Focus on the Family*, and the *Traditional Values Coalition* (TVC). Most of these organizations have their roots in the 1970s and 1980s, and their emergence is directly related to the logic of the culture wars. It is pertinent to list these organizations, as we will meet them in one way or another later, when we consider these conflicts in the global and transnational contexts.

The Christian Right movement, in short, emerges, develops, and gains strength in the American culture wars as a defender of conservative positions—not only through intellectual debates, but also through participation in the real political struggle. The eventual appearance of the global and transnational dimension of the culture wars is a logical continuation of the activities of these organizations in their national context; it is, as one author put it, the "culmination of several trends in [American] religion and civil society over the past few decades" (Butler 2006, 13).

Hunter published his influential book in 1991. At that moment, the culture wars were already taking on a new dimension—they were spilling over the borders of the United States (McCrudden 2015), rapidly becoming transnational and global. Here we should emphasize once more why the American case deserves special attention. Morality conflicts exist not only in the United States (Engeli, Green-Pedersen, and Larsen 2012; Grzymała-Busse 2015); they are a feature of any contemporary pluralistic society. However, it is the American pattern of dealing with these conflicts that reproduces itself in a transnational context. Global value conflicts have a number of typological features that resemble the American ones: they restructure the religious field in terms of the progressive and conservative, they forge interdenominational conservative coalitions, and they polarize. Most importantly, it is American actors, together with the Vatican, who are the motor behind the process of bringing these conflicts to a new transnational level (Buss and Herman 2003; Irvine 2012).

In this book, we argue that one of the main causes of the globalization of the culture wars is the growing significance of the supranational dimension of politics and law in the contemporary world. International treaties, declarations and resolutions, and supranational bodies like the United Nations and the European Court of Human Rights limit the sovereignty of their member states by imposing upon them a universal regime of human rights and of international treaties that previous governments of a country have signed onto, but that later governments may interpret as an impediment to their political power. The fact that decisions taken at the supranational level can have a significant impact at the national level and can directly affect the balance of power in local morality conflicts prompts progressive as well as conservative actors to take their struggles beyond national borders (Finnemore and Sikkink 1998; Nash 2016).

This move beyond national borders can take several forms. In this chapter, we discuss two of these in detail, because they are relevant for our study of Russia in the global culture wars: first, the search by conservative actors for strong allies and the building of transnational alliances; and second, the export of the logic of the culture wars to new regions not yet affected—or not extensively affected—by conflicts over issues such as abortion, homosexuality, and education.

Building Transnational Alliances and Exporting the Culture Wars

The end of the Cold War and of the confrontation between communist and capitalist systems, contrary to Francis Fukuyama's predictions (Fukuyama 1989), did not lead to the "end of history." Instead, it gave rise to new ideological conflicts, of which cultural conflicts between progressives and conservatives are one. This is clearly seen in the case of the United Nations, where the topic of religion has begun to attract more and more attention since the 1990s. Until then, religion had not been an issue for the UN. The lack of religious topics was "due to the 'secular paradigm' that predominated in the post-war era, coloring both thinking and behavior. It was in part a response to the explicit atheism of the USSR and the People's Republic of China, and it muted and even blinded many to religious institutions and issues" (Marshall 2017, 21). However, after the end of the Cold War, two significant processes became visible: first, "a set of dialogues and efforts that have aimed to bring religious topics explicitly into the United Nations system"; and second, "the emergence of a number of contested issues that are perceived as religious in nature, centering on women's rights and particularly reproductive health" (Marshall 2017, 21). Since then, religious freedom, reproductive and sexual health, and family values have become an integral part of the UN agenda (Marshall 2017, 23–24).

At the same time, there was an increase in the number of religious NGOs accredited by the United Nations Economic and Social Council (ECOSOC). In examining the issue of religious NGOs in the United Nations, Karsten Lehman noted that today there are more and more that have a clear social conservative orientation (Lehmann 2016, 74). The conservatives' move into the transnational dimension has, according to Anne Stensvold, been a reaction to a number of SRHR initiatives in the UN context (SRHR is an acronym for *sexual, reproductive, and health rights* in UN documents) (Stensvold 2017a, 2017b). Scholars usually mention two international forums that became a trigger for conservative efforts to become active in the transnational dimension: the International Conference on Population and Development, held in Cairo in 1994, and the Fourth World Conference on Women in Beijing in 1995. The vectors identified at these forums alarmed Christian conservatives and instigated them to establish contacts with similarly minded actors from other religions to organize collective action to counter what they saw as dangerous trends (McIntosch and Finkle 1995, 234). This was a moment of unanimity for key conservative actors: the Vatican, several Islamic states (e.g., the Organization of Islamic Cooperation; see Skorini and Petersen 2017), and Christian Right NGOs.

The move of the Christian Right into the transnational dimension was thus driven by several circumstances (Herman 2001)—first, by the need to respond to the challenges and perceived threats posed by international human rights law to internal American affairs; second, by the feeling that conservatives were losing the American culture wars at home and that "internationalization" and the opening of a second battlefront could be a solution; and finally, by the natural continuation of the success that accompanied the Christian Right in domestic politics during the presidency of George W. Bush, who openly positioned himself as a "newly born" Christian (Marsden 2008, 17). The support of the White House acted as a boost to the leaders of the Christian Right movements, who now sought to expand their influence into the area of foreign policy. As Marsden notes,

> Organizations such as Focus on the Family (FOF), the Family Research Council (FRC), Concerned Women for America (CWA), the Institute on Religion and Democracy (IRD), and the Eagle Forum have turned their attention towards seeking to advance their socially conservative moral values in the United Nations and World Congress of Families. Organizations have been eager to apply for faith-based-initiative funding to deliver humanitarian assistance abroad while evangelizing. (Marsden 2008, 17)

The globalization of the cultural wars leads to the same realignment of the religious landscape that we have already seen in the national American context—but this time on a global scale. Interdenominational and even interreligious alliances are formed—for example, between Muslims and conservative Protestants, who unite against global initiatives to expand the rights of sexual minorities. Bob called this alliance "the Baptist-Burqa network" (Bob 2012) and later, recognizing the emerging role of Russia, extended the phrase to "Baptist-Burqa-Babushka" (Bob 2015). These alliances exist both in the form of situational collaboration—that is, collaboration for the sake of a specific case—and in an institutionalized form. The institutionalization of such alliances can be illustrated by the history of the World Congress of Families, which we analyze in detail in Chapter 6.

The globalization of the culture wars comes in tandem with a split along the lines of conservatism and progressivism, a divide that cuts across religious communities, national borders, and continents. Conservative Protestants in the United States consider themselves as being closer to conservative communities from Africa or Latin America than to progressive North American coreligionists. Philip Jenkins in his book *The Next Christendom* describes this new gaping global division of Christianity:

> As the church became increasingly divided over issues of gender and sexual orientation, North American conservatives found themselves much closer politically to the upstart churches of Africa and Asia than to their own church elites, as they looked to Singapore and Rwanda to defend themselves against New York and Ottawa. (Jenkins 2002, 204)

In large part, the conservative *aggiornamento* in the Russian context is modeled on the response of conservative Christian actors to the secular, liberal order *elsewhere*, rather than being an original and authentic Orthodox Christian response to grievances inside post-Soviet Russian society. This paradoxical outcome is the result of the export of culture wars (Gathii 2006). As Peter Berger writes in "Exporting the American Culture War," much of America's domestic politics revolves around the culture war. But America being not just "any country," but politically and economically hegemonic, its culture has proved enormously influential throughout the world. "Not surprisingly," Berger concludes, "both [the social progressive and the social conservative] subcultures have become export commodities" (Berger 2014). Our book provides evidence that the intellectual resources of the American culture wars are becoming "goods" that are readily distributable worldwide: arguments on abortion, arguments for homeschooling, arguments against gay marriage, a traditional vision of the family, and so on. The Russian case is an example of how the logic of the cultural wars can take root in contexts in which on a societal level there is little or no preexisting moral controversy on these issues.

2

HISTORY

THE SOURCES OF RUSSIA'S TRADITIONAL-VALUES CONSERVATISM

Russia in recent years has joined the global culture wars and has positioned itself as "the last protector of traditional Christian values" and "shield against radical left-wing ideas and ideologies" (Michel 2017). For us, as scholars of post-Soviet Russian society and Orthodox religion, this turn of events raised one simple question: where did all this come from? Even for us, having spent the last fifteen years studying the post-Soviet religious situation in Russia, the rise of the Russian Orthodox Church to become a "new powerful ally for the American Christian Right" (Michel 2017) came as a surprise. What was it we had not seen? What seemed obvious to us was that the Russian traditionalist turn was far from "just natural"; that it was not the inevitable outcome of a peculiar logic of Russian religious and national history and culture, which would allegedly always place Russia on the side of religious Orthodoxy and autocracy (even though the proponents of Russian traditionalism argue just that). Russia's present role in the global culture wars was an empirical puzzle: How—and when—exactly did the Russian Orthodox Church and the Russian government adopt traditional-values conservatism? How did this turn toward moral conservatism fit into the sociopolitical and cultural history and present of post-Soviet Russia? How did it match up with global culture-war dynamics? When precisely did this traditional-values conservatism become a foreign policy agenda? How much of this development should be considered genuinely "Russian," and how much of it stemmed from transnational dynamics? These various questions form the focus of this chapter. First, we examine the logic of the development of Soviet and post-Soviet society that made social conservatism both relevant and in high demand. Following this, we provide concrete examples of the influences of Western actors on Russian conservatism in the early 1990s and analyze the embeddedness of Russia and Russian Orthodoxy in the dynamic of the globalizing cultural wars.

Soviet Roots of Russian Social Conservatism

To make sense of the origins of Russia's traditional-values conservatism, one must study the logic of the development of Soviet society and its transition to post-Soviet society. Victoria Smolkin's *A Sacred Space Is Never Empty: A History of Soviet Atheism* (2018) will be our initial guide in reconstructing the ideological trajectory of Russian society that laid the foundation for the emergence of traditional-values conservatism.[1] The Soviet Union was an atheist state that was determined to get rid of religion and any other of the *ancien regime*'s atavisms. However, as early as the 1970s, Communist Party ideologues noticed two troubling tendencies:

> The first was the growing indifference of the Soviet youth to ideological and worldview questions in general, and to religion and atheism in particular. The second was the growing interest in religion as national culture and spiritual heritage among certain segments of Soviet society—a trend that was led by the creative intelligentsia, but threatened to contaminate young people. (Smolkin 2018, 196)

To a certain extent, Smolkin argues, these two tendencies complemented each other: as the official ideology became less and less attractive, some people totally rejected any ideology and turned to worldly pleasures and consumerism, while others searched for some alternative to fill this spiritual void. In a 1972 essay in the atheistic journal *Science and Religion*, Feliks Kuznetsov wrote, "As our material problems find solutions, questions of moral upbringing and spiritual values become more important" (cited in Smolkin 2018, 202).

Soviet ideologues tried to solve the problem of "moral upbringing and spiritual values" and to counteract the aforementioned tendencies with two moves. First, they tried to reform atheism. Instead of militant atheism

---

1. Following Smolkin, we focus on the developments from the 1970s onward. For the period before, and in particular for the influence of Stalinism on social conservatism in the USSR, see Robinson 2019, 159–62.

aimed at fighting religion, they proposed a positive atheism that "expanded the boundaries of what constituted atheism" (Smolkin 2018, 198). According to Smolkin, "This new kind of atheism—a spiritual atheism—had to address tradition and heritage, lived experience and spiritual needs, and produce its own cosmology and way of life" (Smolkin 2018, 198). The Communist Party's attempts to recreate atheism as a direct replica of religion—with atheistic spirituality and atheistic rites of passage—turned out to be unsuccessful.

Second, the party sought to study religious culture to retain what was useful from religion in terms of values that could be stripped of their suspect religious vestments. Smolkin quotes Anatolii Ivanov, the editor of *Science and Religion*, who wrote, "The main task is to develop research into the spiritual values of the past, in which the religious and the aesthetic are deeply intertwined, in order to free everything historically and aesthetically valuable of its religious wrapping" (cited in Smolkin 2018, 201). The Communist Party's search for religion did not pass unnoticed by those religious dissidents in the Soviet Union who clandestinely studied, taught, and wrote about the Russian religious tradition. "The ones in power started to look for ideological alternatives to Marxism early," Vladimir Bibikhin wrote in an essay entitled "For Administrative Use," in which he revealed a government-sponsored project for the preparation of philosophical digests on Russian and Western philosophy in the 1970s and '80s. Bibikhin recalls critically that the Soviet government was interested in Russian religious thinkers inasmuch as it could shape their ideas into an official canon that could be read in support of Russian nationalism and, as an anti-individualist philosophy, of communism (Stoeckl 2015, 395).

For Soviet party ideologues, there were two aspects to religion: (1) religion as a faith or worldview and (2) religion as a cultural artifact, national tradition, or connection to the past.[2] Religion in the first sense was unacceptable, an ideological enemy that should be destroyed. Religion in the second sense, however, was something that could at least be tolerated and could function as a "pressure valve" for radical thinkers on the right (Smolkin 2018, 201; see also Mikhailovsky 2015).

During the years of *perestroika*, when Marxism-Leninism was crumbling, the Russian Orthodox Church was more than ready to offer itself as

2. This opposition of religion is also found in the contemporary configuration of religion, where religion-as-faith without culture is struggling with religion-as-culture without faith (Roy 2009).

the solution to the problem of moral vacuum. As early as 1985, Metropolitan Aleksii (Ridiger) of Tallinn and Estonia (the future patriarch) wrote a letter to Mikhail Gorbachev asking the state to reconsider the role the church played in the life of society. In this letter, he "assured the Soviet leader that the interests of the church could not be separated from the interests of the Soviet people, and that as a result, the church could and should play a more prominent role in Soviet social life" (Smolkin 2018, 224). Smolkin, in her analysis of this letter (including quotes from the letter), wrote:

> Aleksii proposed that "the main directions of our cooperation" would be the church's contribution to "patriotic and civic education, to the strengthening of the unity of our society, which is so necessary in the difficult current international situation." He noted that de facto, the church was already doing this work. But he suggested that the church could "more actively and decisively combat the various social vices and illnesses—alcoholism, moral depravity, and egoism—to strengthen the family as an essential foundation of Soviet society, and defend the spiritual and moral health of the people." (Smolkin 2018, 224)

This offer was rejected, and the Metropolitan was punished. He lost his position as the head of internal church affairs and had to move from Moscow to Leningrad (Smolkin 2018, 224). Yet the Soviet system was obviously collapsing, not only economically and politically, but also ideologically. And the question of the moral vacuum, of "moral upbringing and spiritual values," remained unresolved.

As the USSR was approaching its end, two main ideological alternatives emerged. These alternatives were well illustrated by a famous letter published in 1988 in a leading Soviet newspaper, *Sovetskaia Rossiia* [Soviet Russia] (Atnashev 2018). The letter became one of the turning points of *perestroika*. Nina Andreeva, its author, a Soviet chemistry teacher, criticized *perestroika* and proclaimed the need to return to "authentic Communist ideals" (Andreeva 1988). In her letter, entitled, "I can't betray principles," Andreeva described two ideological rivals to authentic communism. The first she called "left-liberalism" or "neoliberalism," characterized by adherence to democracy, capitalism, "God-seeking tendencies," and, of course, cosmopolitanism. She called the proponents of the second ideological rival to communism "traditionalists" or "guardians" (*ohraniteli*—those who guard) or "neo-Slavophiles." These people were characterized as those striving to "overcome socialism by moving backwards." According to Andreeva, they wanted to "return to the social forms of the pre-socialist Russia" and were representatives of "peasant socialism" who believed that a hundred years ago the country had lost its moral values that had "accumulated in the foggy mist of centuries by the peasant community" (Andreeva 1988).

It is worth remembering this letter today, because as soon as communist ideology collapsed, these two rival ideologies became dominant. The post-Soviet period has been a period of struggle between liberals and traditionalists. The last decade of the twentieth century was a period of liberal triumph, but the first decade of the next century saw the gradual rise of the traditionalist wing. Hence, the first element behind the rise of traditional-values conservatism was the decline of the official Soviet ideology and the experience of the spiritual vacuum that followed. At the same time there was a growing fascination with religion and the Russian Orthodox Church, which continued to nurture the ambition to fill this moral vacuum.

The second internal source for the rise of traditional-values conservatism can be found in the turbulent transformations the Soviet state and society underwent in the 1980s, ultimately leading to the collapse of the USSR and the emergence of several independent states, including the Russian Federation. This was a real revolution—not merely politically, but also culturally and spiritually. In fact, it was a belated echo of 1968. For decades, Russia had been surrounded by the Iron Curtain, which to a considerable degree prevented the spirit of the sixties from penetrating. By the late 1980s, however, the curtain was no longer functioning, and the country was rapidly flooded with an extraordinary number of new phenomena, including new religious movements, New Age spirituality, new sexual freedom including pornography, Western music, fashion and hairstyles, new drugs, and more (for a good literary portrait of this period, see Carrère 2014). All of this happened against the backdrop of painful economic reforms and inconclusive political transformations that resulted in poverty, increased crime rates, alcoholism, rising abortion rates, and other problems. With these came a growing disillusionment with the liberal transition among ordinary Russians.

The spiritual void and the problem of "moral upbringing and spiritual values" transformed into alarmist moral panics about degradation and degeneration. The comprehensive crisis of late Soviet and post-Soviet society became a hotbed for ideas about moral revival and spiritual regeneration. There are significant parallels here with the emergence of U.S. traditional-values conservatism in the 1970s as a reaction to the social dislocations of the 1960s (Dowland 2015). In his book on Russia's sexual revolution, sociologist

Igor Kon (1995, 269) claimed that Russian society experienced everything that took place in the West in the 1960s with a delay of twenty-five years. If we follow Kon, then Russian moral conservatism emerged as a reaction to the dislocations of the late 1980s and the 1990s—the country's dramatic encounter with the spirit of the sixties. The resulting moral panics and the rise of conservative ideology is not unique to Russia; rather, it is a reflection of the global pattern of a society facing the process "of formation of new sexual-erotic norms and values" (Kon 1995, 268).

As mentioned earlier, Soviet communists were not ready to take the next logical step to connect the challenge of moral upbringing and spiritual values—transformed into the problem of regeneration and overcoming an acute moral crisis—with religious ideology and the Russian Orthodox Church as the purveyor of this ideology. Only later, after the collapse of the Soviet Union, did the post-Soviet Communist Party make this connection. Gennadii Zyuganov, the leader of the Russian Communist Party and a viable candidate in 1996 for president of the Russian Federation, made the question of spiritual-moral values (SMV) one of the top aspects of his political program. According to Jardar Østbø:

> In Gennadii Zyuganov's 1996 election campaign, SMV were mentioned in several programmatic articles. For instance, Zyuganov called for a halt to the "moral genocide" of the Russian people. In his characteristic brand of nationalism and communism, SMV were presented as the opposite of capitalism, self-interest, Western low culture, and Western sectarianism—whose "propaganda" would lead not only to spiritual and moral decay, but also to the "physical demise" of Russia. In this early instance of a securitizing move, Zyuganov explicitly presented what he saw as the materialist decay and Western missionaries' encroachment on traditional SMV as existential threats to Russia. (Østbø 2017, 203)

Russian communists openly merged nostalgia for the Soviet past (a stable social order, a strong position in the system of international relations, etc.) with Orthodox tradition as a substitute for the now-impossible atheist ideology.

The Russian Orthodox Church was also moving in this direction by criticizing the "dashing nineties" and countering the perceived moral decay with the revival of spiritual-moral values. This is particularly evident in the materials of the World Russian People's Council, which since 1993 have been filled with value rhetoric and calls for moral revival of the Fatherland (see Dunlop 1995; Horvath 2016). Alexander Agadjanian calls the continuity between Christian Orthodox and communist spiritual-moral values "a selective reception of the late Soviet conservative ethos" (Agadjanian 2017, 41). This affinity between Orthodox morality and Soviet ethos, he argues, is "based upon a common negative assumption—namely, a rejection of the imagined 'western liberal ethos.'" This position was "deeply shared both by the ideologised moral code which dominated the Soviet public sphere and traditionally anti-western Orthodox rhetoric" (Agadjanian 2017, 42–43). The points of convergence between the late Soviet ethos and Orthodox morality, according to Agadjanian, were many: the rhetoric of the "solid Soviet family" as the basis of a stable society (in spite of, and in contradiction to, the high rates of divorce and abortion); the tacit acceptance of inequality of gender roles (in spite of official propaganda to the contrary); an emphasis on responsibilities rather than rights, on intra-collective social control and solidarity (both as a mechanism of power and an accepted ideal), on the priority of the "spiritual" over the "material," and on sexual (self)-restraint. Also shared were homophobia and the subjugation of individual interests and expressions to the collective good (Agadjanian 2017, 43–44). He concludes:

> All of these elements can be easily given a Christian sacred canopy under the label of "traditional values" which the Orthodox Church has done, but with new interpretations and emphases. The Soviet moral legacy has thus been selectively "sacralised" and subsumed into a longer continuity of Russian Christian history, which has been associated, if only anachronistically, with both the pre-Revolutionary imagined Gemeinschaft and the Soviet collectivistic conservatism. (Agadjanian 2017, 44)

The affinity between communist and new Orthodox values is not a big secret evident only to informed researchers (see also Stepanova 2019, 2015; Tsygankov 2016). It has been openly acknowledged several times by Vladimir Putin himself, including in a speech in 2011:

> We lost certain Soviet-era values that were related to . . . the "Moral Code of the Builder of Communism."[3] But if we look into this "Moral

3. The "Moral Code of the Builder of Communism" was a set of codified moral rules in the Soviet Union that every member of the Communist Party of the USSR was supposed to follow. It was adopted in 1961.

Code of the Builder of Communism," [we see that] it actually [consists of] excerpts from the Bible, and humanity has created nothing better. Our traditional confessions—Buddhists, Christians, Jews, and Muslims alike—generally adhere to essentially the very same positions concerning basic moral and ethical values. And, of course, we must strengthen these values together. We have no other values orientations [than these], and others will likely not arise any time soon. (Regnum 2011)

On another occasion, Putin said that the Code of the Builder of Communism was merely a "sublimation, [with] primitive excerpts from the Bible" (TASS 2018).

One can notice a peculiar ploy here: the connection between contemporary religious values and communist values is acknowledged, but this acknowledgment occurs because communist values are said to have been just a pale copy of authentic religious values. Putin and others thus see today's Orthodox Christian values as deriving from communist values for the simple reason that communist values were nothing more than a shallow imitation of the more original Orthodox Christian values.

Hence, summarizing the logic of the development that made traditional-values conservatism both relevant and in high demand inside Russia, we can see how Russian moral conservatism originated as a reaction to the "dashing nineties" and to the social dislocations of Russia's transition from the Soviet to the post-Soviet context. Traditional-values conservatism emerged out of the moral panics of the late 1980s and the 1990s as a solution to the long-lasting, comprehensive crisis of a new Russian society in desperate need of moral foundations (see also Uzlaner 2017, 2019).

The Outer Sources of Russian Traditional-Values Conservatism

The narrative thus far seems quite logical: the decay of official atheistic ideology revealed a spiritual void that culminated in an acute sense of a comprehensive crisis of the Russian people, with the rising Russian Orthodox Church offering itself and its Christian values as the way out of that crisis. Yet an important element is missing in this sequence. The moral conservatism described previously is related exclusively to Russian history, as an aspiration to revive Russia's past and to restore what was lost during the Soviet and the post-Soviet period. This kind of conservatism is openly anti-Western in nature, and it is difficult to imagine fruitful cooperation between it and its Western analogues. As Nina Andreeva's letter shows, this conservatism is very much backward-looking in that it seeks to restore a "golden age" of the past. As such, its proponents seem to lack the skill, the language, and the arguments to discuss contemporary issues and contemporary challenges. The missing element that must be added to this picture is transnational influence. Its introduction as an element for analysis allows us to understand why the alliance between Russian conservatism and the global right wing in the 2010s became possible.

Traditional-values conservatism is not a unique Russian invention. As discussed in Chapter 1, it was forged in the context of the U.S. culture wars of the 1970s and 1980s. By the end of the 1980s, the American culture wars became transnational. On the one hand, Christian Right NGOs started to be active in international institutions like the UN (Buss and Herman 2003). On the other hand, the agenda of representatives of the U.S. culture wars was to export their beliefs and ideologies to other regions and continents. American conservatives were more than ready to export traditional values or traditional family values to new territories. It is against this backdrop that Russia appeared on the map of the globalizing culture wars in the late 1980s. There is still no comprehensive description of the transnational context of the rise of contemporary Russian moral conservatism. With the few exceptions cited in this chapter (Glanzer 2002; Kon 1999, 1995), most scholars have attributed Russia's conservative turn to traditional Eastern Orthodoxy and the peculiar Russian context. John Anderson, for example, describing the rise of cultural conflicts in Russia, writes that "although the way these issues have been articulated in Russia may owe something to U.S. discourses, the controversies have indigenous roots" (Anderson 2012, 309; see also Anderson 2015). In the remainder of this chapter, we will show that this statement is only partially adequate.

Moral controversies in contemporary Russia do have indigenous roots, but the way they are framed owes much to U.S. discourses. This is visible even at the level of language itself. The very concept of traditional values is quite new in the Russian context. The term was definitely alien to the communist ideology, since communism was strongly opposed to any tradition. The more widespread concept was "spiritual-moral values." Our analysis of the EastView database showed that the first meaningful mention of traditional values in the official Soviet press is from a 1983 article published in *Izvestia*. The article (Matveev 1983), with the telling title, "A Crisis of

Morality and the Morality of a Crisis," was devoted to Jerry Falwell and his "Moral Majority" movement. It described Falwell as a person who is trying to "return to traditional values" blaming the "left," the "liberals," and the "communists" for the moral decay of American society. The article was highly critical of traditional-values conservatism; according to the author, the U.S. Christian Right did not see that the problem was not moral decay but capitalism itself. It was in this context of refutation, therefore, that the concept of traditional values first appeared in the Russian discourse, clearly identified with the American Christian Right. Only a decade later, the assessment of traditional values and of the American Christian Right changed by a hundred-and-eighty degrees: they were now examples to emulate.

CoMission

One case of American Christian Right influence that is well documented is the so-called CoMission program, the subject of Perry Glanzer's book on Evangelical activities in post-communist Russia (2002). This was a program of eighty-three Christian organizations created with the scope of instructing Russian public-school teachers how to teach Christian ethics. Glanzer describes the excitement of the American Christian community as the former Soviet Union opened itself to "Christian enlightenment," with *USA Today* and *Newsweek* running enthusiastic headlines like, "The Former Soviet Republics Are Now Opening Their Public School Doors to Teaching about Christianity" and "U.S. Evangelicals Put God Back in Russian Schools" (cited in Glanzer 2002, 3). Glanzer's well-researched monograph shows that high-ranking Russian officials responsible for education were more than happy to open their doors to American missionaries. These public administrators thought that Americans could help Russia cope with the moral vacuum in which the country found itself after the collapse of the USSR. Glanzer quotes a Russian official, on a visit in Anaheim, California, in November 1992 to meet with American Christian teachers, who used a dramatic picture in his address to the American hosts:

> When a person is in a waterfall and he wants to save his life, and he sees a hand extended to him for help, can he think whose hand is this? He will accept the hand which is first. The first hand was of The CoMission. (Alexander Asmolov, cited in Glanzer 2002, 3–4)

CoMission, endorsed by Russian authorities at the highest levels, initially enjoyed great success, operating until 1997. It entailed more than 1,500 missionary educators not only to Russia, but also to other countries such as Ukraine, Estonia, Latvia, Lithuania, and Bulgaria. The CoMission's activities included training work in schools and missionizing outreach (Glanzer 2002, 5–6). Even the Russian Orthodox Church appears to have welcomed CoMission in the beginning (Glanzer 2002, 9). Eventually, however, the Moscow Patriarchate, alarmed by its proselytizing activities, turned against the program (Glanzer 2002, 195). By 1997, the church had successfully lobbied for a change in the Russian law on religious freedom, which restricted the activities of foreign missionaries in the country and effectively barred the CoMission program from continuation.[4]

Focus on the Family

The American Christian organization Focus on the Family was active in Russia in the late 1980s and early 1990s. Their activities have not yet been described in the literature, and the findings we present here therefore help fill a gap and complete the picture of American influence on Russia traditional-values conservatism. Focus on the Family is an organization that promotes family-values conservatism. James Dobson, a Christian psychologist and the author of popular books on family psychology and raising children, founded the organization in 1977. According to Daniel K. Williams, Dobson "dispensed advice on a wide range of family concerns, including parenting, marital issues, divorce recovery, advice for singles, and caring for elderly parents, all of which he and his cohosts discussed from a Christian perspective" (Williams 2010, 236).

---

4. In 1997, the Russian Duma passed a new Law on Freedom of Conscience and Religious Associations. The aim of the new law was a stricter regulation of the activities of religious communities on the Russian territory, especially of foreign missionary groups. The law introduced the requirement of a fifteen-year waiting period prior to registration as a religious organization, a requirement that effectively barred many foreign missionary churches from providing public worship services or religious teaching. The law also articulated (in its preamble) a hierarchy of religions, with the Russian Orthodox Church in a predominant position. (On the 1997 Law on Religious Freedom, see Froese 2008; Trepanier 2002; Shterin 1998; Davis 1997; and Durham and Homer 1998.)

According to our findings, the first contacts between Russia and Focus on the Family go back to the late 1980s. These first contacts were not with representatives of the Russian Orthodox Church, nor with government structures like CoMission, but with the Russian academic community. The key contact person was Mikhail Matskovsky (1945–2002), a family sociologist at the Soviet Academy of Sciences Institute of Sociology. He visited Dobson for the first time in 1989, and Dobson impressed him. Matskovsky treated Dobson not only as a colleague, but as a guru who had a solution to Russian problems, as revealed by his recollections about this initial encounter, worth quoting at length:

> The first thing that struck me was an army of consultants who, sitting in their cozy offices, answered continuous phone calls. As I was told, husbands, wives, children and grandparents from all over America call to ask how to solve a problem in their family. If the question is simple, they get an answer immediately. When consultants consider the situation as "non-standard," they involve specialists—psychotherapists or psychologists. . . . Having seen the work of the organization, we went outside. There were a lot of cars standing outside. I knew that there was a parking problem in the U.S., but I was not expecting to see this! And if it's a parking lot, why are there people in the cars? What are they waiting for? It turns out that they were waiting for "our James." As soon as he walked out the door, the column came alive. Men and women came out of the cars, they started to thank him for the advice received from books, radio or television, they were shaking his hand one by one. If it hadn't been for the humor with which Dr. Dobson treated this ritual, it might have seemed like he was leading a parade. (Dobson 1991, 8)

Matskovsky played an active role in promoting Dobson's ideas in Russia. In 1991, he published the Russian translation of Dobson's book *Dr. Dobson Answers Your Questions.* The publication of Dobson's book took place under the aegis of an organization founded by Matskovsky called the "Center for Universal Values." In his introduction to the Russian edition of Dobson's book, Matskovsky explains the relevance of Dobson's legacy for Russian post-Soviet context:

> The long-term domination of totalitarian ideology in our country has led to the removal of religion from public life. Instead of eternal

values: don't kill, don't steal, don't make yourself an idol—a relativistic morality began to be planted: kill if it's important for the triumph of the Communist Party's cause; steal ("expropriate the expropriators"), because it's in the spirit of the socialist ideals of justice and equality; don't honor your father and mother, but "betray" them, because the country needs this. It is only now that we are beginning to realize the harmful consequences of this morality for society, the family and the individual. Generations of people have grown up who prefer to feel more like fighters than keepers, more like overthrowers of the foundations than defenders of them. But if there's no one to keep the fire in the family home, because everyone's gone to the barricades, what happens to that fire? What happens to this earth? To preserve the home as an eternal, imperishable value of earthly existence, as a primordial brick of human civilization is the main task of Dobson's conservatism, and we would like to vote with both hands for such conservatism. (Dobson 1991, 8–9)

Matskovsky is not merely repeating the usual lamentations about the moral crisis of Russian society; he also expresses a clear demand for American guidance. After years of atheism, Russian society was ready to receive moral guidance not only from the Russian Orthodox Church, which at that time did not seem strong enough to offer such guidance, but also from anyone who represented respected religious values that had been abandoned by the godless Soviet society.

In the early 1990s, Focus on the Family had huge plans for Russia. We interviewed a functionary of Focus on the Family, who had been active in Russia at the time, to find out more about this period. He recalls that everything started when James Dobson was invited to Washington by Republican congressmen who said that there was a great opportunity to bring Focus on the Family to Russia, since they felt that "there would be an open door to do that" (Interview 2018i). One of the first things that Focus on the Family tried to do was to organize a visit by Dobson to Russia.

Dobson was scheduled to visit Moscow in August 1991. An article about this forthcoming visit, published in *Nezavisimaya gazeta*, was illustrative of Russian expectations of this collaboration. Its title spoke plainly: "Dr. Dobson Could Not Come at a Better Time: An American Conservative Will Advise the Soviet People." The article described Dobson in a highly positive light:

Dr. Dobson is an activist of the conservative movement, but not in the sense of being "outdated." He is one of the most unshakable defenders of what is called "traditional family values" in America. Among them, James Dobson includes marital fidelity, honesty, self-control, premarital abstinence, selfless love for children combined with strict discipline, etc. (NG 1991)

The article went on to discuss Dobson's upcoming visit, including "meetings with deputies of the Supreme Soviet of Russia, with members of the Committee on Marriage and Family Problems of the . . . Council of Ministers, and with sociologists, psychologists, and religious figures. Radio or television broadcasts for the Soviet people are also planned." The *Nezavisimaya gazeta* article included a comment from Svetlana Yampolskaya of the Institute of Sociology of the Soviet Academy of Sciences:

Despite economic differences between our countries, we have common problems: an increasing divorce rate, vulnerable people, family conflicts. . . . But Soviet psychologists and sociologists do not find it easy now to offer recommendations to people. Our country is going through a catastrophe; no one knows what is good or what is bad. In other words, there is no stable system of values. Until 1917, there was faith in God, and after 1917, faith in Communist ideals. And although the norms of communist morality were abstract, discourse took place at the societal level, not the individual level ("don't get divorced; it's bad for the country"), but at least something existed. Right now, it is simply not okay to talk about communism. And every person has a psychological need to believe in something. Dr. Dobson is good for us, because he has a clear system of values based on centuries-old religious tradition. (NG 1991)

The much-anticipated visit did not happen. On his way to the USSR, Dobson's plane was redirected to London because in Moscow the August Putsch of 1991 was unfolding.[5] The failed trip notwithstanding, the activity of Focus on the Family in Russia continued. The organization had am-

5. The August Putsch of 1991 was a failed attempt made by communist leaders of the Soviet Union to take control of the country from Mikhail Gorbachev, who was the Soviet president and general secretary. The Putsch leaders were opposed by civil resistance led by Russian president Boris Yeltsin. The Putsch led to the demise of the Communist Party of the Soviet Union and the dissolution of the USSR.

bitious plans to translate and publish books, to start a radio program like the one operating in the U.S., to have a permanent column in leading Russian newspapers, and to meet Russian officials and religious leaders. The representatives of Focus on the Family made dozens of visits to Russia, receiving significant attention from Russian bureaucrats, including people from the government who were President Boris Yeltsin's advisers on family policy (Interview 2018i).

At that period, the Russian Orthodox Church still generally welcomed such contacts, so it is hardly surprising that representatives of Focus on the Family established contacts with church officials. In our interview, the former activist remembered an encounter with a bishop at Yelokhovo Cathedral (which functioned as the Moscow Patriarchate's main cathedral until 1991), where the organization handed out children's bibles (Interview 2018i). This was, after all, the time when the CoMission program was in full swing and Focus on the Family was certainly not the only conservative Christian organization operating in Russia: "There were lots of other organizations. In fact, probably hundreds of missions and organizations that were working, and there were opportunities where we met together in the United States and talked about supporting each other's activities" (Interview 2018i). A particular feature of Focus on the Family was its very specific focus on promoting "traditional values." It understood itself as an educational organization "from a Judeo-Christian value system perspective." Activists would not preach to people but talk about Christian values and how they could impact family life and childrearing and support husbands and wives in relating to each other (Interview 2018i). By the mid-1990s, however, for reasons probably very similar to those that ended the CoMission program, the activity of Focus on the Family came to an end.

Pro-Life

One important topic for the Christian educators that came to Russia from the West was abortion. Abortion, it should be remembered, was legal and a widely accepted procedure across the former Soviet Union. Legally accessible on demand from 1920 until 1937 and then again from 1955 onward, surgical termination of pregnancy was the most accessible form of fertility control in the Soviet Union, where barrier contraception was hard to come by and hormonal pills were not imported. (For the most important publications on the subject, see Karpov and Kääriäinen 2005; Rivkin-Fish

2013; and Luehrmann 2017b, 2017a.) It was only after the end of communism that abortion became a question of morality politics not only from the perspective of demography (Gal and Kligman 2000), but also as regards women's personal experiences and pastoral practice of the Russian Orthodox Church.

The ethnographic research of Sonja Luehrmann helps us understand that the question of abortion had a completely different status in the USSR than in Western countries. The right to legal abortion had been a key goal of early feminist struggles in the West. In the Soviet Union, on the other hand, the legalization of abortion was the result of state action rather than women's mobilization. Rarely would Russian women speak about their abortion as a "choice" or "decision," as supporters and opponents of legal abortion tend to do in the West. Instead, they would discuss both pregnancy and its termination as something that happens to a woman as a result of external and often unexplained agency. The religious revival of the 1990s presented many of these women with a personal dilemma, because they encountered the notion of abortion as sin for the first time (Luehrmann 2017a, 169).

The Russian Orthodox Church in the early 1990s had no strategy for dealing with abortion; it was simply not on the church's agenda. A Russian Orthodox pro-life activist of the first hour, the priest Maxim Obukhov, remembers how awareness was raised in the early 1990s through contacts with pro-life movements from the West. The Orthodox pro-life activists of the first hour received information material: "When we saw pictures of aborted children who . . . came from the United States, well, from the American pro-life movement, yes, we realized that . . . it is necessary to stop the killing of children" (Interview 2017i).

One influential piece of anti-abortion information imported from the U.S. was the film "Silent Scream" (1984), which was professionally translated into Russian. In 2003, Obukhov's Life (*Zhizn'*) Centre in Moscow also published a translation of John and Barbara Willke's book *Why Can't We Love Them Both*, with the imprinted blessing of Patriarch Aleksii II (Luehrmann 2017b, 111). The priest Obukhov endorses the book by American Catholics as "a wonderful source of information for doctors, teachers, and priests who are responsible for the spiritual and physical health of the Russian nation" (cited in Luehrmann 2017b, 111).

Luehrmann stresses that the Russian Orthodox pro-life strategy indiscriminately adopted arguments of Protestant and Catholic origin. She also observes that Russian Orthodox pro-life activism is often paradoxical:

although many activists are deeply suspicious of Western influences and ecumenical endeavors, they accept psychological expertise that is largely mediated by Catholic and Protestant sources. The Russian activists we interviewed confirm this analysis. They tended to use the anglicized term "pro-life" in Russian (*pro-lajf*), freely admitting to obtaining and translating information material from the West and to discovering topics previously not in the focus of the Russian pro-life movement—for example, the battle against contraceptives that are considered to have an abortive effect. The first plastic dolls of "preborn" children used by pro-life activists to underscore the personification of fetuses also came to Russia as gifts from Western pro-lifers (Luehrmann 2017b, 114).

From these origins in the early 1990s, being pro-life has become a stable feature of Russian social-conservative activism. In our analysis of transnational networks of social conservatives, pro-life groups are always among the players. The Russian Orthodox Church and Orthodox pro-life groups look for ways to promote their cause, often pursuing rival strategies, as we analyze in more detail in Chapter 7.

The World Congress of Families

CoMission and Focus on the Family ended their Russian adventure in the mid-1990s, just around the time when another conservative pro-family organization, the World Congress of Families, started to make headway. As the World Congress of Families will be the subject of analysis in Chapter 6, it is worth introducing this organization and the circumstances of its foundation in some detail.

The WCF was founded in the mid-1990s. Like with Focus on the Families, the circumstances connecting Russians and Americans were academic. In January of 1995, the American college professor and pro-family activist Allan Carlson, then president of the Howard Center for Family, Religion and Society in Rockford, Illinois, traveled to Moscow. The purpose of his trip was to meet the sociologist Anatoly Antonov, professor of family sociology and demography at Moscow State University. It was in fact Antonov who had reached out to his American colleague and proposed the meeting. Antonov was interested in Carlson because he had read his works on family and shared his views. For Carlson, the purpose of the trip was to test the waters and to check out whether the creation of some form of collaboration between Russians and Americans on family issues was feasible.

In his travel diary, which he presumably wrote for colleagues back at the Howard Center, Carlson gave a day-by-day account of his stay in Moscow, of the people he met, the topics treated, and the agreements made (Carlson, personal diary, 1995).[6]

Antonov introduced Carlson to many people in Moscow: to academics, intellectuals, and politicians. He made Carlson visit the Sociology Department of Moscow State University and its Center for Population Study. The American guest received a warm welcome at the Russian Academy of Education's Research Institute for the Family directed by Sergey V. Darmodekhin.[7] Carlson's diary conveys pride when he writes:

> He [Darmodekhin] showed me a copy, in Russian translation, of my 1989 article, "A Pro-Family Income Tax,"[8] which had appeared two years ago in a social science journal. This article, he said, is having "great influence" among Russian Federation officials, as they labor to restructure the nation's income tax. (Carlson, personal diary, 1995, 5)

Darmodekhin invited Carlson to enter a collaboration with the Moscow Research Institute for the Family, for which he had prepared a draft cooperation agreement between the institute and the Howard Centre. The agreement included, according to Carlson's diary, the preparation of joint publications and translations in family sociology, the development of a joint research project, the exchange of material and information, and the nomination of Carlson to the academic board of the Russian Research Institute for the Family. An agreement was reached on all these points, and the protocol was signed "following brandy and toasts" (Carlson, personal diary, 1995, 5).

6. The diary, which we received in copy directly from its owner, has meanwhile been published by investigative journalist Casey Michel (Michel 2019b).

7. In 1995 the Ministry of Social Protection of the Population of the Russian Federation ("Министерство социальной защиты населения РФ [Ministerstvo social'noy zashchity naseleniya RF]") still existed. In 1996 it was merged with the Ministry of Labor of the Russian Federation ("Министерство труда РФ [Ministerstvo truda RF]") to become the Ministry of Labor and Social Development of the Russian Federation ("Министерство труда и социального развития РФ [Ministerstvo truda i social'nogo razvitiya RF]"). Antonov was an advisor to this last, and to the Russian State Duma, during the 1990s and after (Demoscop Weekly 2011).

8. See Carlson 1989. Many texts of Allan Carlson have been translated into Russian.

But not only the Research Institute for Family was interested in cooperation with Carlson; a Russian Orthodox actor also "wanted to talk 'business'" (Carlson, personal diary, 1995, 4). Carlson reported on a meeting with Ivan Shevchenko, who was introduced to him as an artist, chairman of the Orthodox Brotherhood of Scientists and Specialists "Tabor,"[9] and former Duma-candidate. Upon meeting Shevchenko, Carlson felt reminded "of a young Solzhenitsyn" (Carlson, personal diary, 1995, 4). Shevchenko asked Carlson for help in organizing an international conference on the family, planned that summer at an Orthodox monastery near Moscow. Carlson replied that he had himself been thinking about working to convene

> a conference of fairly compatible "pro family" groups from across the globe, to serve as a kind of informal Congress of Families with the purposes of (1) defining the common pressures on families in modern countries, vis-a-vis state and economy, and (2) drafting an "appeal" or "declaration" to the governments of the world including common demands. (Carlson, personal diary, 1995, 4)

He promised to start to organize such an event. The first World Congress of Families took place in Prague in 1997 with the active participation of Shevchenko and Antonov.

The four days Carlson spent in Moscow, as reported in his diary, had been entirely organized by Antonov. One episode in the latter's scholarly biography gives a hint as to the closeness he felt between his views and those of Carlson. During the late 1980s and early 1990s, Antonov was involved in a Russian-American project of family sociologists initiated by the University of Minnesota. The results of the project were published in 1994 under the title *Families before and after Perestroika: Russian and U.S. Perspectives* (Maddock et al. 1994). The project appears to have been a source of disappointment both for the American and the Russian sociologists involved; it definitely was for Antonov, who spoke about it in our interview (Interview 2017f).

Instead of a coauthored article, the volume reproduces at one point the transcript of a discussion between Antonov and an American family soci-

9. This brotherhood was registered in 1991 and existed until 2009. "Tabor" is a reference to Mount Tabor. In Eastern Orthodox Christian theology, the light of Tabor is that revealed on Mount Tabor at the Transfiguration of Jesus.

ologist, Shirley Zimmerman. The discussion reveals fundamental disagreement between the two scholars. During the exchange, Antonov expressed the view that the role of the family is that of "a mediator between the reproductive interests of the personality and the society. The family is a social institution ensuring both demographic and social reproduction" (Maddock et al. 1994, 197), to which the American sociologist replied:

> You must admit that many professional colleagues, both in your society and in mine, do not place primary emphasis upon the family's reproductive function as a cornerstone of family policy. That notion may have some logic from a demographic point of view; however, it is difficult to support from either a feminist or an environmental perspective. (Maddock et al. 1994, 197)

And she continued, "Given the differing histories of our respective societies, it is curious that in our dialogue, you emphasize individual motives while I emphasize social justice—an interesting switch from the traditional stereotypes of Soviet communism and American capitalism" (Maddock et al. 1994, 197).

Antonov recalled the episode years later and said that in this project all the American scholars were "democrats, not republicans." He had sent this publication to Carlson before their first personal meeting in 1995 to make him understand "what they [the American sociologists at Minnesota University] criticize me for" and in order to persuade Carlson that they were "thinking alike" (Interview 2017f).

The episode reveals an ideological alignment between the two founders of the WCF that is rooted in an experience of rejection from the academic mainstream in family sociology. Carlson's work on family policy has received only parochial attention by academic scholars in the West and has been labeled "Christian Right Social Sciences" (Buss and Herman 2003, xxxiii). Carlson, instead, saw himself as a legitimate representative of an alternative sociological school that "ran sharply counter to the primary thrust of American sociology in this era [that was] neo-Marxist in orientation" (Zimmerman 2008, viii). Antonov, in turn, also saw himself as a family sociologist grappling with the Marxist legacy. The views of the two scholars aligned in terms of their anti-Marxism, and they shared an experience of rejection from Western mainstream family sociology.

This academic episode also reveals the main driving motive for Antonov's interest in family sociology: demography. Already in the mid-1980s, he had observed a decline in birth rate in the Soviet Union and advocated state support for the reproductive role of the family as a response. His anxiety about demography only increased when, in the mid-1990s, Russia's economic and demographic crisis was unfolding at full speed (Field 2000). The declining birth rate, the crumbling of the healthcare system, and the dramatic decrease in life expectancy during the years of post-Soviet transition were blamed on the poorly controlled neo-liberal "shock" reforms of the time and the "cultural revolution" of Russian society that had become exposed to Western consumer culture overnight. Antonov, who considered the family "a social institution ensuring both demographic and social reproduction," was looking for Western scholarly literature that would support his views.

The reference to demography demonstrates that Antonov's position on family was largely of a secular and scholarly origin. Even if he was a believer, as professor at MGU during the USSR regime, he had certainly kept his beliefs secret. Also, Carlson in his travel diary does not present his newly found Russian colleague as a religious man. The only Orthodox contact during Carlson's visit to Moscow in 1995 was Ivan Shevchenko, who was not an official representative of the Russian Orthodox Church. The church and its leadership entered the orbit of the WCF only much later, after 2009.

To sum up, then, CoMission, Focus on the Family, pro-life activism, and the World Congress of Families all share the same pattern. In the late years of *perestroika* and the early 1990s, Russian society experienced a moral crisis, but the Russian Orthodox Church was not yet a serious contender on the new free market of ideas—or rather, it was one among several. This allowed foreign actors, especially American Evangelicals, to step in and fill the gap of moral teaching on traditional Christian values. In 1997, Russia adopted a new, significantly less liberal religious legislation, which ended the brief period when the disoriented country had opened itself directly to foreign religious influence. But the period from the late 1980s until the mid-1990s did not disappear without a trace. To a certain extent, Russian moral conservatism as it exists today is a hybrid where national currents and transnational influences have become mixed to the point of indistinguishability. At the same time, Russian conservatism thrives on the demonization of "foreign agents" that are allegedly manipulated by the West to destroy Russia. The situation is paradoxical, because, as our analysis amply demonstrates, one can hardly find a single issue of contemporary Russian moral conservatism that does not bear the marks of transnational influences.

3

INTELLECTUAL ROOTS

THE SHARED LEGACY OF PITIRIM SOROKIN

Societal trends often find their roots in the work of influential individuals. Having considered the ways in which Russians learned about moral conservatism and the culture wars in the 1990s, in this chapter we examine one individual thinker who plays an important role for today's moral conservatism, the Russia émigré Harvard sociologist Pitirim A. Sorokin (1889–1968). As a scholar, Sorokin has been relegated to the margins of his discipline, but his legacy as a public intellectual has persisted in the United States and has soared in Russia over the last three decades. This chapter looks at Sorokin's legacy in the United States and Russia, two countries that have made twenty-first-century moral conservatism a transnational phenomenon. Four aspects are especially relevant here: his emphasis on values, his notion of the "sensate culture," his ideas about the family, and his vision for moral revival. Through a firsthand analysis of moral conservative discourse and documents, as well as qualitative interviews, we show how Sorokin can be seen as a nodal point that binds together individual actors and ideas across national, cultural, and linguistic barriers.

When Karl Mannheim subtitled his 1925 study on conservatism "a contribution to the sociology of knowledge," he did so to emphasize that he was interested in conservatism as a coherent form of reasoning, a style of thinking (*Denkstil*) born out of a specific historical and sociological constellation. He wanted neither to repudiate conservatism nor to side with it. Instead, to bring the morphology of conservative thinking into the open, Mannheim's analysis addressed the historico-political, philosophical, intellectual, and sociological sources of early nineteenth-century German conservatism layer by layer. In this way, he identified the nodal points (*Kno-tenpunkte*) that gave coherence to conservative thought, among them individual writers, intellectual schools, and even publishing outlets. In this chapter, we follow his method of historical and sociological analysis.

Sorokin's life spans the length of the twentieth century. He was born in Tsarist Russia and spent time in prison because of his resistance to the Bolshevik Revolution, eventually being exiled and finding his way to the United States and the halls of the elite institution of Harvard University (see Johnston 1995, 1996; Sorokin 1963a). Many scholars consider him to be a major figure for the sociological theory of the first half of the twentieth century (cf. Ford, Richard, and Talbutt Jr. 1996; Tiryakian 1963; Jeffries 2009; Maquet 1951), but in American academia his work has fallen out of the classical sociological canon, only to be "rediscovered" from time to time (Jeffries 2002; Nichols 2001, 2005, 2012). The situation is different in Russia, where Sorokin was first deprecated as a bourgeois scholar in the Soviet period but was then rediscovered and rehabilitated as a luminary of sociology after the collapse of communism (Kravchenko and Pokrovsky 2001).

Not only was Sorokin a "professional sociologist" who proceeded "via discursive practices among experts trained in its distinctive frame of reference" (Nichols 2009, 28); his legacy has an additional facet that draws together the recent American and Russian reception of his work. In the terminology of Michael Burawoy (2005), this side of Sorokin's work could be called a public sociology that "has an outward orientation toward a broad range of groups that constitute contemporary civil societies." Lawrence T. Nichols (2009, 31), who uses Burawoy's concept, gives a list of Sorokin's works that belong to this field of public sociology, including *The Crisis of Our Age* (1941), *S.O.S.: The Meaning of Our Crisis* (1951), *The American Sex Revolution* (1956), and *The Basic Trends of Our Times* (1964). In this chapter, we argue that it is this public and engaged side of Sorokin that is most alive today, thus making him a nodal point for twenty-first-century moral conservatism.

In what follows, we first analyze the role of Sorokin in today's moral conservative arguments in the United States and Russia, indicating how reference to Sorokin binds these two moral conservatisms together. We then identify four aspects in Sorokin's work that determine his reception among today's moral conservatives: his emphasis on values, his ideas about the family, his notion of the "sensate culture," and his vision of moral revival.[1] We follow this with an evaluation of the differences between Russian and American moral conservatives in their interpretation of Sorokin.

The Reception of Sorokin in American Sociology

Whereas the more recent sociological reception of Sorokin's oeuvre in the United States is limited to a few essays and book chapters (see Tiryakian 1996), his fame as a prophet of social and moral crisis is on the rise. German scholar Susanne Pickel has produced insightful online data that underscore this argument. According to Pickel (2002), while such scholarly sociological works about Sorokin in the United States that do exist drew almost exclusively on his work prior to 1942, among moral conservative and religious authors it is his later works that provide a compass, and this in a highly selective fashion. With regard to Sorokin's rural sociology, however, as we show later, this clear-cut distinction must be qualified, since he initiated this work well before 1942.

In the United States, Sorokin's reputation as a public intellectual is largely based on his post-1942 polemical works. For example, in his book *World Aflame*, Billy Graham (1965) quoted from Sorokin's book *The American Sex Revolution* (1956) and called Sorokin "one of the most astute observers of America's sex scene."[2] This book also became a major source for the documentary film *Perversion for Profit*, which warned against the negative consequences of sexual liberation (*Perversion* 1965). More recently, Southern Baptist leader Albert Mohler (2015, 2004, 2005) has repeated some of Sorokin's claims to argue against the legalization of same-sex marriage. Other writers have concentrated on Sorokin's theory of the sensate culture to decry the effects of secularization and to call for a reconversion to the Christian faith (Dreher 2013, 2015; Berman 2012; Benne 2015).

Besides this reception based on Sorokin's more prophetic works, his early sociological research on rural society has also played an important role in turning him into an author of reference for moral conservatives. Together with Carle Zimmerman, Sorokin developed a particular perspective on

1. An additional line of reception of Sorokin's works, his altruism studies, is discussed in Uzlaner and Stoeckl 2017.

2. For a more detailed analysis of Sorokin's influence on Billy Graham, see Moslener 2015, 71–75.

rural-urban sociology, according to which only a rural lifestyle based on a traditional model of the family, an economy of manual labor and home-based business, and a strong link of the individual to the inhabited territory is sociologically, demographically, and economically sustainable (Sorokin and Zimmerman 1929). Zimmerman (1947) carried this research program further, frequently expressing his intellectual indebtedness to Sorokin (Zimmerman 1968; Zimmerman and Unnithan 1973).

The historian and pro-family activist Allan Carlson, whom we already mentioned in Chapter 2 as the cofounder of the World Congress of Families through his visit to Moscow in 1995, was also, indirectly, a student of Sorokin. He further developed the Zimmerman-Sorokin program of rural sociology through his numerous books on the family. Carlson, who has described his religious stance as "orthodox Lutheranism," has cited Sorokin and Zimmerman as two of three must-reads for pro-family Protestants (the third is Robert Nisbet [2013]). He explains (Interview 2018d) that he discovered Sorokin in the late 1970s when he was writing an article addressing the question of what went wrong with the American family. The first book he read by Sorokin was *The American Sex Revolution*. He then discovered Sorokin's work on cultural cycles and the sensate culture. It was through Sorokin's work that he became acquainted with Zimmerman. Carlson's "manifesto" on the "natural family" in twenty-first-century America takes practical cues from the work of Sorokin and Zimmerman on rural-urban sociology (Carlson and Mero 2005). Two aspects of Sorokin's ideas about the family appear to have influenced Carlson: (a) his idea that small, village-like communities are the best environment for families, and (b) his anti-communism. Sorokin abhorred communism and Bolshevism his entire life. In his (1950) autobiographical writings, he condemned the moral decay under communism, which he had witnessed firsthand before leaving Russia. In Carlson's works (1990, 2007) that are critical of European social-democratic welfare systems, the reader can easily detect the influence of Sorokin's negative judgment of communism.

Sorokin also inspired other authors who represented moral conservatism and gathered around the Howard Center and its predecessor, the Rockford Institute. These include Bryce Christensen and Harold O. J. Brown (1933–2007), the former director of the Center on Religion and Society at the Rockford Institute and former professor of biblical and systematic theology at Trinity Evangelical Divinity School in Deerfield, Illinois. The former wrote an article on Sorokin and Solzhenitsyn (Christensen 1996). The latter published a book-length commentary on Sorokin's *The Crisis of Our Age* (Brown 1996). Together, these authors have created what Doris Buss and Didi Herman call "a secularized, professional discourse on 'the family' that has achieved a wide impact and is rarely associated with their conservative Christian politics" (2003, 140). The professionalization of the discourse also extends to its dissemination. In fact, Transaction Publishers has issued many of Solzhenitsyn's and Sorokin's writings, as well as Carlson's works and new editions of Sorokin's works, with the strong support of its founder, Irving Louis Horowitz, who according to Carlson (Interview 2018d) was a big admirer of Sorokin.

Under Donald Trump's presidency, Sorokin's influence on American Christian pro-family circles became apparent even at the highest political level. The forty-eighth vice president, Michael Richard "Mike" Pence, who is outspoken in his pro-life and pro-family positions, was influenced by Sorokin's ideas. Pence quoted Sorokin while advocating for his failed House Resolution, the Marriage Protection Amendment, in 2006, at the height of debates in the United States about same-sex marriage: "Marriage matters according to the researchers. Harvard sociologist Pitirim Sorokin found that throughout history, societal collapse was always brought about following an advent of the deterioration of marriage and family" (Pence 2006).

Sorokin as a Bridge between the American Christian Right and Russian Conservatives

As an author of reference for moral conservatives in the United States, Sorokin has not only contributed to the professionalization and sociological foundation of the discourse on the traditional family, he has also inspired this discourse's development into a transnational Christian conservative endeavor. This is particularly true for conservatives in Russia. To a certain extent, Sorokin must be seen as one among many towering Russian figures who fled Bolshevik Russia to the West and whose legacy became important both in the Western intellectual landscape and in the Russian intellectual landscape following the collapse of the USSR. The most famous example is Nikolai Berdyaev (Stroop 2014), whom Robert Nisbet cited, together with Sorokin, as "the major prophets of our age" (Nisbet 1953, 8). Another relevant figure in this context is Alexander Solzhenitsyn, who played a role in the formation of late twentieth-century American conservatism. One author has even called Sorokin a "noble forerunner" to Solzhenitsyn (Christensen

1996, 390). Notwithstanding the extensive impact of Berdyaev and Solzhenitsyn on both the West and Russia, it would not be an exaggeration to claim that Sorokin now seems to have exceeded them in terms of his impact on today's transnational conservative movement.

Following the collapse of the Soviet Union and the first decade of social transition, Russian society has undergone a turn toward a conservatism that is associated with Orthodox Christianity, political authoritarianism, and traditional values. As we discuss in this book, this turn toward traditional values was not entirely homegrown but was influenced by contacts between Russian conservatives and like-minded actors in the West. Sorokin occupies a special place in this context, since he is a native intellectual source for both Americans and Russians. He is, therefore, a unique figure.

Sorokin also played a role in the encounter between Carlson and the Russian demographer and sociologist Anatoly Antonov in 1995. Antonov was among those Russian scholars who had already been attracted to Sorokin in the Soviet period, when his name and the study of his works were still forbidden. In an interview with our research team, Antonov (Interview 2017f) recalls that he became acquainted with the works of Sorokin early in his career at Moscow State University when his research advisor brought some of Sorokin's books from abroad and encouraged his students in this clandestine reading. He acknowledged, "Sorokin's writings on the crisis of the family influenced our [Soviet and post-Soviet] scientific way of thinking about the family" (Interview 2017f). Thus, Carlson and Antonov shared an understanding of the crisis of the family and the roots of this crisis anchored in their studies of Sorokin. It is against this intellectual backdrop that they founded the World Congress of Families.

Sorokin continued to play an important role for the working of this organization. We will discuss the World Congress of Families in detail in Chapter 4, but at this point—with reference to Sorokin—it is important to mention one meeting between American and Russian conservatives that took place in 2010. In that year, Larry Jacobs, the managing director of the World Congress of Families, traveled to Russia on an official visit to speak at an event organized by the Russian pro-life organization "The Sanctity of Motherhood." Jacobs recalled, "This was the first official World Congress of Families trip to Moscow since Allan Carlson's visit in 1997 [sic—the trip had taken place in 1995]. We were delighted by the support we found there. Russian pro-life / pro-family forces are eager to cooperate with their counterparts in the West. Given its traditional support for faith and family, Russia will play an increasingly important part in the international struggle to preserve the natural family" (Christian News-Wire 2010).

Participants in the 2010 Moscow meetings between American and Russian moral conservatives frequently mentioned the name of Pitirim Sorokin. Jacobs spoke at the Sixth All-Russia Scientific Conference—the Pitirim Sorokin Annual Sociology Forum, which was organized by Moscow State University's Sociology Department, the Russian Sociology Association, and the Pitirim Sorokin / Nikolai Kondratieff International Institute. Jacobs also met with Vladimir Dobrenkov, the dean of sociology at Moscow State University from 1989 to 2014, who expressed "full support to the pro-Family activities of the World Congress of Families" (Christian NewsWire 2010).

The Americans found their Russian counterparts highly receptive to their ideas about the family and Sorokin's legacy. After the collapse of the Soviet Union, Sorokin became an authority for Russian sociologists. In his interview, Antonov (Interview 2017f) remarked somewhat critically, "This is just what our country is like. We must always have a portrait hanging on the wall. Before, we had Marx or Lenin, and . . . now we have Sorokin instead of Marx." Dobrenkov, a self-proclaimed conservative, promoted Sorokin's status as an important author of reference in sociology. It was Dobrenkov who invited Alexander Dugin to Moscow State University's Sociology Department, despite the latter's mixed reputation as a radical conservative thinker (even by Russian standards).[3] In 2007, the Pitirim Sorokin Foundation at Moscow State University was established. It proclaimed as its mission "the revival of a national ideology based upon values that are traditional for Russia."[4] Dugin (2011, 165) explains the importance of Sorokin's legacy:

> Russian conservatism as yet has not gained a clear structure or a coherent, consistent and systematic expression. Our conservatism remains emotional, rather than theoretical, and impulsive, rather than

3. In the end, Dobrenkov and Dugin had to leave Moscow State University together in 2014 (Safronov and Antonova 2014).

4. The Center is no longer functioning. The archived site can be accessed via https://web.archive.org/web/20150401000000*/www.sorokinfond.ru/ (accessed May 24, 2017).

scientific. In the new historical situation, we must therefore attend to the legacy of Russian thinkers, philosophers, sociologists and economists who, in various historical conditions, have prepared an intellectual foundation for a new Russian conservatism.

Sorokin's book on the American sexual revolution has become an important nodal point for Russian pro-family activists, much as it had been for their American counterparts. Although the Russian translation (Sorokin 2006) had a print run of only several hundred copies and soon went out of stock, the text of the translation is available online and is well-known to Russian moral conservatives.

From the previous discussion it is clear that Sorokin does indeed function as a nodal point (*Knotenpunkt*) for moral conservative thinking in many ways. He has been an author of reference for moral conservative thinkers across time (from the 1950s until today); he tied moral conservative ideas to certain aspects of sociological study through his works on the family, rural life, and the "sensate culture"; and since the collapse of the Soviet Union, his works have united American and Russian moral conservatives into a community of mutual understanding and civil society activism. In the remainder of this chapter, we first consider which aspects of Sorokin's work made him so popular among twenty-first-century moral conservatives. We then examine if and how Russian and American moral conservatives interpret Sorokin differently.

There are four aspects of Sorokin's work that can be seen as crucial for his reception among today's moral conservatives: his emphasis on values, his notion of the "sensate culture," his ideas about the family, and his hope for moral revival. We describe the meaning of each of these in Sorokin's oeuvre before going on to argue that these ideas have since become general features of contemporary moral conservatism.

Culture- and Values-Centrism

When those from the progressive left discuss the Christian Right's moral conservatism, they often express incomprehension as to why conservatives think that culture outweighs economics as a matter of public concern. Why is it that "values matter most" (Frank 2004) in conservative discourse, rather than the redistribution of wealth or equal justice under the law? The focus on values becomes more understandable when we clarify the foundations of the moral conservative approach to the study of society. In this respect, Sorokin is a good guide. An analysis of his works reveals the logic behind moral conservatives' ongoing anxiety over values and their relative neglect of economic issues, which understandably puzzles those scholars and observers who are more materialistically oriented.

Sorokin belongs to the idealistic tradition in sociological theory, which tends to insist that "what differentiates different universes of mind and meaning from each other is not only ostensibly, but even fundamentally—i.e., in the last analysis, the difference in the answer given to the 'last questions'—the twin questions: what is the nature of ultimate reality, and what is the supreme value?" (Stark 1991, 225). For Sorokin, the core of any sociocultural system and its dynamics lay in its "mentality." As he explains in his magnum opus *Social and Cultural Dynamics*, any "logically integrated system of culture" has two aspects:

> The first belongs to the realm of inner experience, either in its unorganized form of unintegrated images, ideas, volitions, feelings, and emotions; or in its organized form of systems of thought woven out of these elements of the inner experience. This is the realm of mind, value, meaning. For the sake of brevity we shall refer to it by the term "mentality of culture" (or "culture mentality"). The second is composed of inorganic and organic phenomena: objects, events, and processes, which incarnate, or incorporate, or realize, or externalize, the internal experience. These external phenomena belong to a system of culture only as they are the manifestations of its internal aspect. Beyond this they cease to be a part of integrated culture. (Sorokin 2010, 20)

Sorokin then concludes that "for the investigator of an integrated system of culture the internal aspect is paramount" (Sorokin 2010, 20). One should stress that his theory "considers the ontological convictions prevailing at a given time, not so much as culture-contents, but rather as culture-premises, from which the culture concerned proceeds and emanates as a whole" (Stark 1991, 226). Or, as Sorokin put it, "If the nature of the major premises of a culture plays such an important part in the qualification of its logical integration, it follows that the key principle by which the character of an integrated culture may be understood should be sought, first of all, in these premises" (Sorokin 2010, 20).

Values are an important part of these premises or "culture mentality." The types of values that are prevalent determine the type of "cultural supersystem" we are dealing with (Sorokin 2010, 676). Frank R. Cowell even claims that the concept of values is Sorokin's most important contribution to sociology, asserting that he was "the first to bring German and continental European sociological thought prominently to the notice of Americans" (Cowell 1970, 25). This claim is open to critical assessment (Endruweit 2002), but it is beyond dispute that values were a central element of Sorokin's understanding of civilizations or sociocultural systems (see also Talbutt 1998). In this values-centered interpretation, culture becomes identical to a "system of values."

Sorokin famously distinguished among three types of cultural systems: (1) ideational culture, (2) sensate culture, and (3) idealistic (or integral) culture. According to his theory, each civilization passes through cycles of change between ideational, sensate, and idealistic phases (Sorokin 2010, 23). Each phase is associated with corresponding sets of values. Ideational values are "absolute," "transcendental," "categoric," "imperative," "everlasting," and "unchangeable." Sensate values are "relativistic," "hedonistic," "eudaemonistic," "utilitarian," and "egoistic." Idealistic values are a "golden middle" between these two extremes (see the table in Sorokin 2010, 39). Cultural change occurs when one set of values is exhausted and is then replaced by another set of values. The period of transition is marked by chaos (Cowell 1970, 474).

Of particular significance for our analysis of the dynamics of culture wars is Sorokin's law of polarization, according to which a cultural crisis on the threshold between one phase and the next is characterized by extreme polarization. Sorokin argued that

> such crises, with their insecurity, instability, anxiety, and sufferings, split human beings into the two opposite extreme types. Some of them are turned into pure eternalists who try to anchor human existence to something solid, lasting, capable of withstanding all the storms of the empirical reality; others are turned into the extreme sensual temporalists of the Carpe diem type, with their tendency to catch the pleasure of the moment for "tomorrow is uncertain." (Sorokin 2010, 315)

Sorokin's categorization of mankind into eternalists and temporalists matches the polarization we observe in many moral conservative writings. Moral conservatives see the ground for existing political cleavages in contemporary societies precisely in the difference in values-orientations and not in social injustice, economic inequality, or other forms of social fragmentation. They take the current debates over same-sex marriage or transgender restrooms as signs of the polarization that, following Sorokin, signifies the crisis of a culture.

Although we can find a direct reference to Sorokin's theory of culture in only a few instances, it is still clear that his writings have helped to create the language of today's culture wars by shaping moral conservatives' vision of social processes and dynamics. Once we understand Sorokin's idealism, we can then begin to see how other elements in his vision of "public sociology" emerge from this theoretical framework.

Sensate Culture and the End of the West

Sorokin's concept of the dying sensate culture is the most visible Sorokinism in recent American conservative discourse. It is also the most attractive aspect of his work for Russian conservatives. They not only recognize traces of Russian Slavophilism in his diagnosis of a deep cultural crisis in the West (which must result in either total collapse or deep cultural transformation), but they also interpret their own situation of post-Soviet transition in a Sorokinian sense, as the doomed demise of sensate culture. For example, Dobrenkov has claimed that Russian society "is living through not simply a period of radical socio-economic and political reformation, but a period of a painful, violent transition from an ideational-idealistic socio-cultural system to a Western-style sensate socio-cultural system" (Dobrenkov 2011, 159).

Sorokin was convinced that Western civilization was in the final stage of the sensate phase in cultural dynamics:

> The organism of the Western society and culture seems to be undergoing one of the deepest and most significant crises of its life. The crisis is far greater than the ordinary; its depth is unfathomable, its end not yet in sight, and the whole of the Western society is involved in it. It is the crisis of a sensate culture, now in its overripe stage, the culture that has dominated the Western World during the last five centuries. (Sorokin 2010, 622)

His sense of doom was so imminent that he did not shy away from predicting that Western civilization would collapse within years. Even though he had to correct this position as time moved on and the expected collapse did not take place (Ivanov 2011), he continued to identify signs of decline. The most important of these was, in his words, the "sex revolution."

In *The American Sex Revolution* (Sorokin 1956), the first version of which was published as an essay in 1954, Sorokin warned of the effects of the liberalization of moral norms for the future of Western culture. His basic position was that at the root of almost all social ills lay "sexual anarchy" and "familial degeneration." The piece was less a scientific essay than a polemical pamphlet, and to many of his contemporaries, it was unacceptably extreme. David R. Mace, for example, reviewed the essay and wrote that Sorokin was "going too far" (Mace 1963, 142). He criticized Sorokin for making statements that lacked "documentation" and for allowing himself, "under the influence of the enthusiasm generated in him by the cause he is espousing, to carry his argument further than prudence would dictate" (Mace 1963, 142). Sorokin was unmoved by such criticism and replied, "In our age of blatant advertising, deafening propaganda, and Gargantuan exaggeration of everything to be sold to the public, one has to hammer his points as hard as he can to be heard by the public, especially if his points are 'unpopular' and run against the prevalent fads and opinions" (Sorokin 1963b, 470).

Sorokin's diagnosis of Western sensate culture has become a recurrent trope in moral conservative discourse, both in America and in Russia. Especially in the Russian context, his authority has become more important than any empirical evidence in support of a more balanced vision of the state of Western society. Sorokin's pamphlet *The American Sex Revolution* was published in Russia as a scholarly edition, with several prefaces (to be discussed later) written by scholars who discuss its theses as if it were a serious academic research paper (Sorokin 2006).

Meanwhile, in America, conservatives widely share Sorokin's vision of a doomed Western sensual civilization. For example, Rod Dreher, the author of the bestseller *The Benedict Option* (Dreher 2017a), has argued that "Sorokin's ideas are absolutely key to the idea that traditionalist conservatives, religious and otherwise, would be wise to take the 'Benedict Option': to consciously withdraw to some extent from a dying cultural order and, in seeking out a way to live faith and virtue out in community, lay the groundwork for what may succeed the current order" (Dreher 2008).

Emphasis on the Family

For moral conservatives, the survival or decline of society depends on the institution of the family. In a time when diverse forms of families not only exist, but are also legally recognized and widely accepted, moral conservatives insist on the superiority of the traditional or "natural" family model. For them, the reality that same-sex marriage is now legally recognized in many Western countries, that divorce rates are high, and that family life is no longer the logical aspiration for many individuals in the West signify that Western society is in crisis. Sorokin was a forerunner for this argument. In 1948, he wrote, "Marriage and the family must be restored to their place of dignity among the greatest values in human life, not to be trifled with. As a socially sanctioned union of husband and wife, of parents and children, the family is to be radically differentiated from all unsanctioned sex association" (Sorokin 1948, 148). He began to express concern about the coming crisis of the family very early in his writings, and, empirically speaking, many of his prophecies on this topic have actually come true (Hillery, Meas, and Turner 1996). As Russell Nieli writes, "Long before the term came into existence Sorokin was a 'family values conservative'" (Nieli 2006).

Sorokin connected his theories about the family with sexual behavior. His experience of the Russian Revolution was a strong source of inspiration for making the argument that sexual license led to social unrest. Sorokin's was a morally conservative anti-communism that seemed to be preoccupied with discussing sexual behavior—something that must have puzzled many of his contemporaries. At a time when Soviet Russia was the quintessential political other to the United States, Sorokin was making the argument that, when all was said and done, Soviet Russia and capitalist America were facing similar challenges that had to do with the regulation of their citizens' sexual behavior. As Nichols writes,

> The emphatic focus on sexual behavior in Sorokin's writings in the U.S. from the 1920s through the late 1950s was another substantive element setting him apart from his American peers. Although some colleagues, particularly demographers and family sociologists such as Kingsley Davis, did address sexual behavior . . . , this was not common among those considered "theorists" or "general theorists." (Nichols 2012, 394)

According to Nichols, Sorokin argued that changes in sexual representations, attitudes, and behavior were key indicators of historical change for the institution of the family and for social relations generally. This general theory allowed him to find similarities between the United States and the Soviet Union at a time when these two countries, in the eyes of most contemporary observers, were antipodes.

Sorokin's moral anti-communism stands behind the aversion of today's moral conservatives to any kind of left-leaning family policy (see Carlson 1990). On the face of it, the opposition of moral conservatives to a number of points on the left's agenda of family policy is somewhat surprising. What could possibly be wrong with day care for children or state incentives for burden-sharing in childrearing between parents, if these policies actually help families? To understand this, we must think through the whole logic of the moral conservative critique of the left's family policy as rooted in Sorokin's condemnation of the early Communist sex revolution, which in his eyes only preceded the American one. Moral conservatives, who share this narrative, consider even seemingly helpful measures for improving the lives of families unacceptable so long as the value of self-determination and liberty of sexual orientation and gender identity stands behind such a measure.

Only much later did Sorokin's works on the family become known and were discussed in Russia. In particular, the demographic interpretation of his work caught the attention of Russian sociologists. Demographic anxiety became a critically important issue of public debate after the fall of the USSR. Take, for instance, the discussions of the so-called Russian cross, concerning the concomitant dramatic rise in the death rate with the radical decline in the birth rate (Khalturina and Korotaev 2006). Sorokin's theses on sexual license as the root of all evil and the natural family as the solution to all ills offered an answer to two highly sensitive questions that Russians were trying to come to terms with in the 1990s: What went wrong with the Soviet Union? And what was wrong with the post-Soviet present? In answer to these questions, they found a Sorokinian answer: one and the same ill ultimately caused the Soviet Union to fail and the post-Soviet democratic transition to derail—sexual immorality. And more importantly, Russia was not unique in this crisis, but was merely following a global trend.

The authors of the introduction to the Russian translation of *The American Sex Revolution* draw direct parallels between the American sexual revolution of the 1960s and Russian events following the collapse of the USSR. In the words of Natalia Rimashevskaya, a corresponding member of the Russian Academy of Sciences, "Astonishingly, *The American Sex Revolution*, written by Pitirim Sorokin exactly fifty years ago, is incredibly pressing for Russia today. . . . P. A. Sorokin destroys the myths of the sexual revolution" (Rimashevskaya and Markova 2006, 6). Yet another preface to this Sorokin edition, written by Yuri Yakovets, president of the Pitirim Sorokin / Nikolai Kondratiev International Institute, claims that "the publication of this book in Russia will facilitate victory over the deepest moral and demographic crisis the country has faced at the end of the twentieth century, which threatens the future of Russian civilization and could lead to its degeneracy and its disappearance from the geo-civilizational map of the world" (Yakovets 2006, 10).

The Promise of a Moral Revival—and the Difference between American and Russian Conservatism

Whereas Sorokin's ideas about the family have allowed moral conservatives from the United States and Russia to recognize each other in a common fate and a common set of shared goals, another aspect of Sorokin's work reveals the difference in their self-perceptions. Despite his alarmism, Sorokin was not ultimately a pessimist. He predicted that at the end of every fading sensate culture, a new idealistic or integralist culture would appear, with new religious values. At the end of the tunnel of the crisis of sensate culture, he saw a light—the emergence of "more religiously communitarian and distinctly nonsensate values of an older Christian integral culture, the latter reasserting itself after decades in decline" (Nieli 2006). Conservatives in both Russia and the U.S. share this vision, at least on a theoretical level; on a practical level, however, their understanding of what this means for their respective contexts differs radically.

For Russian moral conservatives, Sorokin's prediction inspires them to identify post–Soviet Russia as the harbinger of the coming idealistic (or even ideational) culture. In this regard, Dobrenkov has written, "We in Russia hope to escape the clutches of the sensate culture and to create an ideational culture, to fill the foundation with traditional values" (Dobrenkov 2011, 159). He offers a prescription for this to come to fruition: "In the most general terms, the national conservative ideology of Russia must come from a strong hand, from a high collective spirituality, from a Russia that is based upon the traditional values of Orthodoxy and other confessions for the unity of the state and the people" (Dobrenkov 2011, 158). In short, Russian Orthodoxy, traditional moral values, and political authoritarianism are the features of this new, integrated Russian culture. From this perspective, the West represents the dying sensate culture. The West is associated with liberalism and "alien values" *tout court*. In writings that take this perspective, there is no trace of recognition that Sorokin described a mutual East-West predicament. As Dobrenkov puts it, "Western civilization is destined to destruction, and nothing and no one will help it" (Dobrenkov 2011, 161).

If American moral conservatives were ever to become aware of it, this Russian optimism and demonstration of cultural superiority would likely be rather alienating. American conservatives have also creatively proposed ways for people in the West to follow Sorokin's path out of the crisis of sensate culture, mostly calling for a return to Christian values. For example, Brown speaks with delight about Sorokin's idea of moral resurrection and culture conversion from selfishness to altruism and higher values (Brown 1996, 232). Yet he is not very optimistic concerning the possibilities of such a conversion in the U.S. This is where Russian and American conservatives differ. Russian conservatives believe that sensate culture has managed to touch only the superficial layers of their culture; for this reason, it can be easily eradicated along with the liberals who are the bearers of moral decay. In contrast, American conservatives believe that sensate culture has penetrated too deeply into the nation's soil, to the point that there may no longer be any hope of converting the whole culture back to a more idealistic orientation. Dreher provides a good example of this kind of thinking with his "withdrawal strategy," as expressed in *The Benedict Option*, where he advocates for a Christian retreat from a sensate culture that is already doomed. This pessimism about their own culture may explain why American conservatives look with hope to their Russian colleagues.

Understanding the role Pitirim Sorokin serves for contemporary moral conservatism has added one more layer to our analysis of how Russia and Russian Orthodoxy learned about social conservatism after the end of communism. By identifying Sorokin as a nodal point for contemporary moral conservatism and by analyzing aspects of its discourse, we have sought to advance the analysis of the globalization of the culture wars. This globalization is driven by actors and by ideas. Sorokin identified the trench lines of the contemporary culture wars ahead of time. He laid the groundwork for today's transnational coalitions among moral conservative groups such as the World Congress of Families, developing aspects of the conceptual framework and the logic and language used by these conservatives in their discussions of current sociocultural transformations.

4

CONTEXT

THE RISE OF TRADITIONAL-VALUES
CONSERVATISM INSIDE RUSSIA

T he previous chapters have discussed the internal and external sources out of which Russian conservatism of traditional values emerged during the late Soviet period and the first decade of post-communist transition. The conservatism of the Russian Orthodox Church, the moral teachings of Christian educators from the West, and the scholarly rediscovery of the works of Sorokin during this period were, overall, a minority program with little influence on Russian society and politics as a whole and with no direct channels to the government. Before Russia and the Russian Orthodox Church could become an ambitious candidate for leadership in the Moralist International, moral conservative ideas first had to be brought from the margins of social life to the very center of social debate and politics. The culture wars, in other words, had to be introduced to Russian society.

This was by no means a trivial task. In the 1990s, the talk of moral decline and the call for spiritual and moral revival were largely the prerogative of patriotic groups that were acutely experiencing their own marginal status against the backdrop of the dominant post-communist liberal establishment (Shlapentokh, Vanderpool, and Doktorov 1999; Shlapentokh 1999). The patriots, conservatives, and radicals on the right were largely cut off from the mainstream media and felt themselves practically dissidents in the hostile and incomprehensible era of the "dashing 1990s." But starting from around 2000, a gradual transformation has taken place inside Russian society, during which conservative ideas have turned from the worldview of marginal groups to being the dominant ideology, and political legitimacy has increasingly been framed in terms of values of masculinity and patriarchy

(Sperling 2015). The culmination of this process has been the adoption in 2020 of the new text of the Russian Constitution, which has enshrined ideas that would have seemed rather bizarre to most observers in the 1990s, such as the defense of traditional values and marriage as union of man and woman, in the constitution of the Russian Federation.

This chapter discusses the rise of traditional-values conservatism inside Russia to clarify the domestic context of Russia's ascendancy to prominence inside the transnational moral-conservative movement. The chapter functions as a bridge between our analysis of how Russian actors first "learned" about the culture wars and then started "doing" the culture wars. The role of the Russian Orthodox Church and the Russian state inside the global culture wars cannot be understood without an awareness of the gradual conversion to social conservatism and a culture-wars type of public confrontation that took place inside Russia. There can be no doubt that the Russian Orthodox Church has been the key actor in this process, but it could not have been successful if the conservative program had not been picked up and utilized by the Kremlin. In this chapter, we offer a systematic analysis of this process, highlighting four key themes: (1) the rhetorical efforts of the church leadership to explain to the public the conservative *aggiornamento* of the Russian Orthodox Church; (2) the restructuring of Russia's religious landscape around traditional values and spiritual security; (3) the shift of the Russian state toward an ideology of traditional values, both in domestic and foreign policy; and (4) the ideological components of the Russian culture wars. The chapter ends with an outlook on public opinion surveys regarding religiosity and value conflicts.

The Russian Orthodox Church and the "Fundamental Confrontation of Our Age"

At the end of the 1990s, Russian society was tired. The economic-shock reforms and the financial crisis of 1998 had created hardship and unprecedented inequality; many people felt that the promise of greater freedom and wealth had not been kept, and most things Western that had been new, glossy, and interesting at the beginning of the decade had become worn and uninspiring. In this atmosphere, Western ideas and institutions, which in the early 1990s had been portrayed as a "helping hand," were transformed in the public perception into an insidious plan to change Russia's path in history and subvert the spiritual foundations of the people (Malinova 2020).

Ideas about Russian exceptionalism, civilizational uniqueness, and spiritual mission were no longer the prerogative of small circles of conservatives but turned mainstream (for an analysis of the different trends in Russian conservatism, see Suslov and Uzlaner 2019).

One agent of change in the public debate was the Russian Orthodox Church. Throughout the 1990s, the church had been mostly engaged in institutional recovery and internal struggles, but by 2000, the Moscow Patriarchate showed the ambition to become a leading public voice. The new sociopolitical role of the Russian Orthodox Church was primarily related to the figure of Metropolitan Kirill, head of the Department of External Church Relations, who was elected patriarch in 2009. While Patriarch Alexy II had taken a cautious stance regarding the political role of the church, Kirill supported a completely different approach. He illustrated his social vision in a landmark publication entitled *Norms of Faith as a Norm of Life* (Metropolitan Kirill 2000a, 2000b). This article, published in February 2000 in two parts in *Nezavisimaya Gazeta*—a leading Russian newspaper—reflected Kirill's views on contemporary society and its conflicts, as well as on the role that the church should play in these conflicts. Kirill's text is significant here, because it contained a compressed program of the new role that he envisioned for Orthodoxy in Russian society and in the world.

In the article, Kirill presented a roadmap for the church, which was to transform itself into a genuine public religion capable of "defining the future face of human civilization." This new Orthodox path was set in contrast to two existing and, according to Kirill, outdated positions: on the one hand, the secularist liberal position, for which the very existence of a public religion was a scandal and a threat for the dominant liberal consensus; on the other, traditional Orthodox religious and cultural fundamentalism, which, Kirill writes, "has long solved all problems for itself and is deeply convinced that the only way to save itself is to close the door of its house tightly" (Metropolitan Kirill 2000a). Kirill thus basically attacked two positions—one defending secularist liberalism, the other defending fundamentalist Orthodox isolationism. It is symbolic that the article is illustrated by a reproduction of a drawing by Julius Schnorr von Karolsfeld (1794–1872) with the telling title, "Healing the Two Blind Men," depicting the story of Jesus healing two blind persons (Matthew 9:27–35).

The agenda of the conservative *aggiornamento* of the Russian Orthodox Church emerges from the lines of the article in considerable clarity. Russian

Orthodoxy must not retreat from the modern world, nor should it seek accommodation with the secular liberal order, but it should actively engage with the modern world and, if necessary, fight against liberalism and secularism. Kirill sketches out his vision of "the fundamental contradiction of our era and at the same time the main challenge to the human community in the XXI century," by which he means a clash between "liberal civilization standards" on the one hand and "the values of national cultural and religious identity" on the other. He sees the task of Orthodoxy in challenging the hegemony of these liberal civilization standards and criticizing them from the position of "a system of traditional values for Russia," based on a way of life rooted in the tradition of the church (Metropolitan Kirill 2000a). The "fundamental contradiction of our era" that Kirill describes is another way of referring to the culture wars, which he depicts as both a global and a Russian predicament.

Kirill attacks the idea of privatization of religion, according to which religion is "an exclusively internal, inward and almost intimate matter of the human person," and proposes instead that Orthodoxy should become a real public religion capable of halting or reversing mankind's progress along the pernicious road of liberalism:

> We have a lot of accumulated spiritual values, which can brighten up the expectation of an apocalyptic catastrophe that threatens humanity walking past us on the road of "progress." Do we have the right to be tempted to flee from social, cultural, political reality? We are sent by Christ to this world for its salvation (John 17:18). The Lord commanded us not to flee from the world, not to hide from it, but to overcome the world by our faith (1 John 5:14), to walk the whole world preaching the Gospel (Mark 16:15), to be the light of the world and the salt of the earth (Matthew 5:13–16). (Metropolitan Kirill 2000b)

The fallacy of liberalism, according to Kirill, lies in the fact that it ignores the sinful nature of humanity. Humanity is tainted by sin, and therefore the idea of individual freedom, the classical liberal idea of negative freedom, is unacceptable for the church. The Orthodox understanding of freedom is that of positive liberty, which implies the existence of certain limits to individual freedom and of duties of individuals vis-à-vis a community and greater good.

The liberal doctrine encapsulates the idea of emancipation of the sinful individual, and thus the release of the potential of sin in the human person. The free man has the right to throw away everything that constrains him, prevents him from asserting his sinful "Self." All this is an internal affair of sovereign, autonomous, no one but himself, independent of the individual. In this part, the liberal idea is diametrically opposed to Christianity. (Metropolitan Kirill 2000a)

For Kirill, there can be no doubt that this liberal ideology has detrimental consequences for both the individual and society. Therefore, confronting the pernicious influence of liberalism and establishing the "norms of life" based on the Orthodox faith should become the essence of Orthodoxy as a public religion.

The article is an Orthodox call to arms in the culture wars. Published in a leading Russian newspaper, it addressed an audience far larger than Orthodox churchgoers and ordinary believers. It is important to underscore that the article did not stop at a general criticism of liberalism but went so far as to provide a concrete breakdown of the manifestations of liberalism to which Orthodox Christians should be alerted: feminism, the rights of sexual minorities, multiple forms of living together, family planning, and bioethics (Metropolitan Kirill 2000b). This bent toward social ethics and private morality was arguably a new direction for Russian Orthodox critics of liberalism, who usually addressed the issue in a civilizational key, singling out the West with Latin Christianity and the Enlightenment as the main culprit and source of evil. In Kirill's argument, the enemy was not the West, but could potentially be every single member of society—if he or she should stray from the path of "norms of faith as the norm of life."

In fact, Kirill's article reveals a fundamental tension in the Russian approach to the culture wars. On the one hand, from the very first lines Kirill insists that the culture wars are a "fundamental contradiction of our epoch and, at the same time, the main challenge to the human community in the XXI century"—that is, he emphasizes that we are dealing with a universal phenomenon. On the other hand, he describes this conflict in civilizational terms, as one in which the traditions of Russian civilization, "religious-historical identity" based on the Orthodox way of life, are confronted by "alien and destructive socio-cultural factors" (Metropolitan Kirill 2000a). These alien sociocultural factors have penetrated Russia thanks to "the rapid development of communications and means of communication in contemporary times," as well as the fact that "in today's world, the borders that divided national cultures have practically collapsed" (Metropolitan Kirill 2000a). A clear tension, if not contradiction, is constructed here between a universalistic, global logic and a particularistic, nationalist logic. The former pushes toward the search for universal solutions, to which Russian Orthodoxy might make a contribution; the second pushes in the opposite direction, toward self-isolation and the protection of Russia's religious-historical identity from an alien, "Western" civilization.

Kirill tries to solve this contradiction by criticizing both those who "blindly copy" the liberal civilization model and, at the same time, the isolationists, whom he accuses of creating "a narrow national-religious ghetto, where they can shut themselves away from the external enemy, cultivating their own identity and protecting it from the alien harmful influences." Instead, Kirill proposes a middle position: "a model of behavior and social structure that could bring liberal and traditional ideas and values into interaction" (Metropolitan Kirill 2000a). In the context of the religious and public debate at the time, Kirill's middle position was innovative. He suggested criticizing liberalism without completely rejecting it, using instead the resources of the liberal political order to push ideas that are alternative to it. For example, he writes that principles of education and interpersonal relations that reflect Russian traditional values can be affirmed under a liberal principle of "checks and balances" (Metropolitan Kirill 2000a). In Part II, we will give numerous examples of how Russian Orthodox actors have subsequently employed this strategy of searching out and using internal contradictions and paradoxes of liberalism for pushing their anti-liberal ideas.

Though Kirill offers an extremely ambitious plan, he acknowledges that the Russian Orthodox Church has a fundamental problem: it lacks the intellectual and theological resources to perform this task. "We did not know any of this until yesterday" is how Kirill summarizes the experience of Orthodox reflection on the agenda of contemporary cultural wars. He adds that the church may need to "take into account the experience of our Orthodox brothers in the West, who faced similar problems before us," and, he adds, "it may be useful to study the positions of other confessions." Developing an original Orthodox approach to contemporary society is "the creative task of modern Orthodox theology" (Metropolitan Kirill 2000b). Kirill's position accurately illustrates the conservative *aggiornamento* we have discussed in earlier chapters. This conservative *aggiornamento* has allowed the Russian Orthodox Church to enter the international arena and start speaking a language understandable to like-minded conservatives from other countries and religious traditions.

However, it should be noted that the contradiction between the logic of universal conflict affecting all mankind and the logic of Russia's religious-historical identity that is threatened by alien civilization standards did not go away, despite Kirill's attempt to chart a middle way. In fact, Russian traditional-values conservatism has unfolded in two different directions: on the one hand, the direction of active involvement in the Moralist International and participation in the transnational cultural wars; on the other hand, the direction of anti-Westernism and suspicion toward anything foreign. At times these two logics can be reconciled, but at other times they come into conflict and weaken the efforts of the Russian Orthodox Church to become a leading force inside the Moralist International.

Traditional Values and the Restructuring of the Russian Religious Landscape

When we discussed the American culture wars of the 1980s, we mentioned the effect they had on the religious landscape of the country. First, they led to the emergence of new interconfessional and interreligious alliances; second, they deepened internal divisions between progressives and conservatives within confessions; and finally, these ideological confrontations had the tendency to become ever more acute, prompting participants to resort to military metaphors for their struggle. These dynamics can also be observed in the Russian religious landscape.

Inside Russia, new interconfessional and even interreligious alliances have formed around the concept of traditional values. If initially the term "traditional religions"—which started to gain prominence in the 1990s (Fagan 2013, Chapter 6; Rousselet 2020)—only meant those religions that were native to the Russian lands as opposed to nontraditional religions, which were connected to foreign missionary expansion, the concept has by now acquired an ideological meaning: traditional religions are those that adhere to traditional spiritual and moral values.

Again, it was the Russian Orthodox Church that acted as the driving force for uniting religious groups inside Russia round the concept of traditional values. Kirill, in his article from 2000, invited Russia's traditional religions to collaborate in the face of the "fundamental confrontation of our age":

Here I see a wide field for interaction of other traditional religions, of all healthy forces of our society, who love the country and sincerely wish it good, with the Russian Orthodox Church, first of all, with theologians, who are able to help modern man understand the meaning of tradition as a norm-forming factor determining the system of values, including cultural, spiritual and moral orientation of an individual and society. (Metropolitan Kirill 2000a)

Formal cooperation between Russia's traditional religions takes place through the Inter-Religious Council of Russia, established in 1998 on the initiative of the Russian Orthodox Church.[1] The council includes representatives of Islam, Orthodoxy, Judaism, and Buddhism. In the documents of this council one can find a constant refrain: the theme of the unity of religions in defending traditional values from dangerous liberalizing and secularizing tendencies emanating from society. These tendencies include contemporary art, which is accused of desecration of Christian symbols, and anti-religious policies in the sphere of personal and family morality. The activities of the Inter-Religious Council of Russia also include a public-parliamentary commission "in support of Traditional Spiritual-Moral values" that has the task of monitoring the work of the Duma and influencing legislation "in the spiritual-moral sphere of society" (Fagan 2013, 133).

The idea of unity of traditional religions in defending traditional values was a favorite topic of the archpriest Vsevolod Chaplin when he was head of the Synodal Department for Church and Society Relations. Speaking about Buddhists, he noted that Russian Orthodoxy is, theologically, "seriously at odds with the Buddhists," certainly "more divided with them than with Muslims, with Jews, because Buddhists say that they don't believe in 'personal god'" (Chaplin 2015). However, he added, "we and Buddhists, as well as believers of other traditional religious communities, have many similar moral values." Accordingly,

when in Russia or in the world someone tries to overthrow these values, insist that they must be challenged, erased from the lives of nations, traditional Buddhists and Orthodox Christians usually support each other. (Chaplin 2015)

---

1. See official site: http://interreligious.ru/.

Speaking about Muslims, he affirmed a similar tendency, saying that

> Orthodox Christians and Muslims understand that the values of tra-
> ditional morality, the values of the religious dimension of public life
> today, need to be supported, promoted and sometimes protected from
> attempts to reject, humiliate and declare these values to be remnants
> of the past. (Chaplin 2013)

The Moscow Patriarchate also keeps ties with Russian Protestant groups.
Protestant and Evangelical churches have existed inside Russia for centuries, but they are not usually cited among Russia's historical religions. However, as the definition of traditional religions changes from historically
established to supportive of traditional spiritual and moral values, Protestant and Evangelical churches have moved closer to the Moscow Patriarchate. American Evangelical groups appear to have acted as mediators for this
inner-Russian partnership between Orthodoxy and Evangelicalism. The
summit for the defense of Christians in 2016 by the Moscow Patriarchate
and the Billy Graham Evangelical Church, which we discuss in Chapter 5,
was organized with the active participation of Russian Baptists (Interview
2017d).

While the conservative camps inside Russia's major religions converge,
the internal pluralism inside these religions has also increased. In the case
of the Russian Orthodox Church, conflicts between the traditionalist mainstream, represented by the church leadership, and church liberals—as well
as church radicals—have deepened.

Liberal Orthodoxy was initially so called because its representatives were
generally associated with the liberal religious dissident movement of the
1970s and '80s. Toward the end of the Soviet period, church liberals stood
for a Russian Orthodoxy that cherished the reformist ideas of the Russian
religious philosophers of the pre-revolutionary period, that was open to the
advancements made in Orthodox theology in emigration, and that wanted
to build a Russian Orthodox Church independent from the state (Agadjanian 2013). Being liberal in the church context meant being pro-democratic
and somewhat theologically reformist; it did not mean socially liberal or
progressive, as is usually understood in the context of Western debates between religious liberals and conservatives. The meaning of "liberal Orthodoxy" changed after 2012, when church liberals endorsed societal pluralism
and protest, while the church leadership supported traditional values and
the government. The key event that signals the opening of the gap between

a liberal and a traditionalist wing inside the Russian Orthodox Church was the case of the Pussy Riot's "punk prayer" of 2012, which in many ways divided the post-Soviet history of Russian Orthodoxy into a before and an after (Uzlaner 2014; Uzlaner and Stoeckl 2019). Church liberals did not support the hard line of the government, which condemned artists to prison terms, whereas the church leadership welcomed sanctions against the "violation of religious feelings." The priest Pavel Adelheim (1938–2013) was exemplary of the liberal camp inside the Russian Orthodox Church. With his past as a dissident, having served prison sentences for his religious belief during communism, Adelheim criticized the clerical bureaucracy, spoke out in defense of the political opposition, and even petitioned the patriarch for the release of the Pussy Riot activists. When he was murdered by an allegedly mentally ill man in 2013, his death was interpreted by many observers as one more sign of the increasing pressure on liberals inside the church.

However, not only church liberals have been pushed to the sidelines. Those fundamentalists and radicals who do not follow the ideological line represented by Patriarch Kirill and his circle have also been marginalized. The era of ideological diversity and polyphony of Orthodox voices, which has been repeatedly described in the research literature of the post-Soviet decades (Kostjuk 2000; Papkova 2011; Knox 2004; Stoeckl 2020b), appears to have come to an end. The Russian Orthodox Church today speaks through Patriarch Kirill, and all those who disagree with him risk marginalization, if they are not pushed out of the Russian Orthodox Church completely.

The Russian Conservative Turn in Politics

The year 2012 is the key date for the conservative turn in Russian domestic and foreign politics. The passage of power from Dmitry Medvedev to Vladimir Putin, who became president of the Russian Federation for a third nonconsecutive term on May 7, 2012, was not merely a political formality. It coincided with a radical shift of the political agenda from democratization and modernization, the two key themes of the presidency of Medvedev, to political authoritarianism and confrontation with the West under Putin. One of the key elements of Putin's new agenda became the ideology of traditional moral values. For the first time in the history of post-Soviet Russia, moral conservatism moved to the very center of politics (Pomerantsev 2012; Stepanova 2015). In his annual address to the Federal Assembly of

December 2012, Putin pledged to strengthen the solid spiritual-moral foundations of [Russian] society through a series of policy initiatives in the areas of culture, education, and youth policy, with the help of "institutions that are bearers of traditional values." These institutions were, of course, Russia's traditional religions—first and foremost, the Russian Orthodox Church (Putin 2012). The idea that Russia has a mission to fulfill in the contemporary world, that it could become the leader of the new value system, was also clearly expressed in Vladimir Putin's Address to the Federal Assembly of 2013:

> Moral and ethical standards are now being revised in many countries. . . . [The] destruction of traditional values "from above" not only leads to negative consequences for societies, but is also fundamentally antidemocratic, as it is carried out on the basis of abstract ideas, contrary to the will of the popular majority, which does not accept the ongoing change and the proposed revision.
>
> And we know that there are more and more people in the world who support our position to protect the traditional values that for thousands of years have formed the spiritual and moral basis of civilization, of every nation: the values of traditional family, true human life, including religious life, life not only material but also spiritual, the values of humanism and diversity of the world. (Putin 2013)

The two presidential speeches delineated Putin's dual conservative program: in the domestic context, this program was characterized by anti-Westernism, nationalism, and cultural particularism; in the foreign policy context, it became messianic, multilateral, and universalistic, aimed at restoring Russia's status in the world.

One of the tendencies identified by Hunter in the American culture wars was a militarization of rhetoric. The moral disagreement was experienced by Americans as a "war" or "battle"; an association operated a "war room" in its national headquarters, actors described the situation as a "civil war over values," and activists on both sides sought "victory" (Hunter 1991, 64). Similarly in Russia, learning the culture wars has meant a militarization of language. Traditional values—and their alleged enemies—have become an important part of Russian domestic and foreign security policy.

Security (*besopasnost'*) is not only defined in military, but also in ideological and social terms. The term "spiritual security" was introduced in public discourse in the late 1990s as a response to missionary activities of

Protestant groups, which according to the logics of spiritual security were aiming not simply at converting Russian citizens to nontraditional religious confessions, but at "replacing the 'socio-psychological code' of Russia's population" (according to official documents quoted in Fagan 2013, 149). What was under attack, according to this securitizing logic, was Russian statehood itself, which could only be upheld by a population that identified with Russian culture, language, history, and Russian Orthodoxy. Fagan quotes Viktor Zorkaltsev, chair of the parliamentary committee on religion in 2002, for a definition of "spiritual security":

> Spiritual security is key to our national security strategy; it is a shield against the "Fifth Column"; a barrier protecting our multi-ethnic culture, our distinctive, age-old civilization; a guarantee of steadfast identity. To lose the battle for hearts and minds in the modern world is a defeat far more serious than one in military strategy. (Fagan 2013, 105)

The idea that Russian national identity is under siege by relativism, pluralism, and liberalism and has to be defended against Western values and "foreign agents" became dominant after 2011. As Jardar Østbø has argued, the political class reacted to the public protests against the fraudulent parliamentary elections of 2011 with a proposal for a new "social contract" based on traditional values, obedience, and security (Østbø 2017). For this social contract to be persuasive, Russians had to be convinced that they were under threat by extremism and destabilizing foreign powers.

Despite such pledges, the meaning of traditional spiritual and moral values in Russian public discourse remains remarkably vague (Agadjanian 2017). Few official documents try to provide a definition. In 2015, the Russian government adopted a resolution, "On Approving the Strategy for the Development of Education in the Russian Federation for the Period until 2025," which included the following list of traditional values: humanity, justice, honor, conscience, will, personal dignity, belief in goodness, and the desire to fulfill a moral duty to yourself, your family, and your Fatherland (Strategiia razvitiia vospitaniia 2015). The National Security Strategy of the Russian Federation of 2015 refers to a slightly different set of ideals: human life, rights and liberties, family, work, patriotism, moral standards, humanism, charity, mutual assistance, collectivism, the historical unity of Russia's peoples, and the historical continuity of the homeland (Strategiia natsional'noi bezopasnosti 2015, cited in Rousselet 2020, 47). Yet another official document, the Declaration of Values of the Union of the States of Russia and Belarus of 2018, provides the following list: faith, life, love, justice, solidarity, mercy, dignity, power, nation, patriotism, freedom, responsibility, moderation, unity, service, loyalty, and family (Deklaratsiia Tsennostej Soyuznogo Gosudarstva 2018). This last list is followed by a clarification: "Many of these values were proposed by His Holiness Patriarch Kirill of Moscow and All Russia as the basis of national consciousness."

These various lists share, at the bottom line, a priority of collective aims over individual freedom, but how precisely this hierarchy is established and which aspects of social and political life are chosen to communicate this hierarchy differs between groups. Some of the concepts associated with traditional values recall former Soviet values, like solidarity and moderation; others political values, like power, nation, patriotism; others religious values, like faith and mercy; and yet others moral values, like loyalty, family, and love.

It is the last of these moral values, family, that appears as a central category of traditional values in the Russian context, one everybody seems to agree on. However, we find it important to stress that the reason for this convergence on the conservative family model is not only to be found in some intrinsic pro-family logic of Russian traditional spiritual and moral values; nor is it, as suggested by Valerie Sperling, a ubiquitous feature of gendered political legitimization strategies (Sperling 2015). The motivation for the prominence of the conservative family model inside Russian traditional-values conservatism is also to be found in the global culture wars. By the beginning of the twenty-first century, conservative family values had become a global, well-developed ideology with a whole arsenal of different sub-themes (pro-life, anti-gender rights), strategies (networking, conventions, lobbying) and sites of contestation (UN, Council of Europe, European Court of Human Rights). Russian pro-lifers, pro-family activists, and home-schoolers had only to pick up a ready-made global agenda and adapt it to the Russian context. By doing so, they had an advantage over Russian nationalists, patriots, monarchists, or those nostalgic of the Soviet period: they could tap into a powerful transnational network, they presented a positive message, and they had a contemporary, forward-looking appeal that many of the radical groups on the right lacked. And most of all, they could generate a broad consensus among religious groups inside and outside Russia.

The main benefactor of the conservative turn of the Kremlin was the Russian Orthodox Church. For many years it had been promoting the ideology of traditional values and had presented itself as the bearer of traditional spiritual and moral values; now, finally, the agenda that Patriarch Kirill had announced in *Nezavisimaya Gazeta* ten years earlier had found its way into politics. All the key public figures of the conservative turn after 2012 were in one way or the other connected to Orthodoxy: Patriarch Kirill himself; the priest Vsevolod Chaplin (1968–2020) during his time as chairman of the Synodal Department for the Cooperation of Church and Society; the priest Dmitry Smirnov (1951–2020) during his office as chairman of the Patriarchal Commission on Family; Elena Mizulina, chairman of the Duma Committee on Family, Women and Children Affairs; Vitaly Milonov, member of the Legislative Assembly of Saint Petersburg and Orthodox activist; and many others of the actors we discuss in the second part of the book. By 2012, the Orthodox activists finally got what they had been lacking the years before: an open ear in the government.

The Ideological Elements of the Russian Culture Wars

The spiritual-moral revival came along with ideological elements that have since defined the Russian culture wars. We single out four such elements: the concern for symbolic figures of purity, the identification of evil influencers from outside ("foreign agents"), moral anti-Westernism, and Russian messianism.

The first ideological element was the concern for symbolic figures of purity. Public policies in the name of traditional values were presented as ultimately about innocent and vulnerable members of society. These vulnerable elements—children, minors, believers, "the majority of Orthodox believers," "the simple Russian people" or "millions of simple Russians"— had to be defended against extremism and harmful influences. Several laws were adopted that aimed precisely at defending these symbolic figures of purity, such as the law against offending the religious feelings of believers (enacted July 1, 2013) and the law against propaganda promoting nontraditional family values and nontraditional sexual relations among children and minors (enacted June 30, 2013). The underlying logic of these laws was the same: certain figures in society are so innocent and sensitive that the authorities must protect them from harm; the turn toward traditional values is carried out for their sake. Traditionalists often speak in the name of "millions of simple Russians" or "the majority of Orthodox believers." These millions and majorities are opposed to the alien minorities, who in turn represent impurity and a threat to tradition.

Alien minorities constitute the second ideological element of the Russian culture wars—namely, the persecution of symbolic figures of moral decay. The concern for figures of moral purity goes hand in hand with the persecution of those who are perceived as symbolic threats to this purity. These figures of amorality are usually described as "loud minorities" who symbolize moral decay (for instance, homosexuals or the "LGBT-lobby") or are perceived as being responsible for such decay (for instance, liberals or NGOs). On November 21, 2012, the Russian government enacted a law against foreign agents. "Foreign agent," an expression that quickly became part of everyday speech, represents an individual or a group who is an agent of foreign (especially Western) influence and whose activities must be restricted, since these so-called agents seek to destroy Russian traditions by meddling in Russia's social and political affairs.

The third ideological element of the Russian culture wars is moral anti-Westernism. The West becomes the collective symbol of all possible sins and threats. According to Russia's anti-Western thinkers, such things as "immoral" liberalism, SOGI rights, and blasphemous contemporary art all derive from the West. Yet, this anti-Westernism has a clear transnational dimension. Russian conservatives often draw on so-called "depravity stories" (Höjdestrand 2017, 36); these are seemingly factual stories and reports about disastrous effects of social liberalism in the West: how homosexual couples adopt boys and allegedly raise them as girls or abuse them; how governments in some European countries cancel words like "mother" and "father" and exchange them for "parent 1" and "parent 2"; how sexual education corrupts children and puts them on of the path of licentious sexual behavior, and so on. There is nothing uniquely Russian to these stories—most of these have been circulating in conservative milieus in many different countries and languages, some for a long time already (some can be already found in the conservative manifesto *Listen, America!* [1981] by Jerry Falwell). Russian conservatives adopt these stories and make them part of Russian moral anti-Westernism, with an argument that goes routinely like this: Look what happens in the West, which totally surrendered to gender ideology and the agenda of LGBT+ rights. We must do our best to prevent this from happening in Russia; we must uproot the very seeds of these monstrous ideas.

Western civilization, as it is repetitively portrayed by the president and the patriarch, has lost its moral and religious (Christian) foundations; it legalizes sin and transforms itself into an apocalyptic image of "the king-dom of Sodom and Gomorra." This immoral West is portrayed as trying to seduce Russia, which, in turn, becomes the collective symbol of all that is righteous and virtuous. According to Russian traditionalists, Russian civilization, in contrast to Western civilization, still adheres to its religious foundations (tradition) and is the one remaining "stronghold of Christian morality" in the world. Within this Russian civilization, there is no place for antagonists, as all basic elements of this idealized Russia, the people, the state, and, of course, the church fit together harmoniously. Whoever is not in agreement with traditional values and the social consensus around the Russian civilizational model must be a foreign agent, motivated by alien motives. Moreover, this Russia has a mission not only to save itself from subversive influences, but also to help the West to overcome its current moral-spiritual dysfunction. Russia's new moral anti-Westernism, in other words, is no longer isolationist, but instead, expansive.

Russia's expansive anti-Westernism leads to the fourth ideological ele-ment of the Russian culture wars: messianism. While in domestic policy it is security that defines the logic of the Russian culture wars, in foreign policy this logic is dictated by the desire for status recognition and the search for counter-hegemonic strategies. According to Alicja Curanović, "the conservative turn in Russia's foreign policy should be viewed as a re-action to Russians' perception that they have failed to achieve the desired recognition as an equal to the major powers, in other words, the West" (Curanović 2019, 215). The end of the USSR

> reinforced Russia's sense of having been boxed into a corner after 1989, whereas it considered itself a partner in the new system of in-ternational politics. This in turn gave rise to the narrative of Western persecution, "Russophobia" and humiliation, reinforcing traditional narratives about the fundamental incompatibility between Russia and the West. (Sakwa 2017, 327)

This perceived nonrecognition drives Russia's attempts to challenge the he-gemony of the liberal international order and to become a force "to be reckoned with in the management of global affairs" (Sakwa 2017, 324). For the last two decades, the foreign-policy doctrine of the Kremlin has been oriented toward the search for some alternative-value foundation (Curanović 2015). The values that Russia eventually settled on are the values of transna-tional conservatism. This messianism stands in a long tradition of seeing

Russia as having a special mission in this world. What is new, however, is the content of this mission in the twenty-first century. Instead of leading the world to the ideals of communism and classless society, instead of fighting reactionary forces of religion and capitalism—the essence of Russia's mission in the twentieth century—, Russia has shifted to social conservatism and the defense of global "moral majority" against the powers of "godless immoral liberalism."

Public Opinion Surveys on Values and Religiosity

We conclude this chapter with an outlook on public-opinion survey data regarding shifts in religiosity and value orientation in Russian society. After the end of communism, Russian Orthodoxy experienced an undisputed revival. Survey data showed a clear rise in religious affiliation in Russia. The most striking survey data were produced by the International Social Survey Program and included in a widely cited Pew Research Center Report in 2014: according to this survey, in 1991, 31 percent of Russians identified as Orthodox, while 61 percent declared themselves unaffiliated. By 2008, these numbers had reversed, with 18 percent declaring themselves unaffiliated and 72 percent identifying as Orthodox (Pew Research Center 2014, 2017). What the empirical data also show is that self-identifying as Orthodox and as Russian by nationality are linked. Pew Research survey data reveal that 57 percent of respondents said that "being Orthodox" was important for being a "true" Russian (Pew Research Center 2017, 12), and even a quarter of the religiously unaffiliated people in Russia said it was important to be Russian Orthodox to be "truly Russian" (Lipka and Sahgal 2017).

Survey data suggest that Russian Orthodoxy as a marker of identity for society as a whole is attached more to value judgments than to religious practice, which remains at low levels of around 6 percent (Pew Research Center 2017). A clear conservative trend is visible regarding attitudes to gender rights. VCIOM, one of the leading Russian-opinion research centers, published striking figures that show the change in the public attitude to the possibility of same-sex marriages. In 2005, only 34 percent were totally against such marriages, while in 2015 this figure had increased to 70 percent. At the same time, the number of those who hesitated or tended to support same-sex marriage decreased from 31 percent to 14 percent (VTsIOM 2016, 165). These results are confirmed by other major research centers. Levada Center shows that acceptance of same-sex marriages dropped from 15 percent in 2005 to 7 percent in 2015, while rejection increased from 74 to 84 percent (those who are harshly against such marriages are 58 percent in 2015 as opposed to 45 percent back in 2005) (Levada Center 2015). The Public Opinion Foundation (FOM) gives figures for 2019: 85 percent were against same-sex marriage, as opposed to 7 percent who supported such marriages (Public Opinion Foundation 2019). FOM and Levada also show that there has been an increase in the general negative attitude to sexual minorities (answer to the question, "What is your personal attitude to homosexuals and lesbians?"): from 47 percent in 2006 to 55 percent in 2019 (Public Opinion Foundation 2019), from 48 percent in 2003 to 65 percent in 2015 (Levada Center 2015).[2] Pew Research Forum data likewise show that Russia today is among the countries with the lowest acceptance rate of homosexuality across the globe (Pew Research Center 2020).

The attitude to sexual minorities is not the only issue where the conservative turn is visible on the level of public opinion. A similar trend is registered in views concerning abortions. According to the Levada Center, as of 2017 the percentage of those who consider abortion inadmissible has increased from 12 to 35 percent for the last twenty years (Levada Center 2018). Our own calculations based on the European Values Survey confirm the trends just outlined. They also show that Russian society is, overall, more polarized on the questions of homosexuality and abortion today than it was back in 1999. However, the same is not true for other "items" on the conservative agenda, which the European Values Survey regularly tested between 1999 and 2017: the acceptance/rejection rates of practices such as divorce, euthanasia, and prostitution have not significantly changed in the past decades[3] (Pew Research Center 2017; Stoeckl 2020b).

These results show that social conservative and social progressive attitudes in Russia are in flux. The shifting attitudes on some items on the social conservative agenda (homosexuality, abortion) and the stability of others (divorce, euthanasia) are indicative of the fact that today's conservatism of traditional values is not a reflection of some intrinsic stable fea-

2. For Levada, we have combined answers of people whose attitude to sexual minorities is "suspicious," "irritated," and "disgustful or fearful."

3. Polarization was measured by comparing the mid-range answers to extreme answers ("never," "always"). We are grateful to our research assistant Hannah Jordan for the calculations based on the European Values Survey data of 1999 and 2017.

tures of Russian society per se, a broadly shared mentality that has always existed. Rather, it is a result of recent changes in Russian society and politics and the politicization of traditional family and gender norms. These changes are driven not just by national, but also transnational dynamics, and as of late they have become manifested in the Constitution of the Russian Federation.

By 2020, traditional values had transformed from a marginal worldview to the mainstream of Russian domestic politics, a trend that culminated in the new text of the Russian Constitution. In July 2020, the amendment to the Russian Constitution—first proposed by President Vladimir Putin in January, smoothly approved by the State Duma and Constitutional Court in March, and confirmed in a nationwide referendum with 78.56 percent of the votes—took effect. The amended Russian Constitution contains a commitment to traditional family values and precludes the possibility of future legislative changes for the recognition of same-sex marriage. The proposal to define marriage as a heterosexual union was made by Konstantin Malofeev, the head of the conservative Saint Basil the Great Foundation and, since 2018, vice president of the right-wing World Russian People's Council. Malofeev, whose role as sponsor of Russian pro-family groups will be analyzed in Chapter 6, suggested that the constitution should define marriage as being between a man and a woman to create a barrier to the legalization of same-sex marriages (Interfax 2020). He was immediately echoed favorably by the press speaker of the Moscow Patriarchate, Vladimir Legoida, who added that the phrase "traditional family values" should be enshrined in the constitution (Ria Novosti 2020). Both additions found their way into the amended constitution. Paragraph 72 now includes the "defense of the institution of marriage as a union of man and woman," and paragraph 114 mentions the "preservation of traditional family values" among the goals of the Russian Federation. The main purpose of the amendment was to secure Putin the possibility of two more terms in office. But the constitutional amendments also had the effect of introducing traditional-values conservatism into the most important document of the Russian Federation. Russian Orthodox social conservatives and defenders of traditional values were successful in having their priorities reflected in the constitution of 2020.

PART II

DOING THE CULTURE WARS

Russia is a bulwark of Christian values throughout the world and has a special role in the struggle for traditional family values. This is how Alexey Komov, the leader of the Russian chapter of the World Congress of Families, explains it to his audience. Bolshevism was a Western imposition on the Russian people aimed at destroying family values and national unity by introducing feminism and the right to abortion. The Russian people were saved by Stalin, who repressed the progressive Trotskyists and reinstalled patriarchal authority and patriotic values. "Stalin," Komov says, "brought down a destructive revolutionary wave. For this reason, the ideologists of Marxism moved to the West" (AVA 2014). In the West, so the narrative continues, the Trotskyists embraced the program of Antonio Gramsci of a "long march through the institutions" and are now attempting to destroy the traditional family through popular culture and the dissemination of progressive ideas—in particular, the idea of gender. "This happened," Komov explains, "largely due to the activities of the so-called Frankfurt School of Neo-Marxism, which operated in the 1920s–1940s. The theorists of this school (Marcuse, Adorno, Horkheimer, Fromm) combined the ideas of Marx with Freudianism and gave rise to the concept of the sexual revolution of the 1960s" (AVA 2014). Western democracies and international bodies like the United Nations and the European Union, as well as the philanthropists George Soros and Bill and Melinda Gates, are cited by Komov as the agents of this strategy. He cautions his audience against considering the West as an ideological monolith: "In the West, there are liberals and conservatives. Western liberals are socialists and atheists, while conservatives advocate private initiative and Christian and family values." And he ends, "Russia has a real historical chance to become the universally recognized leader of this nascent 'pro-family' movement and regain ideological and moral leadership in geopolitics" (AVA 2014).

This highly problematic rewriting of the ideological history of the twentieth century combines a series of Christian Right ideas—elaborated in the context of the American culture wars—with a positive evaluation of Stalin and the post-Stalinist period. Joseph Vissiaronovich Stalin (1878–1953), just to be very clear, was the general secretary of the Communist Party of the Soviet Union from 1922 until his death. He was responsible for the "great purges" of the 1930s that cost the lives of many hundreds of thousands of Soviet citizens, he was in charge when the Soviet Union defeated Nazi Germany, and he brought large parts of Central and Eastern Europe under communist rule after WWII. Stalin was a communist. So how can a Russian conservative of the twenty-first century be, at one and the same time, anti-communist and pro-Stalin? The "trick" is the identification of communism exclusively with what Americans also refer to as "cultural Marxism." In the eyes of radical Russian conservatives, Stalin is even "saved" from the assessment of atheism, against all odds, because he reopened the churches during the war. In this way, a Russian conservative like Komov can describe himself as anti-communist and pro-Stalinist at the same time. Even inside the Russian Orthodox Church, a positive reevaluation of Stalin is—though not official—not unfrequent. Vis-à-vis a Russian audience, which is already used to a positive public image of Stalin from the annual "Victory celebrations" (marking the victory of the Soviet Union over Nazi Germany, celebrated on May 9), this highly problematic rewriting of the ideological history of the twentieth century is a powerful narrative, because it presents Russia as the true winner of Cold War history. The Soviet Union may have lost the Cold War, but—just like Russia won WWII—it will win the culture wars!

"Doing the culture wars" is the title of Part II of this monograph, where we analyze in four chapters how the Russian Orthodox Church, Russian civil society organizations, and the Russian state start to act as moral conservative-norm entrepreneurs. Their ambitions, networks, strategies, and leadership shape the global culture wars.

CHAPTER

5

AMBITIONS

THE RUSSIAN ORTHODOX CHURCH
AND ITS TRANSNATIONAL CONSERVATIVE ALLIANCES

In Western media, commentators and journalists usually trace Russia's conservative turn back to the Russian government and its instrumental use of religion. The most-told storyline is that the state is using Russian Orthodoxy to pursue socially repressive policy goals domestically and geopolitically reassertive and revisionist goals internationally: "Is Vladimir Putin trying to build a new Orthodox empire?" (Keating 2014), "Putin's Unorthodox Orthodoxy" (Demacopoulos and Papanikolau 2014), "Putin's God Squad" (Pomerantsev 2012), and "Putin's Useful Idiots" (Püttmann 2014) are just some of the titles that made headlines between 2012 and 2014. A video report by *Deutsche Welle* appropriately summed up the sense of disorientation: "Is the Russian Orthodox Church Serving God or Putin?" (DW News 2017). In this chapter, we analyze how the Russian Orthodox Church has developed its profile as moral conservative player in the international context and show that its role is actually more complicated—and less predictable—than the popular storyline of the church as a handmaiden of the Russian state suggests.

We have already shown how among the sources of Russian social conservatism, Russian Orthodoxy is only one, albeit important, source and that transnational influences and the Soviet legacy also play an important role. It was the church's conservative *aggiornamento* that eventually allowed the Russian state to present itself as the defender of traditional values in its domestic policies and external relations and that provided inspiration and connecting points for Christian conservatives inside and outside Russia. However, even though the Orthodox Church effectively may have spearheaded the Russian conservative turn, internal divisions and state policies on religious freedom have put restrictions on the transnational conservative agenda of the Moscow Patriarchate. If Patriarch Kirill of Moscow ever had the ambition to become the new spiritual leader of the global Christian Right, by now it is clear that in the public imaginary this role has fallen to Vladimir Putin—perhaps a defeat for the Russian Orthodox Church.

The Conservative *Aggiornamento* of the Russian Orthodox Church's Human Rights Discourse

The roots of the discourse on traditional values, so pervasive in the present-day Russian context, lie partly outside Russia and outside of the Russian Orthodox tradition—namely, in American evangelicals' proselytizing activities in Russia prior to 1997 and in the Soviet legacy of "The Moral Code of the Builder of Communism." These sources represent two religious and philosophical legacies that traditional Russian Orthodoxy abhors: Protestant Western Christianity and godless Communism. The question is therefore how the fit between Russian Orthodoxy and these other two conceptual legacies became possible. How could these three versions of social conservatism coalesce around a single notion of traditional values?

The answer lies in the conservative *aggiornamento* of the Russian Orthodox Church. The church entered the post-communist period facing enormous internal and external challenges. For one thing, it experienced an undisputed revival. Thousands of church buildings and religious artifacts were restituted to the church by the state, monasteries reopened, many Russians discovered the Orthodox faith, symbols of Orthodoxy proliferated in the public space, and the church restored its role as the representative of public religion in the eyes of Russian citizens (Burgess 2017; Stoeckl 2020b). At the same time, in terms of religious teaching, the church was poorly prepared to address modern life challenges and needed to catch up in almost all areas of pastoral work.

The publication of the document *Bases of the Social Concept of the Russian Orthodox Church* (Social Doctrine 2000) was widely interpreted as a first step in this direction. In particular, Catholic observers looked for parallels between the Second Vatican Council—which had started the new era of *aggiornamento* for the Catholic Church—and the Bishops Council of the Russian Orthodox Church of 2000 (Uertz and Schmidt 2004). Among the central points of the Catholic *aggiornamento* fifty years earlier, there had been freedom of conscience and religious freedom. The Second Vatican Council's document *Dignitatis Humanae* broke with the old ideal of a state religion. Instead, it accepted individual freedom of conscience as God-given and viewed tolerance vis-à-vis other religions positively and in line with Christ's message of nonviolence. On a basic level, *Dignitatis Humanae* cleared away the problems between the Catholic Church and democratic society (Ludwig 2004). The Social Doctrine of the Russian Orthodox Church did not go so far. It retained a negative assessment of religious freedom as a sign of apostasy.

Eight years later, however, the church revised its teaching on religious freedom in the document *The Russian Orthodox Church's Teaching on Human Dignity, Freedom and Rights* (Human Rights Doctrine 2008). In the book *The Russian Orthodox Church and Human Rights* (Stoeckl 2014), one of us has analyzed in considerable detail the process by which the church's teaching on religious freedom shifted from the initial rejection and condemnation to a principled recognition. However, this recognition of freedom of conscience and religious freedom by the Russian Orthodox Church was couched in a discourse on morality and traditional values, which effectively aimed at defining limits to freedoms—only that these limits were no longer described in terms of apostasy, sin, and salvation, but in terms of traditional values and rights.

The conservative *aggiornamento* of the Russian Orthodox Church consisted in the endorsement of the human rights discourse within the limits of a rigid definition of morality and traditional values. For this rigid definition, the drafters inside the Moscow Patriarchate tried to draw on the Universal Declaration of Human Rights itself. At a seminar entitled, "The Evolution of Moral Principles and Human Rights in Multicultural Society" in Strasbourg on October 30–31, 2006, today's Patriarch Kirill—at the time Metropolitan and speaker of the External Relations Department of the Russian Orthodox Church—said:

> I am convinced that the concern for spiritual needs, based moreover on traditional morality, ought to return to the public realm. The upholding of moral standards must become a social cause. It is the mechanism of human rights that can actively enable this return. I am speaking of a return, for the norm of according human rights with traditional morality can be found in the Universal Declaration of Human Rights of 1948. (Metropolitan Kirill 2006)

The norm to which Kirill is referring here is Article 29 of the Universal Declaration of Human Rights.[1] Article 29 mentions "duties to the community" and "just requirements of morality" as possible restrictions for the freedoms granted to individuals through the instrument of human rights. The point was corroborated once more two years after the publication of the Human Rights Doctrine by Metropolitan Hilarion (Alfeyev):

> It should be noted that the postwar human rights instruments did reflect the connection between freedom and moral responsibility. The Universal Declaration of Human Rights from 1948 and the European Declaration of Human Rights and Fundamental Freedoms from 1950 speak about the connection between human rights and morality. It is in later international acts such as the Charter of Fundamental Rights of the European Union from 2000 that the connection between human rights and morality is not mentioned. Freedom is therefore completely divorced from morality. (ROC 2010c)

What these two quotations show is that by 2010, the leadership of the Russian Orthodox Church had acquired a clear understanding of the human rights universe that Russia (and the Russian Orthodox Church) had entered when the Russian Federation joined the Council of Europe in 1996. Consequently, it settled on a new approach for dealing with human rights claims: instead of rejecting them, the church responded in rights terms. Alexander Agadjanian has aptly spoken about "acceptance through rejection" (Agadjanian 2010).

If we recall for a moment Habermas's definition of "modernization of religious consciousness" from chapter 1—(1) "Religious citizens must develop an epistemic attitude toward other religions and world views that they encounter within a universe of discourse hitherto occupied only by their own religion" (Habermas 2006, 14)—then it becomes clear that by 2008 the Russian Orthodox Church had really undergone an epistemic shift. From the rejection of the right to freedom of conscience, the church's stance

---

1. (1) Everyone has duties to the community in which the free and full development of his personality is possible. (2) In the exercise of his rights and freedoms, everyone shall be subject only to such limitations as are determined by law solely for the purpose of securing due recognition and respect for the rights and freedoms of others and of meeting the just requirements of morality, public order, and the general welfare in a democratic society (UDHR 1948, emphasis added).

had moved to an acceptance of modern freedoms but within the limits of a public morality dictated by the traditional values of a society.

According to Hegumen Philaret Bulekov, the Patriarchate's representative in Strasbourg at the time of the publication of the Human Rights Doctrine, the Russian Orthodox Church does not condemn human rights but, rather, seeks to enrich them:

> Offering her own interpretation of human rights and freedoms based on religious ideas, the Church enters as a rightful participant in the lively discussion which is underway on national and international levels and thus becomes a cause for continued evolution of the human rights concept. This involvement of the Church, just as other religious communities, reflects the present stage in this evolution. Because today any discussion on human rights cannot take place only in the "secular irreligious space," considering especially the fact that most of the people on our planet are still religious people. (Quoted in Rimestad 2015, 39)

It is important to understand that this conservative *aggiornamento* has allowed the official Russian Orthodox discourse to incorporate the two rival sources of social conservatism: the American Christian Right and the Soviet legacy. Orthodox traditionalism, family values as preached by American Evangelicals, and the deontology of "The Moral Code of the Builder of Communism" could all blend into the concept of traditional values of society. But maybe even more importantly, the conservative *aggiornamento* led the church to effectively identify as the "enemy" not the international human rights regime as such, not the West as such, not the Enlightenment, nor yet the Catholic and Protestant churches, but the progressive human-rights regime, cultural liberalism, liberal Christians, and secularists. Likewise, the church identified its potential allies, among them American Evangelicals and even ex-communists.

The conservative *aggiornamento*, in short, inserted the Russian Orthodox Church into the discursive and political space of the global culture wars. Today's global culture wars are, to a large extent, conflicts between a progressive, egalitarian approach to human rights and a restrictive, conservative approach that aims to keep human rights out of certain areas of human conduct, such as the family, education, and sexuality. In the eyes of moral conservatives, these areas should remain the domain of laws and mores of specific human communities and not of universal human rights. Universal human rights egalitarianism looks at individuals irrespective of context and status; it "unpacks," so to say, the family, educational standards, and sexual mores and holds them accountable to a universal standard of individual rights and freedoms. For conservatives, this is unacceptable—and what is more, they feel threatened by it. The following quote by American law professor Mark Movsesian summarizes the anxiety of conservatives in front of the expanding international human rights regime very well:

> On the global stage, Western advocates define international human rights in an increasingly progressive way, especially on issues of gender and sexuality. Traditionalist Christians like the Russian Orthodox could genuinely think that their worldviews are quickly becoming inadmissible in human-rights fora. How long will it be, they may wonder, before same-sex marriage is declared an international human right, and countries that refuse to endorse it are labeled human-rights pariahs? (Movsesian 2017)

In order to prevent the expansion of human rights, conservatives argue that areas like family, education, or sexuality, should—in the words of the Metropolitan—"be accorded with traditional morality." What they mean by that is that human conduct and the assessment of what counts as "good behavior" can (and should) be made to conform to views grounded in concrete communities, their habits, and practices, and in religious teachings and traditions.

Traditional morality, as used by the Russian Orthodox Church from the mid-2000s onward, comes to signify past practice rather than a precise social teaching (on this point, see also Chapnin 2020). This conceptual redefinition of traditional morality has allowed the church to integrate different genealogies of social conservatism into its advocacy for traditional values, whether "The Moral Code of the Communist Builder," the "Judaeo-Christian values" promoted by Focus on the Family in the early 1990s, traditional Russian Islam and Buddhism, or Orthodox religious nationalism. It was this redefinition of traditional morality that created the precondition for Russia to become a player in the global culture wars. We provide two case studies that exemplify this dynamic: the collaborations of the Moscow Patriarchate with the Vatican and with the Billy Graham Evangelistic Church. In Chapter 8, we also show how the Russian Orthodox Church has used its refined understanding of traditional values and human rights in foreign-policy initiatives coordinated with Russian state diplomacy.

The Short-Lived "Holy Alliance" between the Russian Orthodox Church and the Catholic Church

Interfaith collaboration between like-minded religious actors at the expense of denominational loyalties is a common feature of conservative norm-mobilization and the American culture wars (Hunter 1991, 86–88). From a Russian Orthodox perspective, however, the interfaith collaboration between conservative religious actors (Orthodox, Catholic, Protestant, Evangelical, Jewish, Muslim, Buddhist) constitutes a novelty, because it entails the Orthodox Church overcoming age-old prejudice against Latin Christians and other faith traditions.

For Russian Orthodox conservatives, collaboration is possible as long as theological questions are set aside. The archpriest of the Russian Orthodox Church, Vsevolod Chaplin (1968–2020), even said, "To be honest, I believe that many Catholics and certainly most Protestants do not actually worship the true God, I mean the God we know from the Bible and from the teachings of the church" (Interview 2018h). This is a remarkable statement from a man who was for a long time the vice speaker of the Department of External Church Relations of the Moscow Patriarchate and the head of the Department for Relations between Church and Society. He went on, however: "But we can have a dialogue. We can cooperate. . . . We must speak out together about how our state works, about the place of faith in politics, about the place of Christian values in law and public decision-making. This is where we can find a lot in common" (Interview 2018h). Chaplin was not alone with this assessment. It is the official line of the Moscow Patriarchate (Interreligious Council 2017) and dictates how the Russian Orthodox Church collaborates with other religious groups inside Russia, with the Catholic Church, and with Protestant churches.

The idea of "Holy Alliance" between the Russian Orthodox Church and the Roman Catholic Church against secularism was born at the end of 2009 and the beginning of 2010. It therefore falls precisely into the period that we identify for the church's conservative *aggiornamento*. In 2009, Patriarch Kirill had just become the new Patriarch of Moscow after the death of Alexey II. For years, he had been the motor behind the new tendencies inside the Russian Orthodox Church in terms of social teaching; he had overseen the process of working out the church's *Social Doctrine* and *Human Rights Doctrine*; he had repeated the argument on traditional morality against individual human rights again and again in his speeches; he had founded the representation of the Russian Orthodox Church to the European Institutions in Strasbourg, the website of which was called "orthodoxeurope .org."[2] Together with Metropolitan Hilarion (Alfeyev), his successor as the head of the Department for External Church Relations, they had great plans for the church.

Inside the Vatican editor Robert Moynihan was so much moved by reading Metropolitan Hilarion's introduction to the Russian-Italian edition of speeches by Joseph Ratzinger as cardinal and pope that he announced that "Rome-Moscow relations begin [a] new era" (Moynihan 2010). In this introduction, Hilarion set forth his vision for the role of the Russian Orthodox Church in Europe:

> The Russian Orthodox Church, with its unique experience of surviving the harshest persecutions, struggling against militant atheism, reemerging from the ghetto when the political situation changed, recovering its place in society and redefining its social responsibilities, can . . . be of help to Europe. The totalitarian dictatorship of the past cannot be replaced with a new dictatorship of pan-European government mechanisms. . . . The countries of Orthodox tradition, for example, do not accept laws that legalize euthanasia, homosexual marriage, drug trafficking, the maintenance of brothels, pornography, and so on. (Cited in Moynihan 2010)

Conservatives in the West who resented the success of social progressive causes in their societies could find a kindred spirit in these words. In fact, Hilarion's invitation came just around the time when conservative Christian leaders in the United States issued the *Manhattan Declaration* (2009), "pledging renewed zeal in defending the unborn, defining marriage as a union between a man and a woman, and protecting religious freedom" (cited in Moynihan 2010). The announcement of a Holy Alliance—a term apparently coined by the Italian journalist Sandro Magister (Magister 2010)—sounded like a call to arms against post-Christian humanism, against secularism, and for a new evangelization of Europe. It was also a call to arms against the achievements of the Catholic *aggiornamento*—the results of the Second Vatican Council, which some conservative Catholics

2. This website went out of use in 2010, but it is still available online. It was replaced by the website of the Department for External Church Relations (mospat.ru), which contains content in multiple languages.

would prefer to wind back sooner rather than later. The Russian Orthodox Church, in short, had now definitely joined the culture wars.

Around the same time, the Saint Gregory the Theologian Charitable Foundation was established in Moscow. The aim of the foundation was to assist the Department of External Church Relations, and especially its head Metropolitan, Hilarion. The executive director of the foundation, Leonid Sevastianov, became responsible for establishing ties with Catholic conservatives in the United States. "We want your help, the help of Catholics, and of Western Europeans and Americans," he is quoted by Moynihan. "We want to try to attract the attention of religious believers, in Russia and abroad, who believe in traditional Christian values, and who want to contribute to making society more just and more moral" (Moynihan 2010). In the context of the analysis in this book, Sevastianov's call for help on behalf of the Moscow Patriarchate is reminiscent of the situation of the early 1990s, when the disoriented ex-Soviet state administration invited Focus on the Family to teach about family, but it also shows that the Russian Orthodox Church has moved on. By 2010, the church was no longer looking for teachers, but for allies in a battle that it had the ambition to lead.

The plan to attract the attention of religious believers abroad and Sevastianov's efforts to connect with wealthy Christian conservative sponsors in the United States proved effective, at least on the financial level. The annual reports of the Lynde and Harry Bradley Foundation show that the Saint Gregory the Theologian Charitable Foundation was awarded a total of 825,000 U.S. dollars between 2009 and 2013 "to support a series of educational and cultural initiatives."[3] The initiatives of the foundation—in order of appearance on its website[4]—include its support for the activities of the Department of External Church Relations of the Russian Orthodox

---

3. This sum is the result of research on publicly available sources: the Annual Report of the Bradley Foundation 2013 ($75,000 U.S.) is available on the foundation's website, the Annual Reports of the Bradley Foundation for the years 2009 ($150,000 U.S.) and 2010 ($300,000 U.S.) can be downloaded from issuelab (https://www .issuelab.org/resources/10147/10147.pdf; https://www.issuelab.org/resources/13081/13081 .pdf), the data for 2011 ($200,000 U.S.) and 2012 ($100,000 U.S.) are reported at https:// www.sourcewatch.org/index.php?title=Contributions_of_the_Bradley_Foundation (all accessed February 25, 2020).

4. The website exists only in Russian: http://www.fondgb.ru/ (accessed February 25, 2020).

Church, its support for the Saints Cyril and Methodius Theological Institute for Post-Graduate Studies of the Russian Orthodox Church, the restoration of the Patriarchal Residence in the center of Moscow, the pro-life organization "Let's Save Life Together" (*Sokhranim zhizn' vmeste*), the publication of free New Testaments and psalm books in the Russian language, the choir of the Moscow Patriarchate, a research award in the humanities, and other cultural programs. From 2010 until 2018, the foundation published the journal *Orthodox Conversation* (*Pravoslavnaya Beceda*), and it produced feature films with the spiritual director of the foundation, Metropolitan Hilarion. The Lynde and Harry Bradley Foundation is listed among its partners, being the only non-Russian partner in the list, and Moynihan also documents a visit to Moscow with a collaborator of the Bradley Foundation (Moynihan 2009).

Moynihan even tried to follow up on the successes of the Saint Gregory the Theologian Foundation, and in 2013, together with the Bradley Foundation and Aid to the Church of the U.S. Bishops' Conference, he announced the creation of a new foundation, the Urbi et Orbi Foundation. Its aim was to help create a strategic alliance among Christians in "defense of the Christian West" (Moynihan 2013). Moynihan mentioned that the Saint Gregory the Theologian Foundation had collected "some $50 million from leading Orthodox Russians . . . used to rebuild Russian Orthodox theological academies, but a certain amount will be available for specific common project with our new Foundation" (Moynihan 2013). However, at time of writing, the Urbi and Orbi Foundation was still collecting its first one hundred founding sponsors.[5]

The John Templeton Foundation also started to collaborate with the Russian Orthodox Church in educational and research programs in this period. Between 2016 and 2018, Templeton's "New Generation of Leaders for the Russian Orthodox Church program" granted 1.5 million U.S. dollars to the Saints Cyril and Methodius Theological Institute for Post-Graduate Studies of the Russian Orthodox Church through the Saint Gregory the Theologian Charitable Foundation (Templeton 2020a). And in the years prior to that, the "Expanding Scientific Training for Religious Leaders" program financed the Saint Gregory the Theologian Charitable Foundation to carry out "a three-year plan to train future theology professors

5. The call for sponsors is posted on the website *Inside the Vatican*: https://inside thevatican.com/product/urbi-et-orbi-foundation/.

and bishops in how to engage their theology with contemporary science and philosophy" (Templeton 2020b).[6] In all these activities, the Saint Gregory the Theologian Charitable Foundation functions as financial administrator of the incoming grants, since in 2012 Russia passed a law that obliges organizations receiving funding from abroad to register as "foreign agents." Technically, this would also apply to the Russian Orthodox Church, which therefore cannot figure as a direct grant recipient.

Despite these impressive numbers, the Moscow Patriarchate undertook only a few concrete initiatives to follow up on the announcements of a strategic alliance between the Russian Orthodox Church and the Catholic Church made by Metropolitan Hilarion in 2009 and reiterated on the pages of *Inside the Vatican* in 2013. For the Catholic Church, the situation changed dramatically with the abdication of Pope Benedict XVI in 2013 and the election of Pope Francis I. The relationship between the Russian Orthodox Church and the Vatican under Pope Francis is not as close as it was under the pope's predecessor, and there is no more sign of a strategic, let alone a "holy," alliance. Pope Francis has made it very clear that he is not interested in supporting strategic alliances in the global culture wars. On the contrary, the editor of the important Roman Catholic journal *Civiltà Cattolica*, the Jesuit Antonio Spadaro called such alliances "an ecumenism of hate" (Spadaro and Figueroa 2017). For the Russian Orthodox Church, too, the situation has changed dramatically: The annexation of Crimea by Russia in 2014, the ongoing war in Eastern Ukraine, and the creation of an autocephalous Orthodox Church in Ukraine against the will of the Moscow Patriarchate in 2019 have put a strain on interfaith East-West relations and weakened the current leadership of the church.

The precariousness of the Russian Orthodox–Catholic relationship became evident in 2016, when the meeting between Patriarch Kirill and Pope Francis in Havana caused unprecedented protests against the patriarch by Russian anti-ecumenists. The meeting between the two church leaders on February 12, 2016, at the Havana airport in Cuba was the first meeting of a Russian patriarch and the Catholic pontifex in history. Their dialogue was mainly devoted to global problems in modern society—in particular,

6. For reasons of transparency, we want to state that we cooperated with the Saints Cyril and Methodius Theological Institute for Post-Graduate Studies of the Russian Orthodox Church in the context of the "Expanding Scientific Training" program in 2013–14.

to the persecution of Christians in the Middle East, the crisis of the family in modern society, military-political conflict, and the religious situation in Ukraine. The Joint Statement between Pope Francis and Patriarch Kirill at this meeting was completely in line with the Moscow Patriarchate's ambition to be an agenda setter on social conservatism. The patriarch concluded the meeting with the statement that "currently the two Churches can cooperate, by defending Christians throughout the world, and they can work together . . . that the foundation of personal, familial and social morality be reinforced" (Vatican 2016). Havana was, to a certain extent, a success for the Russian Orthodox Church—but only in its external relations.

Inside the church, the event caused a storm of protests from anti-ecumenical fundamentalists. The patriarch was criticized by a group of religious nationalists called the "People's Council," a movement with close links to military and paramilitary forces and with branches in almost all Russian regions. According to Boris Knorre (Knorre 2018), the backbone of this movement in the spring of 2016 was made up of military volunteers from the two separatist regions in Eastern Ukraine, the People's Republic of Donetsk, and the People's Republic of Lugansk. The People's Council organized several events dedicated to the implications of the Havana meeting, where some participants debated whether to still commemorate Patriarch Kirill during the liturgy or whether to stop commemorating him because he was a "heretic," while others raised the issue of convening of a local council that should reform the church. Another organization analyzed by Knorre, the "Council of Orthodox Citizens," actually decided to no longer commemorate Patriarch Kirill at Divine Services and to consider the Russian Orthodox Church of the Moscow Patriarchate a "heretic community." The leader of the Council of Orthodox Citizens stopped calling Patriarch Kirill by his clerical title and name and referred to him merely by his civil surname (Gundyaev). Knorre identified at least three more fundamentalist groups who temporarily broke with the patriarch over his meeting with the pope in Havanna. All these fundamentalist movements shared a distinctly nationalistic ideology. One critic of the patriarch, for example, called the meeting of the patriarch with the Vatican "a threat to the sovereignty of the country." He saw the "national security" of Russia at risk and called for the FSB (the Russian intelligence service) to intervene and "defend Orthodoxy" (Knorre 2018; see also Shishkov 2017). By 2016, therefore, the strategic Orthodox-Catholic alliance against secularism and for the defense of the Christian West had, from the Russian side, started to disintegrate into confusion.

Also on the Western side, however, Catholic support for the Russian Orthodox Church waned. In the United States, the question of Ukraine divided the conservative Catholic supporters of the Moscow Patriarchate. George Weigel, one of the signatories of the Manhattan Declaration, cautioned against cooperation with Russia: "Rome must refuse to bend to the Putin storyline," he wrote in 2017 (Weigel 2017). After the annexation of Crimea and the war in Eastern Ukraine, the conservative magazine *First Things* initially disavowed the Russian Orthodox Church by publishing two highly critical articles by former insiders of the Moscow Patriarchate: "The Church in the Bloodlands," by Cyril Hovorun (2014) and "A Church of Empire," by Sergej Chapnin (2015). *First Things* eventually returned, however, to an editorial line supportive of Russian Orthodoxy, if not of the Russian Orthodox Church. The publication of an article by the Russian novelist Evgeniy Vodolazkin (2017) and the discussion of Alexander Dugin as "potential *First Things* author" (Reno 2017) by the editor R. R. Reno signaled that not all conservative Catholics in the United States were willing to give up on Russia as an ally in the culture wars (Reno 2020).

The Moscow Patriarchate and the Billy Graham Evangelistic Association

Catholics aside, there were other Christians in the West with whom the Moscow Patriarchate could weave a network for the support of traditional values. One of these actors was the Billy Graham Evangelistic Association. Relationships between Russians and American evangelicals extend back more than three decades to Billy Graham's well-publicized visit to Russia in the mid-1980s (Jenkins 2018). In October 2015, the current president of the association, Franklin Graham, visited Moscow and met Patriarch Kirill. Half a year later, they announced—in a joint press release—that the Russian Orthodox Church and the Billy Graham Evangelistic Association would hold a World Summit in Defense of Persecuted Christians in October 2016 in Moscow. The summit, they explained, was meant as a response to "the mass persecution of Christians of the Middle East, Africa and other regions in the world, unprecedented in modern history," but also as support for Western Christians who opposed the legalization of same-sex marriage and stood for "Christian moral values" as "confessors of the faith living under various kinds of pressure" (quoted in Shishkov 2017, 76).

However, the World Summit did not take place in Moscow as planned but in the United States. Shishkov gives two explanations for why the event was moved. One is that the Moscow Patriarchate did not want to create another precedent for an anti-ecumenical outcry after the Havana meeting. He quotes Yuri Sipko, the former president of the Russian Union of Evangelical Christians-Baptists, who suggested that the Moscow Patriarchate had canceled the summit under pressure from anti-ecumenical critics (Shishkov 2017, 77). The other explanation is the one given by Franklin Graham himself—namely, that the American partners refused to hold the summit in Russia after the Russian Federation's July 2016 passage of the Yarovaya Laws, which included "anti-evangelism" and "anti-missionary" provisions (Shishkov 2017, 78). Graham wrote, "We were looking forward to this significant event being held in Russia because no one knows modern Christian persecution better than the church that suffered under communist rule. However, just a few weeks ago Russia passed a law that severely limits Christians' freedoms" (Graham 2016). The relocated summit took place in Washington, D.C., in May 2017 and drew more than 800 participants from 136 countries. The patriarch did not attend, but Metropolitan Hilarion headed the Russian Orthodox Church's delegation.

Conservative Ecumenism

In the context of our analysis, the two case studies of contacts between the Moscow Patriarchate and the Catholic Church and American Evangelicals are only one part of the larger picture, which also includes the civil society networks and diplomatic relations that we discuss in the next chapters. However, the church relations are somewhat special, because they take place in the highly regulated world of religious diplomacy. In this world, the ambitions of the Patriarch of Moscow to become a leader in the global culture wars met obstacles of an internal, as well as external, nature.

Shishkov (2017) has described the collaboration between the Russian Orthodox Church and conservative Christians from the West as "conservative ecumenism" because, in contrast to classical ecumenism, this interfaith collaboration does not address issues of doctrine—questions of theology are set aside in such contacts—but issues of ideological affinity. Conservative ecumenism assumes that inside all Christian churches we find progressive and conservative groups that compete in terms of their social and political teaching and influence (see also Cohen 2019). In the event of competition between different ideological wings inside a church, actors can look for cooperation with like-minded actors outside of their faith community to increase their influence—both on society and on decisionmakers inside their own churches. The example of the World Congress of Families, which we discuss in Chapter 6, shows that the strategy of seeking international exposure for greater influence inside one's own church can work: after years of a relative marginal existence as a religious NGO, the Russian section of the World Congress of Families eventually managed to get its position on domestic violence adopted as the official position of the Moscow Patriarchate.

For the Moscow Patriarchate itself, however, the strategy of conservative ecumenism had a more mixed outcome. First, it provoked loud criticism on the part of Orthodox anti-ecumenists and fundamentalists, weakening the position of the patriarch inside the church. Second, the church had difficulties delivering on the expectations of its foreign partners because state policies—as in the case of the Yarovaya laws—counteracted its initiatives. The conflict in Ukraine created a crisis of trust in Russia among conservative Christians in the West, which weakened the influence of the Moscow Patriarchate. But there was arguably a third reason that the strategy of conservative ecumenism had an undesired outcome for the Moscow Patriarchate. In the context of the global culture wars today, it is not Patriarch Kirill nor the Russian Orthodox Church that is seen as the new defender of traditional Christian values, but Vladimir Putin. How did this happen?

We have shown in Chapter 4 how Putin endorsed the conservative agenda of traditional values at the beginning of his third term as Russian president in 2012. He effectively took over the discourse on traditional morality against individual human rights that the Russian Orthodox Church had created in the decade before and started to implement it. During the first six months of this presidency, he signed two landmark laws that caught the attention of conservatives in the West: penalties for the offense of religious feelings and penalties for the public display of symbols of gay lifestyle. This robust defense of traditional values amounted to a slap in the face for Western human rights NGOs and institutions like the European Court of Human Rights and the Council of Europe, which issued warning statements. Conservative Christians in the West—in particular, in the

United States—were impressed. Putin came to stand for something conservatives in the West very much desired: national self-determination
(Caldwell 2017).

It is important to remember that during those years, the years of the
presidency of Barack Obama (2009 until 2017), American conservatives
had become increasingly convinced that they had "lost the culture wars"
(Dreher 2020a, 24, 2017a). By 2016, with the U.S. Supreme Court cases
like *Obergefell*[7] and *Masterpiece Cakeshop*,[8] conservatives felt under siege
and looked for reinforcements (Movsesian 2017; Dreher 2017b, 2017a). In
2017, however, with the election of Donald Trump as president of the
United States, the situation for conservative Christians in the United States
changed again. They now had their own president, who was defiant of the
international human rights regime and willing to pursue a social conservative agenda on issues of abortion, transgender rights, and education. That
the election of Donald Trump came with well-founded suspicion that Russia had meddled with the election did not really create a dilemma for the
Christian Right because it left their priorities untouched (cf. Silk 2019).
Russia was still seen as a stronghold of traditional values—not because the
American Christian Right saw Russians as particularly pious, nor because
the Russian Orthodox Church was seen as a reliable ally, but because the
Russian government had passed one law after the other that was in clear
breach of the progressive egalitarian international human rights regime.
The Russian Orthodox Church's strategy to reinvent traditional morality,
carefully crafted on the discovery of Article 29, had paid off: Russia was
now a player in the global culture wars. Only for the Patriarch of Moscow
the strategy somewhat backfired: from now on, it was all about "How Putin Matters" (Dreher 2017b).

7. *Obergefell v. Hodges* (2015) was a landmark civil rights case in which the Supreme
Court of the United States ruled that the fundamental right to marry is guaranteed
to same-sex couples by the Constitution.

8. *Masterpiece Cakeshop v. Colorado Civil Rights Commission* (2018) was a case in the
Supreme Court of the United States that dealt with whether shopowners can refuse
certain services, like baking a wedding cake for a gay wedding, on the basis of
the owner's religious beliefs.

6

NETWORKS

CIVIL SOCIETY AND THE RISE OF THE RUSSIAN CHRISTIAN RIGHT

The American participant in the Homeschooling Congress in Moscow had no doubt: "You know, when we were coming here, people [back home] were like, 'Are you crazy going to Russia?'" She laughs. "And I'm like: But God wants us there. I mean, go! Because that's where you're supposed to go" (Interview 2018g). Other participants from the United States who attended the world's largest homeschooling event, elaborately organized in St. Petersburg and Moscow in May 2018, also felt that they were there to help Russians. "You know, I have to say, when I sat in that first room here in Moscow that was filled with Russian people . . . I wept!" Our interlocutor remembered how hard it had been for her and her family to legally homeschool in the United States only few decades ago. And see what they had achieved! "I would hope that the thirty-five years of research and experience and freedom fighting, yes, that freedom fighting could be our gift to the Russian people" (Interview 2018e). But she was not only there to share homeschooling expertise; she was also out to learn: "Their [the Russians'] gift to us is this deeper, sometimes richer, understanding of love and the family and the role that that plays in society. Because you've got centuries of tradition in that regard. Hearing Father Dmitry [Smirnov] speak of the child and the family unit, you know, it's this, it's this deep long message that somehow, we've, we have forgotten in the American culture" (Interview 2018e).

In this chapter we continue our analysis of Russia's role in the global culture wars, but we shift the level of analysis from public discourse, the Russian state, and the Russian Orthodox Church to people and civil society. The

actors and organizations we look at in this chapter define Russia's role in
the global culture wars, side by side with the ceremonial declarations by
the Patriarch of Moscow that we analyzed in Chapter 5. The groups we analyze are the direct heirs of the transnational moral conservative networks
of the early 1990s that we discussed in chapters 2 and 3. They develop and
act relatively independently from both religious and state institutions.
These actors and organizations fill the empty container of traditional values with concrete content: the family, pro-life, homeschooling. They
thrive in the moral conservative normative climate that has been created in
Russia in the last decade, and they reinforce this climate by projecting the
image of Russia as the defender of traditionalism to the outside and by
importing topics and practices of social conservatism from the West into
Russia.

The chapter presents two cases: the World Congress of Families and the
global homeschooling movement.[1] We include these two organizations in
this book because they are exemplary of the American Christian Right
going global (the WCF has been described as such in Bob 2012, Buss and
Herman 2003, and Stroop 2016) and a showpiece for Russia's role in the
global culture wars. The analysis of the WCF and Russia's role in the global
homeschooling movement reveals particularly clearly the embeddedness of
Russian conservatism in the dynamic of the global cultural wars and underscore the paradox that, despite the national hysteria about "foreign
agents" and despite claims about Russia's great Orthodox conservative tradition, we can hardly find a single issue of contemporary Russian social
conservatism that does not bear the marks of transnational influences. The

1. The Russian involvement in the WCF has become the subject of investigative
journalism (cf. Levintova 2014; Kane Winter/Spring 2009–10; War Is Boring 2014;
Dornblüth 2019) and has also been analyzed in academic research. Christopher
Stroop's research article (2016) mentions the American-Russian founding moment of
the WCF, and the present-day Russian involvement in the WCF after 2012 is explored
by Kevin Moss (2017), Katharina Bluhm and Martin Brandt (2018), and Anton
Shekhovtsov (2017). Other accounts of the WCF include Masha Gessen's reportage
from the conference of the WCF in Tbilisi in 2016 (Gessen 2017) and several other articles
that deal with particular aspects of the organization (Shekhovtsov 2014; Parke 2015).
The WCF has also been treated in the policy papers and reports of NGOs and think
tanks—for example, by Right Wing Watch, Southern Poverty Law Center, and Foreign
Policy Center (Blue 2013; Southern Poverty Law Center 2015, 2018; Stoeckl 2018b;
Chitanava and Sartania 2018).

actors and institutions analyzed in this chapter act in the name of Russian Orthodoxy, but largely independently from the church leadership. This adds weight to the ironic conclusion of Chapter 5—namely, that the Moscow Patriarchate, which effectively spearheaded the Russian conservative turn, is now no longer fully in control of it. The success of the groups discussed in this chapter is indicative of a highly contingent political dynamic inside Russia, where the notion of Russia as the great defender of traditional values becomes an asset, a trademark, which for now is in the hands of Vladimir Putin, but in principle is ready to be picked up by whoever competes for his succession.

Before we turn to the case studies, it is important to recall the connection between the agenda promoted by the WCF and the overall argument we have been making about human rights in the global culture wars. The WCF advocates conservative family values from a conceptual vantage point that matches the strategy of the Russian Orthodox Church for the promotion of "traditional values": it uses human rights language and human rights instruments, in particular article 16(3) of the Universal Declaration of Human Rights, which defines the family as "the natural group unit of society."[2] The mission statement of the WCF's parent organization, the International Organization for the Family,[3] includes the "Article 16 Initiative," which "empowers leaders in worldwide institutions to protect freedom, faith, and family as the natural and fundamental group unit of society consistent with Article 16 of the United Nations' Universal Declaration of Human Rights" (IOF Mission 2020). In *The Natural Family: A Manifesto*, Allan Carlson and Paul Mero turn the Universal Declaration of Human Rights, more particularly Article 16(3), into a manifesto for the traditional family: "We object to current attacks on the Universal Declaration of Human Rights, a document which proclaims fundamental rights to family autonomy, to a family wage for fathers, and to the special protection of mothers" (Carlson and Mero 2005, 26).

2. "The family is the natural and fundamental group unit of society and is entitled to protection by society and the state."

3. The WCF was founded in 1997 under the umbrella of the Howard Center for Family, Religion and Society in Rockford, Illinois. The WCF works as a series of conferences and as a network of partners in different countries. In 2016, the organization merged with the International Organization for the Family under a new president, Brian Brown. The website of the IOF is profam.org.

Article 16(3) is also the reason pro-family activists fervently oppose policies against domestic violence, the example with which we started our book. As Natalie Davidson has shown, domestic violence moved into the orbit of human rights law only after a long feminist battle to include it under the prohibition of torture (Davidson 2018). Human rights, it should be remembered, were explicitly about individual rights vis-à-vis the state. Domestic violence is something that happens below state level; it happens inside families, and only the redefinition of repeated infliction of gratuitous violence inside the family as "torture" could eventually make the state liable for taking measures against domestic violence, lest it violated its commitment to human rights under the UN Convention against Torture. Pro-family activists, out of principle, are against the move to make the state responsible for something that happens inside families. They see the family as a sealed-off group unit, as a closed box that should not be penetrable to individual human rights or state policies. For this reason—and not because they necessarily support violence in families—they reject policies on domestic violence.

The use of human rights language to oppose the liberal and egalitarian evolution of the international human rights system is a strategy widely adopted by the American Christian Right and originates in what Andrew Lewis has called "the rights turn in conservative Christian politics." He locates the rights turn around 1980, when American anti-abortionists started to use individual rights arguments instead of morality arguments (Lewis 2017). They were only mirroring the strategies that had also been applied by progressivist groups, like the feminist groups cited in the previous paragraph, which used legal instruments rather than moral arguments to force states into action. It was the rights turn that set the scene for the culture wars, in particular the global culture wars as we know them today, waged in front of courts and international institutions (Bob 2019). To our knowledge, the Moscow Patriarchate was the first social conservative actor to stake a claim on Article 29 of the Universal Declaration, while the WCF seems to have the prerogative on Article 16(3).

The World Congress of Families

We have already discussed the founding moment of the WCF in the mid-1990s in Chapter 2. When Allan Carlson came to Moscow in 1995, he was—as he himself very well realized—one American among many others trying to spread new ideas to Russians: "Everybody on the right flooded into Russia. The economic Right, and the Russian experiment of cowboy capitalism, it came with American encouragement, from American support, quite broadly. . . . There were groups like Focus [on the Family] moving in and so on" (Carlson 2020, 42). The official Russian Orthodox Church did not want to have anything to do with the suspected missionaries, and in fact, Carlson's contact with Antonov, professor of demography at Moscow State University, was of a scholarly, academic nature. When the law on religious freedom of 1997 barred the activities of Western Christian groups inside Russia, the WCF was therefore not among the suspects; the collaboration between Antonov and Carlson continued unhindered.

The Russian Orthodox Church and its leadership entered the orbit of the WCF only much later. After 2009, a younger generation of pro-family activists took over from Antonov. These were Igor Beloborodov, Alexey Komov and his wife, Irina Shamolina, and Pavel Parfent'ev. Bluhm and Brand have traced this generation shift back to 2006, when Antonov started a collaboration with Beloborodov, a young sociologist at the Russian Institute for Strategic Studies, and they together founded the Institute for Demographic Research (Bluhm and Brand 2018).[4] It may well have been through this institute and through Beloborodov, by his own account a devout believer, that Antonov—and with him the WCF—came into contact with the Patriarchal Commission for the Family, Protection of Motherhood and Childhood, headed by Archpriest Dmitry Smirnov (1951–2020). Smirnov, formerly responsible for the relationship between the Moscow Patriarchate and the Russian military (Richters 2013, 57–58), was a conservative cleric, but rather progressive in his communication. He ran a multimedia blog and a TV format.[5] It seems safe to say that without him taking an interest in the World Congress of Families, the organization would not have become a part of the Russian Orthodox Church's strategy on family.

Smirnov was instrumental for the intensification of the Russian activity inside the WCF by involving Alexey Komov, who was not a sociologist

---

4. A website of this name (www.demographia.ru) still exists today and runs news and information about the World Congress of Families.

5. Antonov and other members of this institute occasionally figured as interview partners in Smirnov's television-program "Pod Chasy" (*Under the Block*), as did American conservative speakers who visited Moscow in the context of the World Congress of Families or Homeschooling events.

and initially not even a pro-family activist, but a business consultant. By his own account, Komov dates his first contact with the WCF back to 2008, when the financial crisis put him out of business as a consultant and he was advised by Smirnov, whom he called his spiritual advisor, to contact "this organization, this World Congress of Families, to see whether we could not work together" (Dornblüth 2019). In our interview, Komov presented his personal path to the WCF as an autonomous endeavor and the fruit of a religious awakening, in a lengthy narrative that is worth quoting at length:

> I converted to Orthodox Christianity in a deep way maybe eight or nine years ago . . . and decided to do something good in my life. . . . We were hearing a lot of alarming news from the West, that there are gay parades all over, you know . . . and I was wondering that there must be some remaining Christians still in the West . . . and so I bought a ticket and went to Colorado Springs, where they had this World Congress of Families Leadership Meeting and I said "Hello, I'm Alexey Komov from Russia. I'm a business consultant and let us become friends and do a big World Congress of Families in the future in the Kremlin." That was a big dream. I had nothing and that was just a dream and they looked at me and said, "Who is this guy?" (Interview 2017e)

In 2011, Komov set up his own pro-family foundation, Saints Petr and Fevrona Foundation for the Support of the Family and Demography, and he created the Analytical Center *FamilyPolicy.ru*. Komov and Smirnov initiated an American-style fundraising when he posted a plea to support Komov's foundation on Smirnov's blog.[6]

Through the Patriarchal Commission for the Family, the WCF has acted as agenda-setter on family issues inside the Russian Orthodox Church. The pro-family agenda resonates with Russian Orthodox ideas about the family as a "home church," a notion made prominent by the late archpriest Gleb Kaleda (1921–94) (Kaleda 1998). Smirnov was a student of this "family as home church" theological school, and as the head of the Patriarchal Commission for the Family, he was in charge of formulating the patriarch's policy line on the family. Since around the year 2012, the WCF has made slow

6. Website: http://www.dimitrysmirnov.ru/blog/donation/ (accessed December 4, 2018).

but steady progress onto the agenda of the Moscow Patriarchate. The Russian Orthodox Church acted as a co-convener of the Family Congress of 2014 in Moscow and hosted the event in the conference rooms of Christ Saviour Cathedral. Members of the WCF have become involved in church activities like the annual Christmas readings (Pravoslavie 2018b), and WCF activities started to feature regularly as news items on the church's press service (Patriarchia 2018). A particularly evident example of the WCF's increasing influence on policies of the Moscow Patriarchate is the official statement of the Patriarchal Commission for Family against legislative changes in domestic violence issues, with which we started our introduction. On this occasion, the Patriarchal Commission cited an expert report prepared by the WCF (Patriarchal Commission for Family Affairs 2019b; Family-Policy.ru 2019). Inside the church administration, this slow ascendancy of ideas originating in the context of the WCF into the official policy of the patriarchate has met with criticism. Referring to the group around Smirnov and Komov, our interlocutor, who works in the church administration, said:

> What strikes me is that in their writing, they are calling to the authority of each other. They say things like "this is internationally recognized and well-known, and that's absolute truth, and the NGO so and so, and they are very valuable, and very authoritative researchers confirms." But then you go and look and that NGO is the NGO of his wife! You see, they refer to each other. But the rhetoric that they are using is very convincing. And that is, well, a bit misleading, because there is no real authority behind what they present as the absolute truth. (Interview 2017j)

The Russian chapter of the WCF, which has been created around the Commission for the Family, stands for a new development inside the Russian Orthodox Church. It is an organization with equal ties to business, politics, and the Russian Orthodox Church. Its leaders advocate conservative religious positions, but quite independently from the church and Orthodox theology. Their strategies, from fundraising and lobbying to the organization of international congresses, differ considerably from the more traditional workings of the Russian Orthodox Church and the regular church diplomacy that we studied in Chapter 5. They thus represent a new type of religious actor in the Russian context, a Russian Christian Right that is modeled on the strategies and manners of the American Christian Right (Stoeckl 2020a).

The main sponsors behind the new generation of Russian participation in the WCF were (for certain back in 2014) two wealthy and well-connected businessmen, Vladimir Yakunin and Konstantin Malofeev. Yakunin is the former head of the Russian railways and the president of several organizations and initiatives, among them the Russki Mir Foundation, the Dialogue of Civilizations Foundation, and the Saint Andrew the First-Called Foundation. This last foundation includes a pro-life organization called "Sanctity of Motherhood," directed by Yakunin's wife, Natalya Yakunina. Sanctity of Motherhood was founded in 2006 as a pro-life organization with the goal of counseling women against having an abortion. When the WCF organized a congress in Moscow in 2014, Sanctity of Motherhood was among the sponsors, and representatives of the organization have also been present at subsequent congresses.

The second sponsor behind the Russian chapter of the WCF is Konstantin Malofeev. Again, by his own account, Komov used his connections from his time as a business consultant to bring Malofeev on board for the organization of a large WCF event in Moscow in 2014 (Dornblüth 2019). Malofeev is a businessman who owns the Saint Basil the Great Charitable Foundation; his activities include the founding of an Orthodox private school and the TV-station *tsargrad.tv*, which promotes Russian Orthodox nationalism.[7] The Saint Basil the Great Charitable Foundation was registered as an organization in 2007 and then, according to the documentation on the foundation's website, was founded as an NGO in April 2014, just a few months before the WCF conference in Moscow.

Thanks to these wealthy sponsors and the clerical support of Smirnov, the WCF finally came to Russia in 2014, with full backing of the Russian government:

> We managed finally to organize it in the Kremlin and in the Christ the Savior Cathedral's congress hall, which is the official congress hall of [the] Russian Orthodox Church. And we had a meeting at the State Duma, so our people went to State Duma, and we had the Kremlin given to us for basically a private party with a laser show in the ancient cathedral; that was amazing. (Interview 2017e)

---

7. Website: http://fondsvv.ru/about/ (accessed May 14, 2018).

Komov beamed with pride when he said, "Our American friends couldn't believe that there was, you know, a welcome on such a huge scale in Russia" (Interview 2017e).

As a matter of fact, the Moscow congress took place in August 2014, no longer under the official tutelage of the WCF, and despite numerous withdrawals of participants from the West. Russia had annexed Crimea just months earlier and was under international sanctions. The congress's main sponsor, Malofeev, was on the U.S. sanctions list for financing Russian fighters in Eastern Ukraine (Southern Poverty Law Center 2018). Under these circumstances, many of the American participants withdrew their participation. However, this was only a temporary and superficial setback to the cooperation, which intensified again in 2016 and 2017, when the Russian chapter of the WCF was involved in hosting international congresses in two countries of the former Soviet Union, Georgia, and the Republic of Moldova.

For the two wealthy sponsors Yakunin and Malofeev, the WCF is by far not the only initiative geared at creating networks with Russia-friendly actors abroad. Yakunin is also on the board of trustees of the German-Russian Forum, a platform for the elite Petersburg Dialogue with close links to the Kremlin and the German Ministry of Foreign Affairs, and he is the cofounder of the Dialogue of Civilizations Foundation with headquarters in Berlin (Polyakova et al. 2016, 13–14). Malofeev, likewise, has close personal ties with the Kremlin and various networks in Western Europe. Marlene Laruelle has pointed particularly to Malofeev's connections to European aristocracy through French business partners who are descendants of the White Russian emigration of the 1920s (Laruelle 2018). On the ground of such connections, Laruelle has described the agenda of Yakunin and Malofeev as a part of the Kremlin's "white agenda," an ideological agenda with references to Tsarist Russia, Orthodox Christianity, and the anti-communist Russian emigration (Laruelle 2017).

The integration of the Russian chapter of the WCF into the transnational networks of the Christian Right has been facilitated by the personal background of its Russian director, Alexey Komov. Komov studied in the United States, speaks several Western languages, knows Western culture and politics, and has adopted the habitus of American Christian conservatives. Komov also has contacts with politicians on the European populist right and conservative interest groups in Europe. In 2013, he spoke at the party congress of the Italian rightwing party Lega, erroneously introduced as

"Russian Ambassador to the United Nations" (Lega Salvini Premier 2013). He returned to Italy in 2018 for the organization of the WCF in Verona, and he has regular contacts with the Italian organization Pro Vita (Pro Vita 2015). He has also freely admitted to having contacts with members of the Austrian right-wing party FPO (Interview 2017e) and the German right-wing party AfD (Janik 2019).

It is not only the WCF that has managed to move closer to the center of ecclesiastical power inside the Russian Orthodox Church since 2014; Malofeev has also come to play a more central role inside the Moscow Patriarchate. In spring 2019 the World Russian People's Council (Vsemirniyj Russkij Narodnyj Sobor, VRNS) elected Konstantin Malofeev to the position of vice speaker. The VRNS was founded in 1993 as a nongovernmental organization and "civil-society branch" of the Moscow Patriarchate. Its presidency is held by the acting Patriarch of Moscow, and it has its seat in the Danilov Monastery on the premises of the Patriarchate. According to its statutes, the VRNS seeks to "promote the spiritual, cultural, social, and economic revival of Russia and the Russian people," to "contribute to the strengthening of Russian statehood, strengthening the role of the Orthodox Church in the life of society," to "facilitate the moral improvement of Russian society" with the help of Russia's traditional religions, and to "promote the peaceful and nonviolent unification of the Russian people" (VRNS 1993). The VNRS has an openly nationalistic agenda. Its expressed aim is "to promote the peaceful unification of the Russian people," a clear reference to the idea that there exists a sphere of the Kremlin's political influence and interest beyond national borders, extending, in particular, to territories inhabited by ethnic Russians in Georgia, the Baltics, Ukraine, and Belorussia (Richters 2013). Greater Russia, understood in this way, coincides with those areas to which the Moscow Patriarchate lays claim as its historical canonical territory. The fact that Malofeev—reportedly a sponsor of Russian militia groups in the conflict in Eastern Ukraine—became the vice president of the VRNS and occupies a position close to the Patriarch of Moscow is indicative of the recent shift to the right of the Russian Orthodox Church.[8]

8. Malofeev has frequently been presented in Western media as the main sponsor and mastermind behind the WCF and Russia's role in the global culture wars (Michel 2017; Hatewatch Staff 2018; Michel 2019a). Our research did not produce hard evidence for continuous financial support of the WCF by Malofeev, and all the actors obviously deny that there is any link.

The WCF is an example for what Shiskhov (see Chapter 5) calls "conservative ecumenism," a type of interfaith cooperation that sees conservative Christians uniting against common foes (liberalism, secularism, feminism, etc.) while ignoring or taking a distance from doctrinal and theological topics and questions. The Orthodox partners inside the WCF team up with conservative Christians from the West. In the context of the WCF, the Russian Orthodox pro-family activists collaborate not only with American Protestants, but also with champions of the European Catholic right. At the margins of their own church, exponents of conservative Catholicism visibly rejoice about the warm reception they receive. One example is the German Catholic publicist Gabriele Kuby, whose pamphlets against "gender-theory" (Kuby 2012) are presented as serious science in the context of the WCF.

The interdenominational composition of the WCF and its appeal to conservative and nationalist Orthodox groups stand in stark contrast to the widespread anti-ecumenism inside the Orthodox churches of Russia and Georgia, the two churches who have so far most openly expressed official support for the WCF. At the WCF in Georgia in May 2016, Tbilisi's Philharmonic Concert Hall was full—with a third of the seats occupied by Patriarch Iliya and his entourage, who had honored the WCF with his presence—when Elder Robert Gay from the Church of Jesus Christ of Latter-day Saints walked up onto the stage for his speech. Gay began his talk with a personal dedication to his wife (who promptly joined him on stage) and then elaborated the WCF's mission. Adorned with headsets to follow the simultaneous translation from English, the Georgian clerics politely took in this cheerful gospel of the family from a man whom they, in all likelihood, considered a heretic. None of the events by the WCF that we attended during fieldwork included a religious ceremony. Instead, every congress featured a festive moment (a concert or ballet performance), several events also included a street march, and in general the setting was academic and business-like, with keynote speeches, panels, and PowerPoint presentations (for a report about the WCF in Tbilisi, see Gessen 2017).

Komov depicts his organization as a conservative think tank that seeks to influence policymakers, and he describes his transnational connections as "networking for political values." This is the example he gave in our interview about the organization of protests against same-sex marriage legislation in Mexico held in Moscow:

When our Mexican friends . . . I think it was this fall [2016] . . . when their president tried to introduce same sex marriage on the federal level in Mexico . . . our Mexican friends they asked to make a big lobbying rally near the Mexican embassy in Moscow and we did it. With some posters. And we arranged it in Washington, in Madrid, in many countries around the world. (Interview 2017e)

This, he said, was their activity on "street level," and "then we have the intellectual level, the think tanks and then the decision makers, some friendly members of parliaments, etc." (Interview 2017e). The picture of involvement in global Christian Right activism is evident, and it becomes even clearer in the next case: the Russian homeschooling movement.

The Russian Homeschooling Movement

Through the WCF and the emerging Russian Christian Right, ideas and practices more commonly associated with their American counterparts have been imported into the Russian Orthodox milieu. Homeschooling for religious reasons is one of these. Just like the Moscow Patriarchate with Article 29 and the WCF with Article 16(3), the global homeschooling movement champions an article of the Universal Declaration of Human Rights. This is Article 26(3), which speaks of the "right of parents to choose the kind of education that shall be given to their children."[9] The global homeschooling movement confirms the rights-turn in the global culture wars discussed previously. One way in which rights are "used" by transnational conservative networks is through declarations. Both the WCF and the global homeschooling movement have passed "Declarations" and "Principles," in which they stake a claim on a certain topic (family, homeschooling) and a certain argumentative human rights strategy (WCF 1997; GHEX 2016, 2012a). Through these declarations, the activists map the discursive space of international human rights law, locate their claims in relation to specific articles in the human rights documents and treaties, and develop a consistent strategy and terminology in which to present these claims. The fact that the Moscow Patriarchate has also followed this strategy, basing a claim on Article 29 of the Universal Declaration of Human Rights for the

9. Universal Declaration of Human Rights Article 26(3): "Parents have a prior right to choose the kind of education that shall be given to their children."

defense of traditional values, and even managed to implement this strategy through Russian state diplomacy at the United Nations Human Rights Council, suggests that Russian actors have fully arrived as players in the global culture wars.

When the homeschooling movement originated in the United States in the 1960s and 1970s, it was mostly driven by anti-establishment thinkers who advocated homeschooling (or later: unschooling or de-schooling) from a children rights' perspective, criticizing the school system for being too coercive, constraining creativity, putting children under pressure, and not taking children's individuality into account (Holt and Farenga 2003; Gaither 2008a, 117–21). Even today, one part of the homeschooling movement is still driven by countercultural, ecological, humanist, and libertarian ideals. However, starting in the 1980s in the U.S., conservative evangelicals started to avail themselves of the homeschooling agenda (Gaither 2008b). Since the late 1960s, conservative Evangelicals in the United States had been fighting (and losing) a political battle to instill a Christian worldview into school curricula and ensure the legality of prayer and devotional Bible readings in public schools. From the mid-1980s onward, the Christian Right shifted its tactics and started advocating homeschooling as the best model for conservative Christians to educate their children and fight the evils of secularism, moral relativism, defiance of authority, and libertinism that, in their view, plagued the public school system (Dowland 2015, 78–108). By the early 1990s, through a mixture of lobbying and strategic litigation, homeschooling advocates managed to achieve the liberalization of homeschooling in all U.S. states.

For Carlson, the founder of the WCF, homeschooling is a central part of a conservative Christian pro-family agenda. Citing the book by Eric Kaufmann, *Shall the Religious Inherit the Earth?* (2011), he advanced the following argument:

> What communities are having more babies, what are having less? Salafi Islam, Mormons, there's certain ultraconservative groups of Lutherans, even in places like Finland, who have big families. The Old Order Amish in the United States, Hasidic Jews have huge families. And his [Kaufmann's] argument is that, you know, if these current trends continue, in about a century and a half the religious vision is the world's future. Secular liberals are just not having children. (Interview 2018d)

Conservative families would therefore be bound to take over the world, if it weren't for the problem of secular schools: "Secular liberals have found ways to indirectly or directly take other peoples' children by putting them in state schools and teaching them new values" (Interview 2018d). Homeschooling is a way to fight this "indoctrination"; for this reason, Carlson finds the defense of the right to homeschool essential for conservatives and a logical step in the context of the WCF's pro-family agenda. It is therefore not surprising that it was taken up in the context of the WCF. It was again the Russian activists around Komov who intensified connections between the WCF and the American organization Home School League Defense Association (HSLDA)[10] and its international branch, the Global Home Education Exchange (GHEX).[11]

The person most instrumental in promoting homeschooling in Russia from around 2010 onward was Pavel Parfent'ev, lawyer and member of the Patriarchal Commission for Family Affairs, cofounder of the Russian chapter of the WCF, and founder of the Russian "interregional public organization"[12] *Za prava sem'i* (For Family Rights) with offices in St. Petersburg and Moscow.[13]

10. The HSLDA is the single most important U.S. organization promoting homeschooling for reasons of moral and religious conservatism, with over 80,000 members. It is based in Purceville, Virginia (U.S.), and was founded in 1983 with the aim of promoting the legalization of homeschooling in the U.S. and offering legal support to homeschooling families facing prosecution. The international activities of HSLDA include accepting international memberships and publishing reports on the homeschooling situation in other countries, helping to organize global conferences, offering legal advice and support for international homeschoolers facing prosecution, providing support to lobbying initiatives abroad, and helping in the establishment of national homeschooling associations outside the U.S.

11. Based in Canada and founded by the chair of the Canadian Home School League Defense Association, Gerald Huebner, the primary aim of the Global Home Education Exchange (GHEX), is the organization of international homeschooling events. GHEX describes its goals as "advocacy, outreach, and research." Its events have taken place in Berlin (2012), Rio de Janeiro (2016), and St. Petersburg and Moscow (2018), with a future conference scheduled for 2020 in the Philippines.

12. The term "interregional public organization" (*mezhregional'naya obshchestvennaya organizatsiya*) denotes a juridical status for noncommercial organizations with registered offices in more than one Russian region.

13. This organization has an old website, blog.profamilia.ru, and a new website, profamilia.ru.

Parfent'ev, who is a declared Catholic, is also director of the Russian section of CitizenGo, the pro-family organization with headquarters in Madrid, which regularly participates in WCF events and was instrumental in lobbying against the reform bill on domestic violence in November 2019. According to its website, For Family Rights provides support for homeschooling in Russia through lobbying and advocacy and legal advice to homeschoolers. The organization accepts donations and runs a mostly up-to-date news section. Parfent'ev appears to have maintained connections with HSLDA since 2010, when the first reports about Russia appeared on the HSLDA website (HSLDA 2020). He was part of the organizing committees of the first GHEX conference in Berlin 2012 (GHEX 2012b) and of the conference in 2018 in St. Petersburg and Moscow.

It was not Parfent'ev, however, who brought HSLDA and GHEX to Russia, but the much more entrepreneurial Komov and his wife. Through their collaboration with Parfent'ev in the context of the WCF, as they themselves report, they traveled to the GHEX conference in Berlin in 2012. By 2018, they were already on the advisory board of GHEX. The director of HSLDA Global Relations, Mike Donnelly, was invited to Moscow by Komov in 2017 (Donnelly 2017) and met with Archpriest Smirnov for a conversation, available on YouTube (HSLDA 2017), in which they discussed the advantages of homeschooling. At a small homeschooling event in Rome in spring 2017, the plans for the GHEX conference in Russia in 2018, the third global conference after Berlin in 2012 and Rio de Janeiro in 2016 were taking on concrete shape. This is also where we learned about the plans of Komov and his wife to start a Russian version of the American homeschooling curriculum *Classical Conversations*, which went online a year later and about which we write more later.

GHEX is more than a simple grassroots or advocacy organization. Like its partner organization WCF, it is a coalition of actors sharing the same agenda and a transnational advocacy network that uses global conferences as platforms to promote their worldview and gather new members in different parts of the globe. The choice of locations for GHEX events is usually strategic: "We went to Berlin," Gerald Huebner, chairman of the GHEX explained, "because Berlin is a . . . very oppressive place, [homeschooling] is prohibited and we wanted to influence that" (Interview 2017g). Rio de Janeiro was chosen because of the "very large growing interest in the country and very large population to reach out to" (Interview 2017g). Russia became a host because of "the interest in the family by both the Russian government and the Russian Orthodox Church" and as "a way to reach not just Russia but also the former Soviet Union countries" (Interview 2017g).

For GHEX, coming to Russia was a logical continuation of their global activities. The 2018 conference in Russia was the biggest ever international homeschooling event. It brought hundreds of international homeschooling parents, organizations, academic experts, and researchers from over thirty countries to St. Petersburg and Moscow. The Americans even went as far as to "predict Russia will become the second-largest homeschooling population after the United States" (HSLDA 2018, GHEX 2018). The extraordinary scale of the St. Petersburg–Moscow event can be seen from the list of participants, around two hundred in the previous conferences and over one thousand in Russia (see the network graph that is included in Mourão Permoser and Stoeckl 2020). The conference also had global strategic significance, with the creation of an African subcommittee of GHEX with the aim "to advance, connect, and equip the African home education community in exercising the right to home educate" (GHEX 2019). The "biggest ever" event in Moscow thus became a springboard for the expansion of GHEX activities to new countries.

From the perspective of the Russian partners, the prospect of turning Russia into one of the nodes of the transnational homeschooling network, from which new connections were established in different directions, was certainly an important motivation. But there may also have been a second motive behind the decision to organize the Global Homeschooling Conference in 2018. It was a welcome opportunity to organize a successful global conservative gathering after the (relative) failure of the World Congress of Families in 2014 caused by the Crimea crisis. At GHEX Moscow all the key figures of the Russian pro-family movement already involved in the WCF, as well as their main Western contacts, were present. Among the sponsors for GHEX Moscow in 2018 we find again the St. Basil the Great Foundation of Konstantin Malofeev; speakers included Levan Vasadze, the Georgian sponsor of the Tbilisi WCF in 2016, Dmitry Smirnov, the head of the Patriarchal Commission for Family, Ignacio Asuaga, the head of CitizenGo, and of course Allan Carlson, who had traveled to Russia with his wife to talk about their experience as homeschooling parents. Anatoly Antonov, the now retired professor of sociology from Moscow State University, also played an active role. He managed to move the audience with his speech, according to the official report on the GHEX website when he talked about the state of education in the Soviet era. Having survived persecution under the Soviet regime, he explained how the government conditioned Russian families to be distrustful of their community, friends, and anyone other than government officials. Home was just a place to sleep, families were mere cogs in the machine, and children were like "suitcases" dropped off at state schools and then returned. Education was solely the province of the communist state. With evident emotion, Dr. Antonov told GHEC attendees from all over the world he knew there was work to be done, but the emergence of homeschooling was evidence that Russian society was recovering from the deep scars of communism. (GHEX 2018)

The Americans lapped it up. "I am very impressed with this conference in Russia," one participant said, "because many Russian speakers—which we had the interpretation, the translation for—have spoken about traditional moral values" (Interview 2018a). After seventy years of atheism imposed through a Marxist regime, this was remarkable, he thought. And he was even ready to reconsider the role of Stalin, because, after all, he had just learned that "his father was Orthodox" (Interview 2018a).

Many of the participants from the United States and Western Europe, who had traveled to Russia for the first time in their lives to attend the GHEX conference, expressed the sentiment that they could find something in Russia that their own countries were losing. "They removed any reference to the religious heritage of Europe because they didn't want to offend one party or another. They removed the Judeo-Christian history of Europe and that has left a vacuum of spiritual identity," one participant said (Interview 2018a). "Their [the Russians'] gift to us is this deeper, sometimes richer, understanding of love and the family and the role that that plays in society. Because you've got centuries of tradition in that regard" (Interview 2018e). This statement, which we already quoted at the beginning of this chapter, sums up the positive impression many visitors apparently took away with them from the GHEX conference. For the Russian organizers, it could not have worked out better. If 2014 had been a failure, with Russia as the rogue state of the moment, having just annexed Crimea, 2018 was a roaring success: "Russia the great defender of traditional values" had been created as a kind of trademark and had been successfully presented to potential partners and clients on the global culture wars market.

HSLDA, GHEX, and the WCF are welcome fora for the exponents of the newly emerging Russian Christian Right to tighten and extend their transnational networks. Through these platforms, Russia acts as a player in the global culture wars. At the same time, the Russian pro-family and homeschooling activists also have an agenda that is internal to Russia and to their own professional—and even personal—affairs. Our fieldwork and interviews show that Russian homeschoolers and pro-family activists use strategies, topics, and practices of the global Christian Right to carve out their own niche in the Russian religious, educational, and potentially even political system. It is these activities we examine in more detail in the remainder of this chapter: the creation of a Russian homeschooling curriculum.

Homeschooling is very rarely practiced in Russia, and it is even more rarely chosen for religious reasons.[14] According to a recent report, Russian parents choose family education for their children for a variety of reasons. The most popular are: low quality of school education (66.4 percent); the desire to preserve the health of the child and to avoid excessive workloads (55.6 percent); and the ability to bring up the child in the tradition of family continuity (39.8 percent). Religious views of the family as a reason are also present but are in one of the lowest places (only 4.1 percent) (Zhuikova, Lialikova, and Karpova 2018, 20). Even Komov had to admit that homeschooling in Russia was more a phenomenon of necessity and not religious convictions.

> In our country, of the 100,000 Russian children who are educated at home, about 70,000 are disabled children who simply cannot go to school. There are also a large number of athletes and musicians, i.e., children who must devote almost all their time to developing their talent. There aren't that many "pure homeschoolers." (Pravoslavie 2018a)

Constructing homeschooling for religious needs as a practice in Russian society therefore means, basically, starting from scratch. Both Komov

14. According to the report, homeschooling has been legal in Russia since 1992. By 2007 there were 3,940 registered homeschoolers in Russia, and by 2015/16 their number had doubled (8,452 people), amounting to 0.058 percent of the total number of people receiving general education at that time (Zhuikova, Lialikova, and Karpova 2018, 6–7). Russian homeschoolers present a much higher number, speaking of 100,000 children being educated at home (Agranovich 2012).

and Shamolina worked in business before turning to activism, and they have now turned homeschooling into their enterprise. Every product needs a market, and in the case of homeschooling, this market still must be created. The second Russian-language homeschooling conference in May 2019, one year after the GHEX conference, provided the opportunity to do so.

"We're a dying country," Archpriest Smirnov gloomily declared to the audience gathered in Moscow's Holiday Inn Sokolniki. "The Russian people are dying out. Overcoming this trend is the main task." Despite this clarion call, the audience seemed somewhat reluctant to accept homeschooling only for the sake of the preservation of the Russian nation. At the conference at the Holiday Inn, which we here reconstruct from our field notes, many questions focused on the quality and level of home education, its advantages in terms of school achievement, and everyday challenges for families and affordability. The excessive enthusiasm of the American guest speaker Philip Mamalakis, author of the book *Parenting toward the Kingdom: Orthodox Christian Principles of Child-Rearing*, appeared quite exotic to some potential homeschooling parents who were present. The speakers on the podium were clearly trying to make a point for homeschooling for religious reasons. And for those who were not already convinced, the book tables outside the conference hall sold advanced science courses for children—that is, books for parents for whom family education is not a matter of faith and religious education, but of providing their children with unique competencies that are superior to those in the average school curriculum.

In the United States, one reason for religious parents to choose homeschooling is science classes—homeschooling is a way to avoid children being taught Darwinian evolutionary theory. In the Russian Orthodox context, the debate on creationism and intelligent design theory, its corelative, is quite new. In what is to our knowledge the only article that exists about this topic so far, Anderson identifies the roots of creationism in Russia in the early 1990s (Anderson 2012). He writes that promotion of creationism was largely the work of individuals and Protestant church groups influenced by American debates, using books by American creationists translated into Russian. Books by Henry Morris, a leading U.S. advocate of young-earth creationism, already were circulating in the Soviet Union during the 1980s, and a group registered as the Moscow Creation Society in the early 1990s began to hold meetings and organized a symposium that was attended by leading international creationists in 1992 (Anderson 2012,

314). Creationism, in short, was part of the moral education that Western Christian activists bestowed on Russians in this period, which we've discussed in Chapter 2.

Creationism became the subject of public debate only in 2006, when a Russian Protestant family went to court to argue that the Ministry of Education should allow alternatives to evolution be taught in high schools. Anderson reconstructs the public debate and writes that some of the arguments in court resonated with the Russian Orthodox Church's own concerns about teaching religion in public schools. After 2007, more and more Russian hierarchs spoke out in defense of creationism, and in 2010, Metropolitan Hilarion (Alfeyev)—head of the Department of External Church Relations and rector of the Saints Cyril and Methodius Theological Institute for Post-Graduate Studies of the Russian Orthodox Church—said that it was time to "end the monopoly of Darwinism," because "Darwin's theory remains a theory" (cited in Anderson 2012, 317). Anderson notes that in Russia, in contrast to the U.S. heartland, there do not exist whole regions of the country where the support for creationism is high. In addition, in his opinion the Russian school system and Russian elites were still supportive of a strong materialist scientific tradition (Anderson 2012, 218). The Russian homeschoolers discussed in this chapter carry forward the challenge of Darwinian evolutionary theory in public school curricula. Komov called for the creation of a scientific committee that should introduce "Intelligent Design" as an alternative to evolution. Scientific creationism, a formerly Protestant idea, has found its way into Orthodox thinking.

Among the specific educational programs presented both at GHEX in 2018 and at the Moscow Holiday Inn in 2019 was *Classical Conversations*, or rather the Russian version of it, *Klassicheskie Besedy*. *Classical Conversations* is a curriculum, created in 1997 by Leigh Bortins, for parents who homeschool their children. It is a fee-paying program with a kind of franchise model that aims at the creation of homeschool communities with licensed directors, mostly in the United States, but also abroad. *Klassicheskie Besedy* is not the first non-American program; there also exists a Brasilian *Classical Conversations*. The Russian creators and directors of *Klassicheskie Besedy* are Komov and Shamolina.

It is worth looking in some detail at Shamolina's account of her path to homeschooling and her discovery of *Classical Conversations*. Her experience, described in her article *My Way to Homeschooling*, echoes the conversion-and-awakening narrative of her husband, Komov, before joining the WCF.

Everything starts with a moment of crisis—in her case, the idea that something is wrong with the Russian school system. This moment of crisis is resolved by new knowledge about a foreign experience:

> For the first time I heard about family education from our family friend Pavel Parfentyev. To my great joy, in 2012 Berlin hosted the International Conference on Homeschooling (ghec2012.org), which I attended together with Pavel, who represented Russia in the conference organizing committee. (Klassicheskie Besedy 2020a)

Next, Shamolina recounts, she decided to do something in this direction. However, in the absence of a Russian homeschooling tradition itself, the most reasonable thing to do, it seemed to her, was to look at what is already available: "I went over the Berlin conference once again . . . on the cover of one of the catalogues, I saw the name of the community *Classical Conversations*" (Klassicheskie Besedy 2020a). At this point, Shamolina also had a dream: a Russian *Classical Conversations* curriculum:

> My husband and I started dreaming that something similar would be created in Russia: a society that would provide guidance and support on the path of homeschooling. Adhering to it, the family would no longer feel like "lone sailors" in the raging sea of education, but would have a reliable lighthouse and tugboat. (Klassicheskie Besedy 2020a)

The Komovs got in touch with the rights holder, the Bortins Company, and were given the go-ahead for the development of a Russian adaptation of the material. This adaptation would, according to Komov, "be better than the original American website and then they will kind of copy it probably afterwards" (Interview 2017e). He was convinced: "We'll set the new standard in this area."

The philosophy of *Klassicheskie Besedy* is based on the idea of reiterating educational programs from late antiquity that will fit with the Christian worldview (Shamolina and Geda 2018). Even though *Klassicheskie Besedy* is explicitly not positioned as exclusively Orthodox, the visual design of the program website includes icons and quotes from Orthodox saints. The developers of the program present their curriculum as "Christian" (Klassicheskie Besedy 2020b).

A fundamental point in the program is the rejection of the theory of evolution and of Darwinism. On the project's website, there is a reference to a separate website of a "Scientific Community of Supporters of the Theory of Intelligent Design" (Biolar 2020).[15] In his 2018 interview, Komov tries to explain the program's stand on evolutionary theory:

> *Klassicheskie Besedy* is not a catechism program, but an academic program. Nonetheless, in our materials, for example, there is no postulate that man came from an ape and that this is supposedly proved by science. This is a cliché, which is pseudo-religious in nature and in fact has been refuted by science many times. There is much scientific evidence that contradicts this theory. We also have a chronology of world history that begins with the Creation of the World. (Pravoslavie 2018a)

The rejection of evolutionary theory and the support of intelligent design theory is, as we pointed out, a novelty in the Russian Orthodox context. Russian creationism is one more example of how purportedly traditionalist Christian topics and strategies inside Russia are taken over from the American culture wars. The debate on what can be legitimately taught in schools resonates with the church's own bitter experience during communism, when religious topics were banned from schools in favor of scientific atheism. In this sense Anderson's conclusion that the Russian cultural conflicts are indigenous rather than imported is correct; what is important for our argument, however, is that this conflict is constructed in a way that clearly derives from a culture-wars dynamic. By presenting creationism and homeschooling as solutions, an emerging Russian Christian Right is carving out an argumentative space for itself inside society and inside the church.

In fact, both Komov and Shamolina, as well as Smirnov, their mentor, were at pains to explain that *Klassicheskie Besedy* was in no way officially connected with the Russian Orthodox Church. In 2019, the Patriarchal Commission on Family Affairs published a special document on the curriculum, where, on the one hand, the program was praised, while on the other it was very clearly emphasized that it was an independent enterprise:

---

15. Navigating the maze of websites created in Russian around the WCF and homeschooling, we have noticed that the web design of many of these pages is very similar. The font, location of the drop-down menus, use of pictures, and flash functions are identical.

The fact that Irina Shamolina and Alexei Komov work pro bono at the Patriarchal Commission has nothing to do with the *Klassicheskie Besedy* program. As specialists in protection of family values, international cooperation and family education, who maintain contacts with colleagues in Russia and abroad, they provide great assistance to the Commission's work. (Patriarchal Commission for Family Affairs 2019a)

That the Patriarchal Commission had to publish a separate document disavowing any connection to this curriculum is not surprising: despite all its Orthodox fanfare and references to antiquity and the church fathers, the program is completely new, and it is taken over from an American model. This fact was and is of concern to anti-Western and anti-ecumenical conservative Orthodox believers, as we already saw in the harsh criticism of contacts between the Patriarchate and the Vatican in Chapter 5.

In concluding this chapter on the WCF and the Russian homeschooling movement, it is worth stressing once again how these two examples clearly reveal the embeddedness of Russian conservatism in the dynamic of the global cultural wars. Present-day Russian moral conservatism is constructed around topics that owe more to the global struggle over the definition of human rights than to Russians' lived experience. The two examples also show that even though Russian pro-family conservatives act in the name of Russian Orthodoxy, especially vis-à-vis their foreign interlocutors, they are in fact largely independent from the church leadership. The actors that we have encountered in this chapter have hitched their professional and indeed personal fate to the trademark "Russia the great defender of traditional values."

CHAPTER

7

STRATEGIES

THE RUSSIAN ORTHODOX ANTI-ABORTION
DISCOURSE IN A TRANSNATIONAL CONTEXT

Even though Russia's history of abortion can hardly be compared with
that of Western countries, the anti-abortion discourse of the Russian
Orthodox Church closely follows that of the Western Christian Right.
During the twentieth century, the very nature of the legal and political
system of the Soviet Union prevented the emergence of any constitutional
struggle over abortion or any conceptualization of abortion as a right (Luehrmann 2017b). Whereas abortion was *the* central topic for culture-war
struggles in the West, in communist Russia it was treated as an issue of
public health, and its space was determined chiefly by material considerations and demographic preoccupations: abortion as a form of birth control made women available to take part in the workforce, and the temporary
ban on abortions under Stalin was aimed at population growth. The absence of religion in the Soviet public sphere and the collectivistic socialist
philosophy prevented any public discourse concerning the morality of abortion. After the end of the USSR, however, it quickly became a central
topic for both the Russian Orthodox Church and for lay religious actors.
In Chapter 2 we have already pointed out that abortion was among the
topics that Christian educators from the West introduced to the Russian
public in the early 1990s. Today, the Russian Orthodox pro-life stance is—
thanks to the internet—even more closely connected with organizations
in the West, many of them from the Catholic Church, but also with American Protestants and Anglicans. In this chapter, we provide an overview of
the theological considerations and different actors and discursive strategies
behind the Russian Orthodox anti-abortion discourse. These strategies, we

argue, are in part contradictory, because they start from different assumptions about the relationship between the state and religion. The Russian Orthodox Church is not unified in its position on abortion. Whereas the church leadership acts as a partner of the state and tries to influence state policies through cooperation, individual clerics and lay Christian activists see their actions as an anti-state activity and position themselves against the strategy of collaboration of the Moscow Patriarchate (Stoeckl 2020c).

The anti-abortion activities described in this chapter take place against the background of changing trends regarding reproduction inside Russia. In terms of a general trend, the abortion rate in Russia has sharply decreased since the end of the Soviet Union. According to researchers, during the period between 1992 and 2015, the abortion rate has gone down more than eight times and now resembles that of other industrialized countries such as Sweden and France (Lipman and Sakevich 2019). This decrease is explained by researchers as the result of changed habits in the use of contraceptives and better knowledge about family planning and not primarily related to more conservative or religious attitudes (Lipman and Sakevich 2019; Sakevich and Denisov 2014).

The Moscow Patriarchate's Pro-Life Strategies

The teaching of the Russian Orthodox Church on abortion has been elaborated in detail in the document *The Basis of the Social Teaching of the Russian Orthodox Church* (2000). The cardinal point of the church's position is the rejection of abortion as murder: "From the moment of conception any encroachment on the life of a future human being is criminal" (Social Doctrine 2000). In a situation where abortion continues to be legal in Russia and accessible through the public healthcare system, the Russian Orthodox Church has elaborated two strategic attitudes vis-à-vis abortion,

These attitudes appear contradictory at first because one consists of active engagement of the Christian with public and political life to "improve" society and change existing laws, whereas the other includes strategies of retreat and conscientious objection of the Christian living in a society judged as apostatic. From the church's perspective, however, the two attitudes are complementary and mutually reinforcing through a division of tasks: the clerical hierarchy commits to an active dialogue with state authorities with a view to guiding public morality, also in legislative terms;

the lay Christian believer is called to bear witness to his or her faith through conscientious objection.

The Social Doctrine dedicates Chapter 11 to "Personal and National Health." The very fact that national health is correlated with personal health in the heading of the section suggests that the Russian Orthodox Church sees individual health as instrumental to the health of the people. This becomes especially clear in the section dealing with abortion, which is introduced by an assessment of Russia's demographic crisis:

> The Russian Orthodox Church has to state with deep concern that the peoples she has traditionally nourished are in the state of demographical crisis today. . . . The Church has been continually occupied with demographic problems. She is called to follow closely the legislative and administrative processes in order to prevent decisions aggravating the situation. It is necessary to conduct continuous dialogue with the government and the mass media to interpret the Church's stand on the demographic and healthcare policy. (Social Doctrine 2000)

By making explicit that the church "is called to follow closely the legislative and administrative processes," the passage elaborates a strategy of dialogue between the church and state. This strategy presupposes cooperation.

The second, alternative strategy is the opposite of cooperation—namely, that of refusal to cooperate. This is the strategy of conscientious objection, which is brought into play only as a last resort: "The Christian, following the will of his conscience, can refuse to fulfill the commands of state forcing him into a grave sin" (Social Doctrine 2000). Conscientious objection, therefore, is contemplated as a last resort rather than a preferred strategy. It is evaluated by the church in the first place as a negative principle because it "testifies that in the contemporary world, religion is turning from a 'social' into a 'private' affair of a person. This process in itself indicates that the spiritual value system has disintegrated" (Social Doctrine 2000). Conscientious objection is recognized as a positive principle only in that it "has proved to be one of the means of the church's existence in the non-religious world, enabling her to enjoy a legal status in secular state and independence from those in society who believe differently or do not believe at all" (Social Doctrine 2000). This is especially relevant for medical personnel, as the document explains: "The Church calls upon the state to recognize the right of medics to refuse to procure abortion for the reasons of conscience."

With these two strategies, the Moscow Patriarchate successfully influenced Russian state policy on abortion. According to Denisov and his co-authors, the church managed to reverse the federal target program on family planning implemented in the 1990s by shifting the focus of government policies from reproductive rights and sexual education to the teaching of traditional values (Denisov, Sakevich, and Jasilioniene 2012, 8). The researchers quote from the address by the minister of Health and Social Development to participants of the second All-Russian Congress of Russian Orthodox doctors:

> One of the important moments, where the role of the church is especially significant, is the protection of family traditions and values and the prevention of and the reduction of abortions. We need to further pursue the campaign notifying about the harm caused to health by abortion, to inform people, particularly the youth, about potential complications, to talk about the psychological impact of abortion on women, and to create a proper mental attitude to motherhood. (Cited in Denisov, Sakevich, and Jasilioniene 2012, 8)

In fact, legal initiatives geared toward restricting access to abortions in Russia started around the same time the Social Doctrine was published. The Russian law "Fundamentals of the Healthcare of Russian Citizens" from 1993 had legislated that abortion can be performed upon a woman's request up to twelve weeks of gestation or up to twenty-two weeks in the presence of certain "social reasons." The definition of what constituted valid social reasons changed several times during the 1990s and 2000s. In 2003, the list of valid reasons for legal abortions after week twelve (except for medical reasons) was reduced drastically (Myers 2003) before finally being reduced, in 2012, to only one point—namely, rape (Denisov, Sakevich, and Jasilioniene 2012, 4).

In the literature, the gradual tightening of reproductive rights in Russia over the last two decades has been associated with the official rhetoric of traditional family values and demographic crisis (Denisov, Sakevich, and Jasilioniene 2012; Erofeeva 2013). In 2006, President Putin made Russia's demographic decline a major point of his annual address to the nation. One year later, the Russian government launched a program entitled, "Demographic Policy for the Russian Federation—Present to 2025." The program included monetary incentives for women to have more children and was almost exclusively built around a one-time monetary measure called "maternal capital" (Rivkin-Fish 2010). During the same years, several legislative proposals were discussed—for example, a complete ban on abortions and the requirement to get a husband's approval for abortions, none of which made it beyond the proposal stage (Erofeeva 2013, 1,931–32). However, things began to change, according to Erofeeva, when in 2010 the Russian State Duma installed a Women, Family and Children Issue Committee with the participation of the Russian Orthodox Church. Participation as a religious actor in this committee was the exclusive privilege of the Russian Orthodox Church; no other religious groups were invited (Ponomariov 2017, 174). The committee had a decisive impact on the new Russian health law, changing access to abortion significantly in 2012.

The new law "On the Fundamental Healthcare Principles in the Russian Federation" of 2012 included measures such as establishing a mandatory "week of silence" from seven days to forty-eight hours between the visit to a medical facility and the termination of pregnancy, depending on gestational age (Article 36), and the right of the doctor to refuse to perform medical "termination of pregnancy if it does not directly threaten the patient's life and health of others" (Article 70) (Stella and Nartova 2016, 8–9). The draft bill submitted to the Duma had gone even further and had stipulated, among other things, that before signing a consent form for abortion, a woman was required to visualize the fetus by means of ultrasound, to listen to the fetal heartbeat, and to consult with a psychologist, who "has to explain the right to refuse abortion" (Stella and Nartova 2016, 8). This rhetoric and language previously had no place in the Russian legal system, whereas it is widespread in the American pro-life discourse, and analogous provisions have been adopted in several U.S. states' law. It is also interesting that, after the first Demographic Summit in Moscow in 2011, organized by the Russian chapter of the World Congress of Families (see Chapter 6), promotional materials of the WCF claimed that the summit "helped pass the first Russian laws restricting abortion in modern history" (Federman 2014).

Despite the deep divergences in the history of abortion in Russia and the West, and despite the different significances of contemporary anti-abortion struggles, current strategies against abortion in Russia and the West show surprising similarities. In both cases anti-abortion activism targets simultaneously the legal frame that allows for abortion and de facto access to abortion services. Moreover, in all cases, anti-abortion movements exhibit an incremental strategy: they pursue a particular legal change, but, once they obtain it, the conflict is not settled. On the contrary, each victory galvanizes pro-life activists to raise the threshold and engage in new battles. In the case of the Russian Orthodox pro-life, there is a major rift between clerics and activists who advocate an incremental strategy of small steps, making abortion rare and difficult, and those clerics and lay activists that call for a full-out ban on abortions.

For now, the incremental strategy has been more successful: Several legal initiatives have followed the 2012 health law reform in Russia, all of which sought to further restrict access to abortion. In 2014, legislation on advertising made advertisement for abortions illegal, and in 2015, there was an initiative to exclude abortions from the public health service. This last resulted from a joint effort by the social conservative members of Parliament Elena Mizulina and Vitaly Milonov and the Russian Orthodox Church, with Patriarch Kirill arguing that believers must be "liberated" from their obligatory compliance with the murdering of children through the state-imposed social security tax (ROC 2015). This last initiative failed to gain support from the government.

Another legal initiative in 2017, which required all medical facilities in Russia that offer abortions to obtain a special license, was successful. Interestingly, while the U.S. and Russian health systems can hardly be compared, the strategy aimed at drastically reducing the number of abortion providers through clinic licensing has been in play in the United States for many years. Such restrictions have been traditionally defended by conservative politicians and pro-life activists on the grounds that they aim at protecting women's health (Greenhouse and Siegel 2016). In Russia, the new government decree on clinic licensing was interpreted in the media as a bargain of the government with the pro-life movement: the government did not take abortions off the list of free social healthcare services, but it did tighten control over abortion facilities. However, the licensing policy creates the preconditions for taking abortions away from public health care in the future, since it will allow, for the first time, the obtaining of precise statistics and information on abortions performed in Russia. It may also lead to banning private clinics from offering abortions. Consequently, the law could, in the long run, pave the way for even more restrictions (Ivanov 2017).

The church has also used human rights arguments—the right to life of the unborn—in a recent document dedicated to abortion. This document, published on the website of the Moscow Patriarchate as a discussion paper by the Theological Commission, is entitled, "On the Inviolability of Human Life from the Moment of Conception" (Patriarchia 2019). It establishes "the right to identity, life, and development" of the human embryo and calls for legal instruments to be created for the recognition of these rights. The rights-argument in the document echoes an expert position paper published years earlier on the website run by the Representation of the Moscow Patriarchate in Strasbourg entitled, "On the Legal Bases for Legal Recognition of the Value of Life, Human Dignity, and the Right to Life of a Child at the Stage of Prenatal Development" (Ponkin et al. 2014).

The anti-abortion discourse is one area where the Russian Orthodox Church has undergone a conservative *aggiornamento*, bringing its discursive strategies against abortion up to date with modern circumstances: the right to life, conscientious objection, public health, taxes, abortifacient contraceptives, ultra-sound checks, and psychological consultations—all of this has become a part of the church's pro-life repertoire. The Social Doctrine of 2000 still argued against abortion with the church fathers and on the grounds of demographic concerns, but the strategies subsequently pursued by the Moscow Patriarchate tackled concrete legal and social challenges in a language that owed more to the modern human rights system and the organization of the secular state and public healthcare institutions than to theology and soteriology.

Twenty years after the publication of the Social Doctrine, the Moscow Patriarchate has been quite successful with its strategies to influence state policy on abortion by consultation with the government. At the same time, however, one could also argue that the Russian Orthodox Church has achieved little compared with other items on the traditionalist agenda. The Russian state has written the concept of marriage as being between a man and a woman into the Constitution of 2020, it has banned the public display of "nontraditional relationships," and it has criminalized the offense of religious feelings and the excessive use of swear words. The Kremlin has not hesitated to rule in an autocratic fashion on many occasions; it could ban abortions tomorrow. The fact that it has not taken this step, which would with all likelihood be widely unpopular among Russians, can be interpreted as a sign that the government uses the traditional-values discourse only when it is politically convenient. The lay Christian pro-life activists, to whom we turn now, seem more aware of this fact than the Moscow Patriarchate and consider the government not a partner, but an antagonist.

Russian Orthodox Lay Associations' Pro-Life Strategies

There are, by now, hundreds of Russian pro-life organizations and groups, and it was not within the scope of our research to survey them all. Only those organizations that had connections to transnational pro-life networks were included in our analysis. Among these was the organization *Zhizn'*, led by the priest Maxim Obukhov, who is a member of the Patriarchal Commission for Family, Protection of Maternity, and Childhood. It is widely recognized to be the first Russian Orthodox pro-life organization and was started with Western help (see Chapter 2). The large charitable foundations discussed in chapters 5 and 6, each well-connected to the Christian Right in the West, the Kremlin, and the Moscow Patriarchate, also have their own pro-life organizations. The Saint Gregory the Theologian Charitable Foundation, which supports the workings of the Department for External Church Relations of the Moscow Patriarchate, runs an organization called *Zokhranim zhizn' vmeste* (Let's Save Life Together); the Saint Andrew the First-Called Foundation, directed by Vladimir Yakunin, includes the pro-life organization Sanctity of Motherhood (*Svyatost' Materinstvo*), which is run by the director's wife, Natalya Yakunina; and the Saint Basil the Great Foundation of Konstantin Malofeev gives high priority to pro-life activities.

The Russian pro-life movement is divided in strategic terms, with large charity foundations like the one just mentioned, and the Moscow Patriarchate focused on pastoral care, women's support and education, and legislative lobbying in small steps and a civil society branch aiming at maximalist solutions. Some of the Russian Orthodox lay organizations pursue a much more radical anti-abortion strategy than the Moscow Patriarchate itself. In 2015, the association For Life (*Za zhizn'*, not to be confused with the already mentioned organization *Zhizn'*) launched a popular referendum to ban abortions completely in Russia. The referendum gained little support among politicians, but it gathered around half a million signatures, according to the organizers. The Patriarch of Moscow, Kirill, was among the signatories. Obukhov, the founder of Russia's first pro-life organization, on the contrary expressed doubt about the usefulness of such a referendum. He did not think that a ban on abortion was realistic in Russia at this time. "Talking about the prohibition of abortion . . . is a waste of material and human resources," he said. And even though he frequently attended events by radical anti-abortionists, he said that he sometimes felt "sorry for fifty rubles on the metro there and fifty back, because for these hundred rubles you can buy a bun or something useful" (Interview 2017i).

In the pro-life strategy of *Za zhizn'*, a cult of the Russian nation is apparent. Vladimir Potikha, at the time the vice president of the organization, argued that the prohibition of abortion in Russia should contribute to making Russia a great power again, much like the Soviet Union had been in the past. For this purpose, he even created an emblem based on the state emblem of the Soviet Union, replacing the hammer and sickle in the center with a baby inside a uterus, his organization's symbol. He explained that the slogan "Proletarians of the World Unite" had a hidden meaning, because the Latin term *proles* originally meant "offspring." Potikha glossed over the paradox that abortion in the Soviet Union had been legal; as a matter of fact, he blamed the legalization of abortion in the Soviet Union on Jewish doctors and hailed the Stalinist period of criminalization of abortion as a successful project and as a response to eugenics in Nazi Germany (Potikha 2017).

All the pro-life activists we interviewed showed awareness of anti-abortion struggles in the West, in particular in the United States, and appeared well-informed about social conservative political strategies. One interviewee hailed the former American president George W. Bush, who endorsed an abstinence-based approach to HIV prevention, the so-called ABC-strategy ("Abstinence, Be Faithful, Use a Condom") and gave examples from abortion-preventive policies in U.S. states he thought Russia should emulate (Interview 2018b). The same interviewee also explained his understanding of the global culture war against abortion: there was, on the one side, "a worldwide pro-life movement, which is probably largely shaped by what is happening in the United States" and, on the other side, "the culture of death," organized by—according to this interviewee—Planned Parenthood International and the United Nations Population Fund. "They advocate the legalization and imposition, literally the introduction of abortion, euthanasia, the sexualization of consciousness, contraception with and without an abortive effect, the legalization of same-sex relationships and their promotion" (Interview 2018b). It is important to realize that many of these activists did not feel that they had the Russian government on their side; rather, they saw themselves as lobbying and mobilizing the public for their ideas to force the government into action (a point also confirmed in Luehrmann 2017b). However, they also felt in a minority position inside their own society. One activist interviewed by us lamented the fact that an anti-abortion rally in Moscow collects no more than two to three thousand people, whereas the March for Life in Washington regularly gathers large support (Interview 2017c).

The election of Donald Trump as president of the United States was interpreted by Russian pro-life activists as an opportunity for anti-abortionists in Russia and worldwide. Our fieldwork happened to take place only a few days after President Trump signed an executive order on January 23, 2017, barring federal funds from organizations that promote abortion around the world, including the International Planned Parenthood Federation (the policy, known as the Mexico City Policy or the Global Gag Rule, was first ushered in under Ronald Reagan and bars federal funds from going to foreign organizations that perform abortions overseas or lobby for the practice's legalization in other countries). During a recorded meeting, which is also available online, one Russian activist expressed the hope that Trump's action will have beneficial effects on Russia, preventing "such organizations from destroying family values here in Russia." The Global Gag Rule, according to this activist, was an opportunity for Russian pro-life organizations, which should fill the void left by the no-longer-funded international pro-choice organizations (Chesnokov 2017). For Russian pro-life activists, the global culture war over the abortion question was a reality, and they felt that Russia had a special role to play. "You see," one activist we interviewed explained, "pro-life for Russia is an element of its national idea, of its important universal mission. Russian has always succeeded in universal missions. Whether it's the salvation of the world from fascism or the idea of pro-life and protection of traditional family values" (Interview 2018b).

In the interaction between Western and Russian moral conservatives, the topic of abortion appears almost pedagogical—it is easy, intuitive, and well suited for the identification of who is on the progressive and who is on the conservative side. For a lay believer in the Russian Orthodox Church, it is not common knowledge that Christian churches in the West are split between a progressive and a conservative wing. Many Russian activists learned about the existence of such divisions and about the culture wars in the West for the first time from Western pro-lifers and through the topic of abortion. Through the global pro-life movement, they are presented with a normative map, which guides them on this and other morally controversial topics. This normative map largely reflects a Western experience, and taking it over precludes other ways of approaching and formulating solutions to moral conflicts.

8

LEADERSHIP

RUSSIAN TRADITIONAL-VALUES CONSERVATISM
AND STATE DIPLOMACY

In the previous chapters we have analyzed the role of the Russian Orthodox Church in the global culture wars on the level of church diplomacy and of transnational NGOs and civil society networks. In this chapter, we add to this picture the level of Russian state diplomacy. Religion is a factor that shapes Russian foreign policy (Curanović 2012). The Russian state acts as a moral conservative actor not only domestically through laws in support of traditional values, but also internationally through its state diplomacy in international institutions. In this chapter, we look at two international fora, the United Nations Human Rights Council (UNHRC) and the Parliamentary Assembly of the Council of Europe (PACE), to show how Russian diplomats carry the Russian traditionalist agenda into the arena of international human rights politics and thereby influence the dynamics of the global culture wars.

The chapter examines two cases: Russian-led debates on traditional values and on family in the UNHRC between 2009 and 2016 and Russian diplomatic efforts on the topics of internet safety in PACE in 2013. These cases are not only a showpiece for Russia's emerging leadership role in the global culture wars; they also demonstrate that Russia, still a great power in international relations, effectively changes the dynamic of global norm debates and increases the leverage of conservative positions in the international human rights arena. The two cases also show that the Russian administration's conservative position in international human rights debates is the fruit of the conservative *aggiornamento* of the Russian Orthodox Church, whose ideological priorities are handed on to the Russian government through a formal coordination between the Moscow Patriarchate and Russian state diplomacy.

Promoting Traditional Values and Family in the UNHRC

Ever since its foundation, the workings of the UNHRC have been characterized by a struggle between universalists, actors who have promoted the implementation of universal human rights standards on the one hand, and contextualists, actors who have argued that human rights have to be realized—and thus relativized—according to specific religious, cultural, and political contexts on the other (Alston and Goodman 2012, Chapter 7; Lenzerini 2014). These two groups battle over the appropriate interpretation and global implementation of human rights. Universalists promote the active inclusion of all individuals and causes subject to potential human rights violations that have hitherto not been addressed in a specific human rights language: women, children, LGBTQ, disabled persons, and other marginalized and stigmatized groups. Contextualists argue against such a universal application of ever more detailed definitions of human rights and their potential violations. They refer to religious, cultural, and historical traditions as legitimate sources of norms governing a society and advocate a restrictive application of human rights law. Both universalists and contextualists make active use of the UN's human rights discourse and its procedures and institutions, but contextualists do so with a restrictive purpose that is diametrically opposed to the cause of universalist advocates of human rights and, arguably, the UN bureaucracy itself. The contextualists' cause is therefore frequently interpreted by universalist critics as an attack on and backlash against human rights (Marshall 2017, 129). Though contextualist arguments are rooted in an intra-Western debate,[1] the human rights skeptical view is mostly associated with African, Asian, and Middle Eastern countries (the Global South). Universalist positions are *prima facie* associated with Western liberal democratic countries, even though some countries—in

---

1. The contexualist, cultural-relativist, and rights-skeptical positions on human rights was first formulated in a 1947 statement by the Executive Board of the American Anthropological Association, which set the tone, stating that rights must be integrated in different cultures by "the only right and proper way of life that can be known to them, the institutions, sanctions and goals that make up the culture of their particular society" (cited in McCrudden 2014, 4).

particular, the United States—have advocated both contextualist and universalist positions depending on the political orientation of the government. In the period under scrutiny in this chapter—2009 until 2016—the Democratic administration under President Barack Obama took a universalist stance, whereas the administration under President Donald Trump effectively advocated positions similar to the Russian position. The Russian intervention analyzed in this chapter challenges the universalist-contextualist debate by presenting the conservative position as "truly" universal and the progressive universalist position as partisan.

The Traditional Values resolution promoted by the Russian Federation in the UNHRC between 2009 and 2013 had its origin in the Russian Orthodox Church's discourse on human rights described in Chapter 6— that is, in the church's interpretation of Article 29 of the Universal Declaration of Human Rights, with its emphasis on duties and just requirements of morality. The Patriarch of Moscow and other members of the church had reiterated time and again the argument that Article 29 legitimizes contextual parameters as guiding norms for the interpretation of human rights. They thereby interpreted human rights not in an individual, but in a social and public light. The focus was not on how human rights protect individuals, but on how they enable them to do certain things. The Russian Orthodox Church wanted to set a limit to the enabling side of human rights, and it defined this limit in terms of "traditional morality." However, Article 29 of the Universal Declaration, which was usually cited as the source for this idea by church officials, does not contain the term "traditional morality"; it speaks instead of "just requirement of morality . . . in a democratic society." In other words, the Universal Declaration indeed envisions limits for human rights, but these limits are understood as the fruit of a democratic process. The speakers of the Moscow Patriarchate interpreted the meaning of Article 29 differently when, by using the term "traditional morality," they sealed public morality off from change through democratic deliberation, preferring instead past practice and traditional mores as sources of legitimacy. Nonetheless, the argument has gained traction inside the UN human rights system in ways we now analyze in more detail.

The Russian-led traditionalist agenda before the UNHRC in the period under scrutiny mobilized a stable coalition of supporters from among non-Western UN member states—in particular, the countries of the Islamic Organization and from the Global South. It has also acquired considerable support from conservative, mostly Christian, civil society actors in the West. These groups formed a conservative coalition that presents itself as more in line with the original intention of the Universal Declaration than contemporary progressive promoters of human rights. The traditionalist coalition has prevailed in all the UNHRC resolutions discussed in this chapter, and as a result, the liberal egalitarian human rights position of Western states has become a minority opinion.

The seminars, reports, and submissions connected to the resolution "promoting human rights and fundamental freedoms through a better understanding of traditional values of humankind" span a period from 2009 until 2013 (see also Horvath 2016). The first resolution, 12/21, was presented by Valery Loshchinin, the representative of the Russian Federation to the Human Rights Council at the time. It requested

> to convene, in 2010, a workshop for an exchange of views on how a better understanding of traditional values of humankind underpinning international human rights norms and standards can contribute to the promotion and protection of human rights and fundamental freedoms. (UNHRC 2009)

This resolution was adopted against the votes of the Western countries and, one year later, on October 4, 2010, the requested workshop entitled "Traditional Values and Human Rights" took place at the United Nations Commission on Human Rights in Geneva. The press service of the Moscow Patriarchate reported extensively on the workshop and the preceding resolution, presenting it as the outcome of Kirill's address to the General Assembly of the United Nations in March 2008. Among the participants at this workshop was Igumen Filip Ryabykh, representative of the Moscow Patriarchate in Strasbourg. In his speech at the seminar, he expressed the view that religious views on matters of human rights should be considered in the development and establishment of international human rights standards to counteract efforts to promote a new generation of human rights, such as "the right to sexual orientation, euthanasia, abortion, experimentation with human nature" (Ryabykh 2010). He specified the intention of the resolution as follows:

> It is about time that the ideological monopoly in the sphere of human rights is over . . . from the point of view of democracy, it is important

to provide an opportunity for representatives from different philosophical and moral views to participate in the development of the institution
of human rights." (Ryabykh 2010)

At the seminar, the Permanent Mission of the Russian Federation in Geneva organized a reception that was attended by representatives of the diplomatic corps and the seminar participants. At the ceremony, Ryabykh
thanked Loshchinin "for his help for the Russian Orthodox Church" and
praised the many years of cooperation between the diplomat and the Russian Orthodox Church (ROC 2010a).

   In fact, Loshchinin had acted as cochair of the Working Group on Cooperation between the Moscow Patriarchate and the Ministry of Foreign
Affairs since 2003, the year in which he helped to create this group with
Patriarch Kirill, at the time head of the External Relations Department of
the Russian Orthodox Church (MID 2003). The Working Group on Cooperation between the Moscow Patriarchate and the Ministry of Foreign
Affairs does not have a website, but the press service of the Moscow Patriarchate regularly reports on the annual meetings. The minutes of these
meetings are not public, and the annual press releases do not give away
information on the topics discussed. The only exception is the year 2010—
that is, the year of the aforementioned seminar in Geneva—where we
read that Metropolitan Hilarion (Alfeyev) and the deputy minister discussed the interaction of the church and the ministry on human rights
issues (ROC 2010b). The distribution of ceremonial awards by Patriarch
Kirill to high-level diplomats inside the ministry appears as a permanent
feature of this interaction (cf. ROC 2016).

   From this interaction it is already evident that the Russian diplomatic
effort on promoting human rights through traditional values was the fruit
of cooperation between the Foreign Office and the church. The coordination
became even more evident in the next steps: In March 2011, the Human Rights
Council again adopted a resolution entitled, "Promoting Human Rights and
Fundamental Freedoms through a Better Understanding of Traditional
Values of Humankind" (UNHRC 2011). Resolution 16/3 affirmed that
"dignity, freedom and responsibility are traditional values." It also noted "the
important role of family, community, society and educational institutions in
upholding and transmitting these values." Resolution 16/3 contained the request to the Human Rights Council Advisory Committee to prepare a study
on how a better understanding and appreciation of traditional values could

contribute to the promotion and protection of human rights and to present that study to the council before its twenty-first session.

By the time the twenty-first session started in September 2012, the study had not been finished, but the Russian rapporteur for the report, the diplomat Vladimir Kartashkin, presented a preliminary study (UNHRC 2012a). This study repeated the argument advanced by the Russian Orthodox Church based on Article 29 of the Universal Declaration of Human Rights, stating:

> Any society or State has a system of "law—obligation—responsibility," without which the fundamental rights and freedoms of the individual cannot be guaranteed. This close link is underlined in Article 29 of the Universal Declaration of Human Rights. (UNHRC 2012a)

The link between Article 29 and traditional values was not well received by the Advisory Committee of the UNHRC. In response, it presented its own "Study of the Human Rights Council Advisory Committee on Promoting Human Rights and Fundamental Freedoms through a Better Understanding of Traditional Values of Humankind," substantially rewriting Kartashkin's study and interpreting the traditionalist agenda strictly in contextualist terms, associating traditional values with debates on rights of indigenous people, and not even mentioning Article 29. Already with its first sentence, the study sank the ship of the traditional-values agenda:

> There is no agreed definition of the term "traditional values of humankind." The study invents a new term, "positive traditional values," in order to emphasize that only some forms of traditional values consistent with the Universal Declaration of Human Rights can be instrumental in the promotion, protection and implementation of international human rights in diverse social and cultural contexts, whereas others can be harmful. (UNHRC 2012b)

The European Union also submitted a statement in response to the Traditional Values resolution, rejecting the whole concept:

> Traditional values are inherently subjective and specific to a certain time and place. Human Rights are universal and inalienable. To introduce the concept of "traditional values" into this discourse can result in a misleading interpretation of existing human rights norms and undermine their universality. (European Union 2013)

Judging from these reactions, which basically dismantled the argument of promoting human rights through traditional values, the carefully crafted strategy of the Moscow Patriarchate and the Russian Ministry of Foreign Affairs between 2009 and 2012 appeared wholly unsuccessful.

Nevertheless, the resolutions had sent out a powerful signal to conservative actors across the globe (McCrudden 2014). Horsfjord concludes that, from the point of view of the traditionalists, the advisory board's dismissive study was "the hegemonic international human rights discourse reasserting its power. It is the voice of 'these fellows' who reflect 'the opinion of a narrow circle of experts, functionaries, or noisy but well-organized minorities'" (Horsfjord 2017). This view—that the international human rights regime is in the hands of a progressive elite—is shared by moral conservatives in many Western countries and by many actors in countries of the Global South, where it becomes intermingled with the postcolonial critique of Western hegemony. Through the Traditional Values resolutions (and even through its failure), Russia sent a message to all of them that it was now on their side and ready to lead their cause.

And indeed, conservatives did not need to wait long for a new cause under Russian leadership: Protection of the Family—a standard topic on the conservative agenda, this time with no risk of misunderstanding. At the 26th Session of the UNHRC on June 25, 2014, the council was asked to vote on Resolution 26/11, entitled "Protection of the Family" (UNHRC 2014a). The resolution, which was presented by a group of countries including Egypt and Russia, set forth a general aim to "strengthen family-centered policies and programs as part of an integrated, comprehensive approach to human rights." A group of countries that included the U.S. and Western European states tabled an amendment emphasizing that "in different cultural, political, and social systems, various forms of the family exist." This amendment was not discussed after Russia brought into play a no/action motion that was adopted by a 22–20 majority. Resolution 26/11 was eventually adopted by a recorded vote of 26 to 14, with 6 abstentions. In the resolution, it was stated that "the family has the primary responsibility for the nurturing and protection of children," that family is "the fundamental group unit of society and entitled to protection by society and the State," and that the UNHRC should convene a panel discussion and prepare a report.

The Moscow Patriarchate does not seem to have been instrumental for this topic at the UNHRC—at least our research did not reveal the same type of involvement as with the previous one. What we did find, however, is an active involvement of individuals and groups associated with the World Congress of Families, which we discussed in Chapter 7. The Howard Center for Family, Religion and Society (at the time the American headquarters of the World Congress of Families) took part in a requested panel discussion, held on September 15, 2014, during the 27th session of the UNHRC (a report on this discussion was published on December 22, 2014) (UNHRC 2014b), and the Russian CitizenGo website published a call on its website to support the Group of Friends of the Family coordinated by Russia (CitizenGo 2015).

The Russian involvement in the Protection of the Family resolution in the UNHRC can be read as evidence for the fact that Russia is successful in taking over strategies and topics that are deeply rooted in the global culture wars—and maybe less successful in proposing topics of its own, like traditional values for the promotion of human rights. Russian actors have become part of a continuous process of sharing ideas, texts, and background information through which expertise on argumentation before the UN is being actively built up by conservative actors[2] (United Families International & World Congress of Families 2017).

What is remarkable about the resolutions on Traditional Values and Protection of the Family is that they mobilized a stable coalition among the UNHRC member states made up of Russia and the post-Soviet states, the countries of the Organization of Islamic Cooperation, and countries from the Global South. They were met with consistent opposition from Western European countries, the United States, and a few others.[3] Coalition-making over universalist-contextualist topics is, as we have already pointed out, not a novelty in the UN context (Stensvold 2017c; Hug and Lukács 2014). In the past, the debates on defamation of religion (cf. Baumgart-Ochse 2015; Belnap 2010; Blitt 2011; Marshall 2011; Angeletti 2012; and Kayaoglu 2014) or dialogue of civilizations (Bettiza and Dionigi 2015) pursued similar causes. Additionally, the campaign and coalition for family values are not novelties. Conservative mobilization against topics of sexual

2. For a similar observation on the professionalization of religious NGOs, see Lehmann 2013.

3. A map of the cumulative voting results is included in Stoeckl and Medvedeva 2018.

orientation and gender identity in the human rights context goes back to 1994, when the Vatican, together with religious and nondenominational conservative NGOs and Islamic States, raised arguments about the natural and traditional family at the Cairo Conference on Population and Development (Bob 2012). Together with the 1995 UN Conference in Beijing, these two large UN conferences are considered by scholars as the starting point for global activism by the Christian Right network (Buss and Herman 2003; Haynes 2013).

What is new about the resolutions studied in this chapter is that the leader of this debate was Russia, supported by Muslim states and countries from the Global South. Heiner Bielefeldt, former UN Special Rapporteur on Freedom of Religion, confirmed to us that Russia has taken over the leader's position in a discussion that, ten years ago, was associated with Muslim states (Interview 2017h). Indeed, Muslim states are still actively involved in the traditionalist agenda, and it was Egypt, not Russia, that tabled the resolution on the family. However, Russia appears to have been acting behind the scenes. One interviewee from the diplomatic corps of a post-Soviet country explained to us that it was Russia that initiated the Group of Friends of the Family in 2014[4] (Interview 2017a).

Russia's leadership role was corroborated by two interviewees from the NGO sector, one of whom said, "Russia is taking over. This is quite clear" (Interview 2018f). Russia is taking over the conservative agenda not only from the American Christian Right and the Muslim states, but, as this other interviewee made clear, also from the Holy See:

> You have had the last four years a constant, a constant research by the Russians to create bridges and to gain a Holy See voice . . . to support some of the agenda of Russia. And with some success. (Interview 2017b)

Russia's leadership role in the promotion of a traditionalist agenda in the UNHRC has opened a new phase in moral-conservative-norm protagonism at the UN. This new phase is characterized not by new topics, but by a new argumentative strategy of the conservative camp, directly related to the human rights debate of the Russian Orthodox Church. The Rus-

---

4. This group included Bangladesh, Belarus, China, Côte d'Ivoire, Egypt, El Salvador, Mauritania, Morocco, Qatar, Russian Federation, Saudi Arabia, Tunisia, and Uganda.

sian Traditional Values initiative between 2009 and 2013 tried to present itself as having a universalist agenda; it sought to blur and redraw the conceptual boundaries between the universalist and contextualist positions in the human rights discourse by calling into question the habitual distinction between the universalist position as liberal, egalitarian, and progressive and the contextualist position as illiberal, restrictive, and relativist. Instead, the traditionalist agenda presented itself as conservative, but as equally universal as the liberal position promoted by Western states or, indeed, the UN bureaucracy itself. This reversal is most poignantly expressed in the following statement by the American Center for Family & Human Rights (C-Fam):

> Only a few developed countries have changed their laws to recognize a special status for homosexual relationships, yet they argue this requires a change to the universal, longstanding understanding of family for all UN member states and UN policy. (C-Fam 2015)

The individualist egalitarian approach to human rights, which has habitually been associated with the Western liberal position on human rights, is depicted here as elitist and sectarian ("few developed countries") and the traditionalist position, which stands in the lineage of contextualist arguments, is presented as truly universal ("all UN member states"). In this way, the traditionalist agenda turns around the liberal egalitarianism of its opponents into a restrictive, elitist, and anti-pluralistic position.

The case study of the UNHRC demonstrates that from learning the culture wars, Russia and the Russian Orthodox Church have moved on to doing the culture wars, aspiring to lead the conservative camp with their own ideas and initiatives. Yet our research has revealed that there are also conservative actors who disagree with the Russian strategy. Not only have the resolutions on Traditional Values and Protection of the Families put Western states on the defensive; they have also put many traditionalist civil-society organizations from Western countries in the awkward position of siding with a coalition of illiberal actors from Russia, the Islamic States, and the Global South. The traditionalist agenda polarizes and effectively blocks a broader debate about the sources and evolution of human rights, reducing it to a "zero-sum clash of cultures and values" (McCrudden 2014, 43). This is a problem for some actors who find the traditionalist agenda important and in part persuasive, but do not agree with its strategy or want to side unconditionally with the states that promote it.

One American interviewee from the NGO sector explained to us that his conservative Christian organization supported the traditionalist agenda promoted by Russia since 2012 but preferred not to appear too closely associated. Was it really a good idea to have the country that locked out their missionaries book a room in the New York UN headquarters for a pro-family gathering? It was preferable, he explained, to ask Samoa or Vietnam for cosponsorship (Interview 2018f). Another NGO stakeholder remarked that in his view, Vatican diplomacy was cautious not to be associated too closely with the Russian agenda:

> The Holy See has wanted to play always in the sense that it won't be only Russia, but a couple of other countries too, especially to support [a] resolution, so that it doesn't appear that the Holy See is [unintelligible] to the interest of Russia. (Interview 2017b)

The view was corroborated by one further interviewee from a UN diplomatic delegation who said that, while he actually supported the goals of the resolutions on Protection of the Family, he did not support the "unhelpful and intense, prescriptive language" in which the debate had been couched (Interview 2018c). This interviewee admitted to finding the work of a lot of conservative NGOs who intervened in support of the Protection of the Family resolution "unhelpful," and specified, "I want everything they want, but I disagree a hundred percent about their strategy" (Interview 2018c).

These actors, as we have argued in detail elsewhere (Stoeckl and Medvedeva 2018), find themselves in a communicative deadlock, or better put, a communicative double bind. A communicative double bind is a situation in which an individual is confronted with two conflicting demands, neither of which can be ignored or escaped. A subject in a double-bind situation is torn both ways, so that whichever demand he or she tries to meet, the other demand cannot be met. Developed in the context of clinical psychology (Bateson 1972), the communicative double bind describes well the situation of a particular group of actors in the context of debates inside the UNHRC over items on the traditionalist agenda—namely, the position of moderate conservative stakeholders. These are, as expressed in the statements presented earlier, often religious NGOs supportive of the goals of the traditionalist agenda but unwilling to be associated with the illiberal and anti-democratic credentials of the leaders of the discussion. The existence of a communicative double bind was confirmed by Bielefeldt during our interview, when he said:

The opposition created by the launching of the traditional values agenda is destructive. These resolutions create a situation in which you are told "either you buy traditionless freedom and a completely contextless, abstract freedom, or you buy tradition" and then you are per se in an anti-liberal context. This is appalling. Neither does it do justice to the real question, nor is it good for the discourse constellation. But they [the traditionalists] have launched this divisive strategy very cleverly and I believe there is a lot of confusion. (Interview 2017h)

From the perspective of sociology of religion, these statements reveal the multivocality of religion and the need to make differentiations inside the religious camp, instead of identifying religions exclusively with the conservative position. The global culture wars have an effect on religions themselves, dividing them into a conservative and a liberal wing, and forcing moderates to take a side. In this way, a middle ground for compromise disappears. The traditionalist agenda inside the UN, spearheaded by Russia since 2009, has created a communicative situation in which moderate conservative actors stand to lose. It has pulled nonliberal views on human rights out of the contextualist and culturalist corner into a universalism of its own making, directly in contrast with the individualistic egalitarian universalism of the liberal view on human rights.

Russia's Conservative Agenda in the Parliamentary Assembly of the Council of Europe

In the second part of this chapter, we add the case of the Council of Europe to this analysis about the role of Russia and the Russian Orthodox Church in the international human rights regime.[5] The Russian interaction with the Council of Europe was put on hold in 2014 after the unlaw-

---

5. The Council of Europe (founded in 1949 and not to be confused with the European Union) is an international organization whose stated aim is to uphold human rights, democracy, and the rule of law in Europe. It has its seat in Strasbourg and 47 member states (27 of which are also EU members). The European Court of Human Rights is a body of the council, as is the Parliamentary Assembly (PACE), which is made up of 324 members of Parliament, delegated from the national parliaments of the member states. Russia, which joined the Council of Europe in 1996, has a delegation of eighteen members of parliament.

ful annexation of Crimea from Ukraine. Relations resumed in 2019. The material analyzed in this section dates from the time before 2014. Russia's relationship with the Council of Europe and the European Court of Human Rights has already been analyzed in the literature (see Mälksoo and Benedek 2017; Henderson 2018; Holzhacker 2013; Jordan 2003); what we want to add in this short subchapter is a closer appraisal of the connections among Russian diplomatic initiatives in the Parliamentary Assembly of the Council of Europe, the Russian Orthodox Church's discourse on traditional values, and the transnational moral conservative networks studied in this book.

The interaction of Russia and the Council of Europe repeats the pattern already revealed by the previous case of the UNHRC. The Russian government uses the Council of Europe as a forum to advance its traditionalist agenda. One instance was the debate on social services and child welfare, which essentially saw Russia as an opinion leader inside PACE for a restrictive approach to the legislation and practice of the removal of children from families by public authorities. Inside Russia, this debate was discussed under the heading of "juvenile justice." Since we have already discussed this case in other publications (Stoeckl 2016; Uzlaner 2019) and it has also been analyzed by others (see, for example, Höjdestrand 2016), we will not reiterate our analysis here. What is important to stress, in essence, is that in the juvenile justice debate there was a clear link between conservative groups inside the Russian Orthodox Church (at the time led by Archpriest Vsevolod Chaplin) and members of the United Russia Party delegated to the Council of Europe. The Russian diplomats promoted the position that state authorities should interfere as little as possible with families. The idea that families should be treated as units and the rejection of specific individual human rights instruments for the protection of children and women echoes the social conservative position on family that we have already encountered in previous chapters. Whether it is child welfare or domestic violence, the social-conservative position is always the same: the family should not be "split up" by individual human rights instruments.

However, Russian delegates to PACE not only pushed topics on the traditionalist agenda; they also used the strategy of reversing topics that, at first sight, appear neutral and bipartisan. Our new case concerns such an initiative. In July 2013, the Russian delegate to PACE, Robert Shlegel, submitted a Motion for a Recommendation entitled, "Coordinated Strategies for Effective Internet Governance." The motion stated a goal that appeared to invite broad consensus:

> . . . growth of cyber-crime, theft of money and personal data, fraud, unpunished defamation, threats, dissemination of extremist information, child pornography and malicious software have led to a slowdown in the use of the Internet compared with the rate of its expansion. . . . The task of creating legislation in this area should be systematic and international, and should be accomplished by concerted action of all member States of the Council of Europe. (PACE 2012)

Shlegel was subsequently nominated a rapporteur on "coordinated strategies for effective Internet governance" and in this function participated in the UN Internet Governance Forum (IGF) held in Bali, Indonesia, in October 2013 (PACE 2014). He did not end up writing a report on the subject, however, because in 2014 the work of the Russian delegation at the Council of Europe was suspended. In 2016, the topic was handed over to an Estonian member of Parliament, Andres Herkel, who completed the report by 2019 (PACE 2019a). Herkel announced that in his report "the emphasis of the report, laid by Shlegel, would have to be changed," and he raised the accusation that "this topic has been seen as a hidden attempt to probe the possibilities for restoring Russia's rights [inside the Council of Europe]" (Press Release 2016). The news was reposted on Russian websites, where Herkel was promptly accused of being an Estonian nationalist hostile to Russia (Regnum 2016).

Around 2012 and 2013, Shlegel, the Russian rapporteur, was an important figure in the Kremlin's ideological turn to traditional values.[6] As a member of the youth organization "Nashi" [*Ours*], he supported this turn. His path also crossed with actors from the Russian Christian Right. In February 2013, he took part in a conference organized by the League for Safe Internet (*Liga Besopasnogo Interneta*). This organization, founded in 2011, is part of the conservative enterprise set up by Konstantin Malofeev around his Saint Basil Foundation. Since 2018 it has been directed by Ekaterina Mizulina, the daughter of the conservative Duma member Elena Mizulina.

For the Russian government, controlling the internet is a priority, and in the last years the Kremlin has developed laws and tools for doing so

---

6. In 2019, Shlegel reportedly left Russia and took German citizenship (Meduza 2019a).

(Sherwin 2019). For the Russian Orthodox Church, the topic of "internet safety" is relevant in the context of control of public speech and freedom of expression. In 2016, for example, the YouTube blogger Ruslan Sokolov-skiy was prosecuted for uploading a video in which he plays Pokémon Go in the "Church on Blood in Honor of All Saints Resplendent in the Russian Land in Yekaterinburg" and was convicted of charges that included incit-ing hatred and insulting the feelings of believers (see also Uzlaner and Stoeckl 2019). In short, in the context of Russia's traditional-values discourse, internet governance to prevent the dissemination of extremist informa-tion can amount to limitations of the freedom of expression more gener-ally. PACE's final recommendation based on the Herkel report expressed awareness of this hidden agenda behind the topic of internet governance when it demanded that Council of Europe regulations should "prevent user protection and security requirements from becoming pretexts for silencing dissenting views and undermining media freedom" (PACE 2019b).

This spotlight on internet safety at the Council of Europe highlights two things: first, the Russian social-conservative agenda does not stop at the clas-sical culture war topics of family, pro-life, and education. It actively creates new topics and politicizes them in a way that strategically fosters polariza-tion between a liberal progressive and an illiberal restrictive understand-ing of human rights. The aim of Russian actions in international political fora is to put a brake on progressive human rights universalism, and almost any area of human rights activism is suitable for this strategic goal.

Second, the case also highlights that at the level of Russian state admin-istrators, mid-level politicians and diplomats, and civil-society actors, the domestic and transnational dynamics of the Russian traditional-values agenda becomes increasingly complicated. Several scholars have tried to analyze these groups to find out who controls whom and what their goals are. Schlegel, for example, has been called one of "the Kremlin's Trojan Horses" in Western Europe (Polyakova et al. 2016). The evident connections between these actors and the populist right in Western Europe have also attracted the attention of scholars and investigative journalists (see, for example, Shekhovtsov 2017; Pomerantsev 2012, 2013). Like puzzle pieces, these studies add to the complex picture of Russian transnational conservative-norm mobilization.

From our analysis in this book, the map of Russian transnational conservative-norm mobilization is characterized by one generalizable trajectory: from "learning the culture wars" to "doing the culture wars." This way of looking at things places the Russian conservative turn firmly in a global dynamic of social progressive–social conservative polarization rather than looking for the roots of the traditional-values discourse exclusively in the Orthodox tradition or in Russian civilization. The motor behind this process of inscribing Russia and Russian Orthodoxy into the global culture wars was, as we have shown in this book, the conservative *aggiornamento* of the Russian Orthodox Church. It was the church that defined the climate of debate, the topics and the habitus of the Russian social conservatives. However, it was not the Moscow Patriarchate that turned this program into a pervasive domestic and foreign political agenda, but the Kremlin. Once the Russian government picked up the traditional-values agenda in 2012, this became a call to arms for all sorts of actors, politicians, bureaucrats, and diplomats to become culture warriors. The result is the vast array of NGOs, foundations, networks, events, policy initiatives, and declarations we have described in the last four chapters, all ready to claim Russian leadership of *The Moralist International*.

Epilogue

We conclude this book in a time of war. Russia has waged a military invasion on Ukraine, and Western countries have imposed sanctions on Russia. The current events will change the fortunes of the Moralist International in ways that are difficult to predict, but just like a car in full speed covers a certain breaking distance before it stops, Russia's weight inside the global culture wars produces a momentum of continuity. When the Patriarch of the Russian Orthodox Church motivated the Russian aggression in the language of global moral conservatism, saying that a military intervention was justified because Russia needed to fight off a powerful liberal West that wanted to impose gay parades on the Orthodox, commentators on the Christian Right in the West thought he actually had a point (Dreher 2022).

The story of the *Moralist International*, which we have told in this book, qualifies the myth of Russia as a stronghold of Christian values rooted in a thousand-year history. It sheds light on Russia's recent past, when it was not the powerful defender of conservative values as it now presents itself, but a disoriented, demoralized society imagining itself as a man falling into a waterfall and happy to receive any possible help from foreign partners. The story of *The Moralist International* is at odds with the view current among many people on the Christian Right in the West who see Russia as a dreamland of authentic Christian tradition, unspoiled by left-liberal influences. In fact, what they—in particular, American Evangelicals—see in Russia today is to a certain extent the harvest of a seed they planted thirty years ago. Pro-life and pro-family activism, homeschooling, and the rejection of gender rights are four concrete policy areas in which Russians have taken lessons from Western actors. Around these topics, the Russian Orthodox Church, Russian lay activists, and state actors developed a consistent domestic and international moral conservative agenda that turned Russia into a key player on the conservative side of the global culture wars.

The close entanglement of moral conservatives from Russia, Europe, and the U.S. has been built over years, during which Russian actors operated transnationally through different institutions and organizations: the Russian Orthodox Church, civil society organizations, and Russian state diplomacy. These three institutional levels were related to each other, but this relation was not one of a simple command chain with the Kremlin on the top. The *conservative aggiornamento* of the Russian Orthodox Church is the key to understanding this development. Yet not all the developments described in this book took place under the umbrella of the Russian Orthodox Church, and we are thus confronted with a maze of actors, initiatives, policies, organizations, and networks that worked both with and against each other in the name of moral conservatism. The "Moralist International" in the title of our book is precisely this field of actors, initiatives, policies, organizations, and networks that, on the one hand, represent Russia in the global culture wars and, on the other hand, represent the global culture wars to Russia.

For many years, moral conservatives across Russia, Europe, the U.S., and the Global South have seen themselves as struggling with the same "enemies": secularism, liberalism, and sexual and reproductive rights. In the period that we describe in this book, the greater international visibility and outreach that they achieved, thanks to joint efforts, played to everybody's advantage. Before February 2022, we would therefore have concluded that the motivation to continue to follow this path was likely to remain strong and that Russian actors would continue to play a special role in the World Congress of Families, the global homeschooling movement, the Catholic-Orthodox alliances, or inside the UN's Friends of the Family group. In which ways does Russia's war against Ukraine change this picture?

The Moralist International has always been a complex and paradoxical phenomenon, consisting of unexpected partners with their own goals and different domestic agendas. As a matter of fact, the Moralist International has already changed faces many times. The Vatican, which was the first international leader of the conservative camp, has by now become a great disappointment for the American Christian Right: against the backdrop of sexual scandals, Pope Francis replaced the socially conservative stance with a more moderate rhetoric vis-à-vis progressive social and cultural trends. Another conservative alliance, that between the American Christian Right and Muslims (which Clifford Bob called the "baptist-burqa" network), turned out to be no less fragile. Just like 9/11 put an end to the collaboration between the Christian Right and Muslims, the war against Ukraine is likely to halt the vertiginous rise of Russia inside the Moralist International. As a consequence of this war, Russia will have lost moral credibility to act as a leader and reference point inside the Moralist International in the future. The warmongering of the Patriarch of Moscow disqualifies the Russian Orthodox Church for dialogue with Western churches and inside the Orthodox world; the trademark "Russia as a stronghold of conservative values," which was so carefully constructed by the Russian partners of the World Congress of Families and pro-life activists, loses persuasiveness in the light of indiscriminate violence, and Russia's weight in international institutions diminishes. However, in ultraconservative Christian Right circles (Riccardi-Swartz 2019), Russia's aggression—and the Western sanctions in response—may also have a galvanizing effect. Actors on the Christian Right both in Russia and in the West will be receptive to the justification of Russia's war against Ukraine in moral conservative terms ("fighting off gay parades"). With the decision to attack Ukraine, Russia has turned the culture wars into a real war, adding a new, terrifying dimension to the Moralist International.

From a culture-wars perspective, a society is the battleground for two social forces, one progressive and one conservative, that are in a bitter contest over the future and destiny of the people. The perspective that we have taken in this book, on the contrary, is that the culture-wars perspective itself creates this polarization. Most observers of the (global) culture wars have assumed that in transnational value conflicts there will always be a progressive and a conservative camp in competition with each other and that these two camps are kind of co-constitutive. Inevitably some readers of our book will point out that we have omitted the LGBT and other progressive NGOs that poured into post-Soviet Russia during the 1990s; that we have ignored the power of foundations like the Open Society Institute, which funded liberal educational programs and civil society activism in Russia just like the Bradley Foundation or Templeton funded conservative ones—that we have, in short, not told both sides of the story.

As a matter of fact, it was not our intention to tell both sides of the story; further, the empirical evidence that we found did not support the presence of a robust progressive movement. With regard to Russia, the view that we are confronted with a situation of "progressive action–conservative reaction" does not correspond to the reality on the ground. Russian conservatism developed and flourished without strong socially progressive forces on the national horizon. Instead, the progressive groups and liberal NGOs that existed inside Russia since the 1990s were sidelined, if not shut down, and conservatism has become the dominant social imaginary. The public hysteria inside Russia about "foreign agents" has created a situation in which liberal and pro-democratic groups were marginalized and alternative visions of the political identity and destiny of Russian society were silenced.

In conclusion, we want to stress that the division of the public into two camps that is characteristic of the culture wars is just one possible response to the deep pluralism of contemporary societies. Polarization as a response to pluralism is highly problematic and "learning the culture wars" has meant that other aspects of civil and Christian life in Russia have not been learned or that they run the danger of being unlearned, forgotten. The human rights activism of Orthodox dissidents during the Soviet period, the religious philosophical writings of the underground, or the demands to open church archives in a search for truth on Soviet-time collaboration are today no longer present in the public discourse of the Orthodox Church. Instead, the church leadership has fully backed up an autocratic Russian state that uses the protection of traditional values as a pretext for war, for censorship and repression of freedoms. In this book, we have analyzed how Russia and how the Russian Orthodox Church arrived at this point. At the end of our reconstruction of Russia's culture war story—we find a Russia at war.

ACKNOWLEDGMENTS

A great amount of traveling, fieldwork, discussions, personal exchanges, transcription time, and desk research has gone into this study. We conducted qualitative empirical research as observers in the gatherings of the World Congress of Families in Tbilisi (2016), Budapest (2017), Chisinau (2018), and Verona (2019) and in international homeschooling events in Rome (2017) and Saint Petersburg and Moscow (2018). At these and other occasions we conducted dozens of interviews with social conservative activists from Russia, the United States, and Europe. Most of these interviews are confidential, but some interview partners agreed to disclose their identity, and we cite them with their clear name in the text. We are grateful to our interlocutors for taking the time to speak to us.

This book would not have been possible without the precious collaboration of our research assistants Caroline Hill, Olena Kostenko, Ksenia Medvedeva, and Hannah Jordan at the University of Innsbruck. Our team and advisory board members Alexander Agadjanian, Phillip Ayoub, Clifford Bob, Thomas Bremer, Sergei Chapnin, José Casanova, Ingeborg Gabriel, Sergey Horujy (†), Julia Mourão Permoser, Elena Namli, Aristotle Papanikolaou, Vera Pozzi, Olivier Roy, Andrey Shishkov, and Chrissy Stroop provided challenging comments and feedback throughout the research process, for which we are immensely grateful. Pasquale Annicchino and Susanna Mancini joined us for field trips and opened our eyes to the important legal and juridical aspects of our analysis. Thanks also go to our kind and encouraging language editor, John Harbord, who was our first reader, to Nathan Wood for his precious feedback on the complete manu-script, and to our peer-reviewers and editors at Fordham University Press.

We have anticipated some of the findings included in this monograph in previous publications. Chapter 3 has been published as "The Legacy of Pitirim Sorokin in the Transnational Alliances of Moral Conservatives," in the *Journal of Classical Sociology* 18(2) (2017): 133–53. The first section of Chapter 6 includes excerpts from an essay published by Kristina Stoeckl as "The Rise of the Russian Christian Right: The Case of the World Congress of Families," in *Religion, State & Society* 48(4) (2020): 223–38; the second section of Chapter 6 draws on research for the essay "Advocating Illiberal Human Rights: The Global Network of Moral Conservative Homeschooling Activists," published in *Global Networks* 21(4) (2020): 681–702, by Julia Mourão Permoser and Kristina Stoeckl. The first section of Chapter 7 uses excerpts from the book chapter "Transatlantic Conversations: The Emergence of Society-Protective Anti-Abortion Arguments in the United States, Europe and Russia," by Susanna Mancini and Kristina Stoeckl, published in the edited volume *The Conscience Wars: Rethinking the Balance between Religion and Equality*, by Susanna Mancini and Michel Rosenfeld (Cambridge: Cambridge University Press, 2018), 220–57. The first section of Chapter 8 draws on the essay "Double Bind at the UN: Western Actors, Russia, and the Traditionalist Agenda," by Kristina Stoeckl and Kseniya Medvedeva, published in *Global Constitutionalism* 7(3) (2018): 383–421. We want to thank our coauthors and the publishers for granting permission to include these materials in the monograph.

Kristina Stoeckl acknowledges the important input for the interpretation and writing up of the results that came from her participation as Senior Fellow in the "Orthodoxy and Human Rights" project sponsored by Fordham University's Orthodox Christian Studies Center and generously funded by the Henry Luce Foundation and Leadership 100. The research for this book was funded by the European Research Council (ERC) under the European Union's Horizon 2020 research and innovation program (POSEC, grant agreement no. 676804), as well as by the Austrian Science Foundation (FWF) (grant agreement no. Y-919).[1]

---

1. A complete list of publications from the POSEC project and open access to all published articles can be found here: https://zenodo.org/communities/postsecularconflicts/?page=1&size=20.

BIBLIOGRAPHY

Interviews

Interview. 2017a. Interview conducted in the context of the POSEC project with a member of the diplomatic corps to the UN of a post-Soviet country. Place: The interview was conducted via Skype. Original language: Russian (all quotes have been translated by April French). Date: February 23, 2017.

———. 2017b. Interview conducted in the context of the POSEC project with a European stakeholder from the NGO sector. Place: The interview was conducted via Skype. Original language: English. Date: June 16, 2017.

———. 2017c. Interview conducted in the context of the POSEC project with a pro-life activist. Place: Moscow. Original language: Russian (translation by the authors). Date: January 28, 2017.

———. 2017d. Interview conducted in the context of the POSEC project with a Russian Evangelical leader. Place: Moscow. Original language: English. Date: 03.02.2017.

———. 2017e. Interview conducted in the context of the POSEC project with Alexey Komov. The interviewee agreed to waive confidentiality. Place: Moscow. Original language: Russian (translation by the authors). Date: January 31, 2017.

———. 2017f. Interview conducted in the context of the POSEC project with Anatolij Antonov, Russian cofounder of the World Congress of Families. The interviewee agreed to waive confidentiality. Place: Moscow. Original language: Russian (translation by the authors). Date: February 3, 2017.

———. 2017g. Interview conducted in the context of the POSEC project with Gerald Huebner at Homeschooling Congress in Italy. The interviewee agreed to waive confidentiality. Place: Rome. Original language: English. Date: May 19, 2017.

———. 2017h. Interview conducted in the context of the POSEC project with Heiner Bielefeldt, former UN Ambassador for Religious Freedom. The interviewee agreed to waive confidentiality. Place: The interview was conducted via Skype. Original language: German (translation by the authors). Date: January 16, 2017.

———. 2017i. Interview conducted in the context of the POSEC project with Maxim Obukhov. The interviewee agreed to waive confidentiality. Place: Moscow. Original language: Russian (translation by the authors). Date: January 14, 2017.

———. 2017j. Interview conducted in the context of the POSEC project with church administrator. Place: Moscow. Original language: Russian (translation by the authors). Date: January 14, 2017.

———. 2018a. Interview conducted in the context of the POSEC project with a participant at the Homeschooling Congress in Russia. Place: Moscow. Original language: English. Date: May 5, 2018.

———. 2018b. Interview conducted in the context of the POSEC project with a pro-life activist. Place: Moscow. Original language: Russian (translation by the authors). Date: February 9, 2018.

———. 2018c. Interview conducted in the context of the POSEC project with a UN diplomat. Place: New York. Original language: English. Date: February 23, 2018.

———. 2018d. Interview conducted in the context of the POSEC project with Allan Carlson. The interviewee agreed to waive confidentality. Place: Moscow. Original language: English. Date: May 19, 2018.

———. 2018e. Interview conducted in the context of the POSEC project with an American Participant at the Homeschooling Congress in Russia. Place: Moscow. Original language: English. Date: May 19, 2018.

———. 2018f. Interview conducted in the context of the POSEC project with an American stakeholder from the NGO sector. Place: The interview was conducted via Skype. Original language: English. Date: February 23, 2018.

———. 2018g. Interview conducted in the context of the POSEC project with two anonymous American participants in the Homeschooling Congress in Russia. Place: Moscow. Original language: English. Date: May 18, 2018.

———. 2018h. Interview conducted in the context of the POSEC project with Vsevolod Chaplin. The interviewee agreed to waive confidentiality. Place: Moscow. Original language: Russian (translation by the authors). Date: February 7, 2018.

———. 2018i. Interview conducted in the context of the POSEC project with former American NGO leader. Place: The interview was conducted via Skype. Original language: English. Date: November 21, 2018.

Secondary Sources

Agadjanian, Alexander. 2010. "Liberal Individual and Christian Culture: Russian Orthodox Teaching on Human Rights in Social Theory Perspective." *Religion, State, and Society* 38 (2):97–113.

———. 2013. "Reform and Revival in Moscow Orthodox Communities: Two Types of Religious Modernity." *Archives de Sciences Sociales des Religions* 162:75–94.

———. 2017. "Tradition, Morality and Community: Elaborating Orthodox Identity in Putin's Russia." *Religion, State & Society* 23 (1):39–60.

Agranovich, M. 2012. "Kto ne khochet khodit' v shkolu? Vse bol'she semei v Rossii berutsia uchit' svoikh detei samostoiatel'no i doma" [Who Doesn't Want to Attend School? More and More Families in Russia Make a Decision to Teach Their Children at Home]. *Rossiiskaia Gazeta*, April 10, 2012. https://rg.ru/2012/04/10/obuchenie.html. Accessed February 24, 2020.

Alexievich, Svetlana. 2016. *Secondhand Time*. New York: Random House.

Alston, Philip, and Ryan Goodman. 2012. *International Human Rights*. Oxford: Oxford University Press.

Anderson, John. 2012. "Rock, Art, and Sex: The 'Culture Wars' Come to Russia?" *Journal of Church and State* 55 (2):307–34.

———. 2015. *Conservative Christian Politics in Russia and the United States: Dreaming of Christian Nations*. London and New York: Routledge.

Andreeva, Nina. 1988. "Ne mogu postupat'sia printsipami." [I Cannot Let Go of My Principles]. *Sovetskaia Rossiya*, March 13, 1988.

Angeletti, Silvia. 2012. "Freedom of Religion, Freedom of Expression and the United Nations: Recognizing Values and Rights in the 'Defamation of Religions' Discourse." *Stato, Chiese e pluralismo confessionale: Rivista telematicai*, October 8, 2012.

Atnashev, Timur. 2018. "Pereklyuchaya rezhimy publichnosti: Kak Nina Andreyeva sodeystvovala prevrashcheniyu glasnosti v svobodu slova" [Switching Regimes of Publicity: How Nina Andreeva Facilitated the Transformation of Glastnost into Freedom of Speech]. *Novoe Literaturnoe Obozrenie* 3. https://www.nlobooks.ru/magazines/novoe_literaturnoe_obozrenie/151/article/19758/. Accessed February 16, 2020.

AVA. 2014. "Aleksej Komov v Kishinyove: 'Pora postavit' poslednuyu tochku v otnoshenii k kommunizmu.'" [Alexey Komov in Chisinau: It Is Time to Put a Full-Stop to the Relations with Communism]. *AVA News Portal Moldova*, April 12, 2014. https://ava.md/2014/04/12/aleksey-komov-v-kishineve-pora-postavit/. Accessed October 21, 2019.

Ayoub, Phillip M. 2013. *When States "Come Out": The Politics of Visibility and the Diffusion of Sexual Minority Rights in Europe*. Ithaca, N.Y.: Cornell University Press.

Bateson, Gregory. 1972. *Steps into an Ecology of Mind: Collected Essays in Anthropology, Psychiatry, Evolution, and Epistemology.* London: Intertext.

Baumgart-Ochse, Claudia. 2015. *Which Gets Protection—Belief or Believer?* [Elektronische Ressource]: *The Organisation of Islamic Cooperation and the Campaign against the "Defamation of Religions" / Claudia Baumgart-Ochse, PRIF Reports 136.* Frankfurt am Main: Hessische Stiftung Friedens- und Konfliktforschung.

Belnap, Allison G. 2010. "Defamation of Religions: A Vague and Overbroad Theory That Threatens Basic Human Rights." *Brigham Young University Law Review* 2010 (2):635–85.

Benne, Robert. 2015. "How a Decadent Culture Makes Me Think like Sorokin." *First Things*, January 19, 2015. https://www.firstthings.com/web -exclusives/2015/01/how-a-decadent-culture-makes-me-think-like-sorokin. Accessed May 16, 2017.

Berger, Peter. 2014. "Exporting the American Culture War." *American Interest*, August 20, 2014. https://www.the-american-interest.com/2014/08/20 /exporting-the-american-culture-war/. Accessed February 7, 2020.

Berman, Morris. 2012. "Pitirim Sorokin." *Blog Dark Ages America*, April 28, 2012. http://morrisberman.blogspot.co.at/2012/04/pitirim-sorokin_28.html. Accessed May 16, 2017.

Bettiza, G., and F. Dionigi. 2015. "How Do Religious Norms Diffuse? Institutional Translation and International Change in a Post-Secular World Society." *European Journal of International Relations* 21 (3):621–46.

Biolar. 2020. "Nauchnoe coobshestvo storonnikov teorii razumnogo zamysla" [Scientific Community of Supporters of Intelligent Design Theory]. http://id .biolar.ru/. Accessed January 28, 2020.

Blitt, Robert C. 2011. "The Bottom Up Journey of 'Defamation of Religion' from Muslim States to the United Nations: A Case Study of the Migration of Anti-Constitutional Ideas." *Studies in Law, Politics and Society* 56:121–211.

Blue, Miranda. 2013. "Globalizing Homophobia, Part 4: The World Congress of Families and Russia's 'Christian Saviors.'" *RightWingWatch*, October 4, 2013. https://www.rightwingwatch.org/post/globalizing-homophobia-part-4 -the-world-congress-of-families-and-russias-christian-saviors/. Accessed January 29, 2020.

Bluhm, Katharina, and Martin Brand. 2018. "'Traditional Values' Unleashed: The Ultraconservative Influence on Russian Family Policy." In *New Conservatives in Russia and East Central Europe*, edited by Katharina Bluhm and Mihai Varga, 223–44. London and New York: Routledge.

Bob, Clifford. 2002. "Merchants of Morality." *Foreign Policy* (129):36–45.

———. 2012. *The Global Right Wind and the Clash of World Politics.* Cambridge: Cambridge University Press.

———. 2015. "Religious Activists and Foreign Policy in the West." In *Faith, Freedom and Foreign Policy: Challenges for the Transatlantic Community*, edited by Michael Barnett, Clifford Bob, Nora Fisher Onar, Anne Jenichen, Michael Leigh, and Lucian N. Leustean, 94–111. Washington, D.C.: Transatlantic Academy.

———. 2019. *Rights as Weapons: Instruments of Conflict, Tools of Power*. Princeton, N.J.: Princeton University Press.

Brown, Harold O. J. 1996. *The Sensate Culture*. Dallas, Tex.: Word Pub.

Burawoy, Michael. 2005. "For Public Sociology." *American Sociological Review* 70:4–28.

Burgess, John P. 2017. *Holy Rus': The Rebirth of Orthodoxy in the New Russia*. New Haven and London: Yale University Press.

Buss, Doris, and Didi Herman. 2003. *Globalizing Family Values: The Christian Right in International Politics*. Minneapolis and London: University of Minnesota Press.

Butler, Jennifer. 2006. *Born Again: The Christian Right Globalized*. London and Ann Arbor, Mich.: Pluto.

C-Fam. 2015. "Submission to the Office of the High Comissioner for Human Rights from the Center for Family and Human Rights (C-Fam)." *Office of the High Commissioner of Human Rights*, October 28, 2015. http://www.ohchr.org/EN/HRBodies/HRC/Pages/ProtectionFamily.aspx. Last accessed April 5, 2017.

Caldwell, Christopher. 2017. "How to Think about Vladimir Putin." *Imprimis* 46 (3). https://imprimis.hillsdale.edu/how-to-think-about-vladimir-putin/. Accessed February 20, 2020.

Carlson, Allan C. 1989. "A Pro-Family Income Tax." *National Affairs* 37 (Fall): https://www.nationalaffairs.com/public_interest/detail/a-pro-family-income-tax. Accessed October 9, 2018.

———. 1990. *The Swedish Experiment in Family Politics: The Myrdals and the Interwar Population Xrisis*. New Brunswick, N.J.: Transaction.

———. 1995. "Personal diary of Trip to Moscow and Prague." Gift to the author.

———. 2007. *Third Ways: How Bulgarian Greens, Swedish Housewives, and Beer-Swilling Englishmen Created Family-Centered economies—and Why They Disappeared*. Culture of Enterprise Series. Wilmington, Del.: ISI.

———. 2013. "Interview." *Calvinist International*, May 29, 2013. https://calvinistinternational.com/2013/05/29/carlson-interview/. Accessed May 18, 2017.

———. 2020. "The Great Battles Lie Ahead." Interview with Allan Carlson. In *Postsecular Conflicts: Debates from Russia and the United States*, edited by Kristina Stoeckl and Dmitry Uzlaner, 37–51. Innsbruck: Innsbruck University Press.

Carlson, Allan C., and Paul T. Mero. 2005. *The Natural Family: A Manifesto.* Dallas: Spence.

Carrère, Emmanuel. 2014. *Limonov.* Paris: P.O.L. Gallimard.

Casanova, José. 2019. "Global Religious and Secular Dynamics: The Modern System of Classification." *Religion and Politics* 1 (1):1–74.

Chaplin, Protoierei Vsevolod. 2013. "Religioznaia kul'tura i nravstvennost' po-nastoiashchemu formiruiut cheloveka." [Religious Culture and Morality Shape Man]. *Website Islam.Ru*, January 1, 2013. http://islam.ru/content /analitics/30290. Accessed August 24, 2020.

———. 2015. "O traditsionnom rossiiskom buddizme." [On Traditional Russian Buddhism]. *Website of the World Russian People's Council*, March 23, 2015. http://www.rg.ru/2013/06/30/chuvstva-anons.html. Accessed August 24, 2020.

Chapnin, Sergej. 2015. "A Church of Empire." *First Things*, November. https:// www.firstthings.com/article/2015/11/a-church-of-empire. Last accessed March 3, 2016.

———. 2020. "The Rhetoric of Traditional Values in Contemporary Russia." In *Postsecular Conflicts: Debates from Russia and the United States*, edited by Kristina Stoeckl and Dmitry Uzlaner, 128–38. Innsbruck: Innsbruck University Press.

Chesnokov, Sergey V. 2017. "Sovremennaya diskusiya o prave rebenka na zhizn' do rozhdeniya." [The Contemporary Discussion about the Right of Life of the Child before Birth]. [Video]. YouTube. Uploaded by Festival Za Zhizn' on March 2, 2017. Registered January 27, 2017, in the context of the XXV Christmas Readings, Hotel Salyut, Moscow. https://www.youtube.com /watch?v=NzrbZ3xXMO8&t=307s. Accessed April 20, 2017.

Chitanava, Eka, and Katie Sartania. 2018. "Public Space: The Battleground in the Revanchist City." In *The Rise of Illiberal Civil Society in the Former Soviet Union*, edited by Adam Hug. https://fpc.org.uk/wp-content/uploads/2018/07 /The-rise-of-illiberal-civil-society-in-the-former-Soviet-Union.pdf. Accessed October 15, 2018. London: Foreign Policy Think Tank.

Christensen, Bryce J. 1996. "Pitirim A. Sorokin: A Forerunner to Solzhenitsyn." *Modern Age* 38:386–90.

Christian NewsWire. 2010. "Jacobs Finds Support for International Pro-Family and Pro-Life Movement in Moscow." *Christian News Wire*, December 13, 2010. http://www.christiannewswire.com/news/4302615709.html. Accessed May 24, 2017.

CitizenGo. 2015. "Podderzhivayem Gruppu druzey sem'i v OON!" [We Support the UN Family Friends Group!]. *Website of CitizenGO Russia*, March 14, 2015. https://www.citizengo.org/ru/20029-podderzhivaem-gruppu -druzey-semi-v-oon. Accessed March 13, 2020.

———. 2019. "Ostanovim antisemejnij zakon o 'domashnem nasilii'" [Let Us Stop the Law on "Domestic Violence"]. *Website of CitizenGO Russia*, October 23, 2019. https://www.citizengo.org/ru/fm/174541-ostanovim -antisemeynyy-zakon-o-domashnem-nasilii?fbclid=IwAR1yxvm6aIHgaxnI0 0DetiQFfiNV7dHj3ti703NWda3zzzaSbJTInn_k590. Accessed February 18, 2020.

Cohen, Will. 2019. "Whether and How Ecumenism, Anti-Ecumenism, and Conservative Ecumenism Are Politically or Theologically Motivated: A View from the United States." *State, Religion and Church* 6 (1):20–43.

Cowell, F. R. 1970. *Values in Human Society: The Contributions of Pitirim A. Sorokin to Sociology*. Boston: Porter Sargent.

Curanović, Alicija. 2012. *The Religious Factor in Russia's Foreign Policy*. London and New York: Routledge.

———. 2015. "The Guardians of Traditional Values: Russia and the Russian Orthodox Church in the Quest for Status." In *Faith, Freedom and Foreign Policy: Challenges for the Transatlantic Community*, edited by Michael Barnett, Clifford Bob, Nora Fisher Onar, Anne Jenichen, Michael Leigh, and Lucian N. Leustean, 191–212. Washington, D.C.: Transatlantic Academy.

———. 2019. "Russia's Contemporary Exceptionalism and Geopolitical Conservatism." In *Contemporary Russian Conservatism: Problems, Paradoxes and Dangers*, edited by Mikhail Suslov and Dmitry Uzlaner, 207–33. Leiden: Brill.

Davidson, Natalie. 2019. "The Feminist Expansion of the Prohibition of Torture: Towards a Post-Liberal International Human Rights Law?" *Cornell International Law Journal* 52 (1):109–36.

Davis, Derek H. 1997. "Russia's New Law on Religion: Progress or Regress?" *Journal of Church and State* 39:645–56.

Deklaratsiya Tsennostej Soyuznogo Gosudarstva. 2018. "Deklaratsiya Tsennostej Soyuznogo Gosudarstva Rossii i Belarusi." [Declaration of the Values of the Union of Russia and Belarus]. *Website of the Obshchestvennaya Palata Soyuznogo Gosudarstva*, June 5, 2019.https://op-soyuz.ru/декларация -ценностей-союзного-гоцуд/. Accessed August 24, 2020.

Demacopoulos, George, and Aristotle Papanikolau. 2014. "Putin's Unorthodox Orthodoxy." *blogs.goarch.org—An internet ministry tool of the Greek Orthodox Archdiocese of America*, June 25, 2014. http://blogs.goarch.org/blog/-/blogs /putin-s-unorthodox-orthodoxy?p_p_auth=IpTqHq5b&_33_redirect =http://blogs.goarch.org/home?p_p_id=101_INSTANCE_Z7aQ1f5b QmL4&p_p_lifecycle=0&p_p_state=normal&p_p_mode=view& p_p_col_id=column-1&p_p_col_pos=1&p_p_col_count=2. Accessed July 16, 2014.

Demoscop Weekly. 2011. "Anatoliyu Ivanovichu Antonovu—75 let." [Anatolij Antonov Turns 75]. *Demoscop Weekly*, 475–76. http://www.demoscope.ru /weekly/2011/0475/nauka01.php. Accessed October 9, 2018.

Denisov, Boris P., Victoria I. Sakevich, and Aiva Jasilioniene. 2012. "Divergent Trends in Abortion and Birth Control Practices in Belarus, Russia and Ukraine." *PLoS ONE* 7 (11). http://doi.org/10.1371/journal.pone.0049986.

Dobrenkov, Vladimir I. 2011. "Krizis nashego vremeni v kontekste teorii sotsiokul'turnoi dinamiki P. A. Sorokina: Prorochestvo o sud'bakh mira i Rossii" [The Crisis of Our Times in the Context of the Theory of Socio-Cultural Dynamics of P. A. Sorokin: Prophecy about the Fate of the World and Russia.] *Nasledie* 1:150–63.

Dobson, Dzhejms Ch. 1991. *Roditelyam i molodozhenam: Doktor Dobson otvechaet na vashi voprosy* [To Parents and Newly Wedded: Doctor Dobson Answers Your Questions]. Moscow: Centr obshhechelovecheskih cennostej.

Donnelly, Mike. 2017. "Why Homeschooling Is Gaining Respect in Russia." *HSLDA Advocates for Homeschooling since 1983*, April 4, 2017. https://www .hslda.org/hs/international/Russia/201704040.asp. Accessed June 11, 2019.

Dornblüth, Gesine. 2019. "Religiöse Recht in Russland un den USA." *Deutschlandfunk*, November 19, 2019. https://www.deutschlandfunk.de /netzwerk-konservativer-christen-religioese-rechte-in.724.de.html?dram:article _id=463836. Accessed January 29, 2020.

Dowland, Seth. 2015. *Family Values and the Rise of the Christian Right.* Philadelphia: University of Pennsylvania Press.

Dreher, Rod. 2008. "Pitirim Sorokin and the Benedict Option." *Beliefnet*, May 25, 2008. http://web.archive.org/web/20081011141535/http:/blog .beliefnet.com/crunchycon/2008/05/pitirim-sorokin-and-the-benedi.html. Accessed May 24, 2017.

———. 2013. "Sorokin & Twilight of the Sensate." *American Conservative*, August 14, 2013. https://www.theamericanconservative.com/dreher/sorokin -twilight-of-the-sensate/. Accessed May 16, 2017.

———. 2015. "Terrorism & This Religious Century." *American Conservative*, November 18, 2015. http://www.theamericanconservative.com/dreher /terrorism-religious-century-isis-faith-christianity-islam/. Accessed May 16, 2017.

———. 2017a. *The Benedict Option: A Strategy for Christians in a Post-Christian Nation.* New York: Sentinel.

———. 2017b. "How Putin Matters." *American Conservative*, November 21, 2017. http://www.theamericanconservative.com/dreher/how-putin-matters -russian-orthodoxy-evangelicalism/. Accessed May 14, 2019.

———. 2020a. "'All the Great Renewal Movements Came from below': Interview with Rod Dreher." In *Postsecular Conflicts: Debating Tradition in*

Russia and the United States, edited by Kristina Stoeckl and Dmitry Uzlaner, 24–36. Innsbruck: Innsbruck University Press.

———. 2020b. *Live Not by Lies: A Manual for Christian Dissidents*. New York: Penguin Random House.

———. 2022. "War & Culture War: Patriarch Kirill & LGBT." *American Conservative*, March 8, 2022. https://www.theamericanconservative.com/dreher/war-culture-war-patriarch-kyrill-lgbt-russia-ukraine/. Accessed March 9, 2022.

Dugin, Alexander G. 2011. "Konservativnaia paradigma i kritika teorii progressa v sotsiologii Pitirima Sorokina: Aktual'nost' dlia sovremennoi Rossii" [The Conservative Paradigm and the Critique of the Theory of Progress in Pitirim Sorokin's Sociology: Relevance for Contemporary Russia]. *Nasledie* 1:164–70.

Dunlop, John B. 1995. "The Russian Orthodox Church as an 'Empire-Saving' Institution." In *The Politics of Religion in Russia and the New States of Eurasia*, edited by Michael Bourdeaux, 15–41. Armonk, N.Y.: M. E. Sharpe.

Durham, W. Cole, and Lauren B. Homer. 1998. "Russia's 1997 Law on Freedom of Conscience and Religious Associations: An Analytical Appraisal." *Emory International Law Review* 12 (101):101–246.

DW News. 2017. "Is the Russian Orthodox Church serving God or Putin? / DW English." YouTube, April 26, 2017. https://www.youtube.com/watch?v=Ja_awL1nsJE&feature=youtu.be. Accessed June 11, 2019.

Endruweit, Günter. 2002. "Theorieimporte von Europa nach Amerika am Beispiel Pitirim A. Sorokins." In *Pitirim A. Sorokin: Leben, Werk und Wirkung*, edited by Bálint Balla, Ilija Srubar, and Martin Albrecht, 65–84. Hamburg: Krämer.

Engeli, Isabelle, Christopher Green-Pedersen, and Lars Thorup Larsen. 2012. *Morality Politics in Western Europe: Parties, Agendas and Policy Choices*. Basingstoke: Palgrave Macmillan.

Erofeeva, Lyubov Vladimirovna. 2013. "Traditional Christian Values and Women's Reproductive Rights in Modern Russia—Is a Consensus Ever Possible?" *American Journal of Public Health* 103 (11):1,931–34.

European Union. 2013. "Contribution of the European Union: Traditional Values." *Office of the High Commissioner of Human Rights*, February 15, 2013. http://www.ohchr.org/EN/Issues/Pages/TraditionalValues.aspx. Last accessed April 5, 2017.

Fagan, Geraldine. 2013. *Believing in Russia: Religious Policy after Communism*. London and New York: Routledge.

Falwell, Jerry. 1981. *Listen America!* New York: Bantam.

FamilyPolicy.ru. 2019. "Pravovoi analiz proekta Federal'nogo zakona 'O profilaktike semeino-bytovogo nasiliya v Rossiiskoi Federatsii'" [Legal Analysis of the

Draft of the Federal Law "On the Prevention of Domestic Violence in the Russian Federation"]. *Website of FamilyPolicy.ru*, December 2019. http://www.familypolicy.ru/rep/rf-19-051-01.pdf. Accessed February 18, 2020.

Federman, Adam. 2014. "How US Evangelicals Fueled the Rise of Russia's 'Pro-Family' Right." *National Interest*, January 7, 2014. http://www.thenation.com/article/177823/how-us-evangelicals-fueled-rise-russiaspro-family-right. Last accessed April 6, 2014.

Field, Mark G. 2000. "The Health and Demographic Crisis in Post-Soviet Russia: A Two-Phase Development." In *Russia's Torn Safety Nets: Health and Social Welfare during the Transition*, edited by Mark G. Field and Judyth L. Twigg, 11–42. New York: Palgrave Macmillan.

Figes, Orlando. 2008. *The Whisperers: Private Life in Stalin's Russia*. London: Penguin Allen Lane.

Finnemore, Martha, and Kathryn Sikkink. 1998. "International Norm Dynamics and Political Change." *International Organization* 52 (4):887–917.

Ford, Joseph B., Michel P. Richard, and Palmer Talbutt Jr. 1996. *Sorokin & Civilization: A Centennial Assessment*. New Brunswick, N.J.: Transaction.

Frank, Thomas. 2004. *What's the Matter with Kansas? How Conservatives won the Heart of America*. New York: Owl.

Froese, Paul. 2008. *The Plot to Kill God: Findings from the Soviet Experiment in Secularization*. Berkeley: University of California Press.

Fukuyama, Francis. 1989. "The End of History?" *National Interest* 16:3–18.

Gaither, Milton. 2008a. *Homeschool: An American History*. New York: Palgrave Macmillan.

———. 2008b. "Why Homeschooling Happened." *Educational Horizons* 86 (4):226–37.

Gal, Susan, and Gail Kligman. 2000. *The Politics of Gender after Socialism: A Comparative-Historical Essay*. Princeton, N.J.: Princeton University Press.

Gallaher, Brandon. 2018. "Tangling with Orthodox Tradition in the Modern West: Natural Law, Homosexuality, and Living Tradition." *Wheel* 13/14:50–63.

Gathii, James T. 2006. "Exporting Culture Wars." *U.C. Davis Journal of International Law and Policy* 13 (1):67–93.

Gessen, Masha. 2017. "Family Values: Mapping the Spread of Antigay Ideology." *Harper's Magazine*, February 20, 2017. https://harpers.org/archive/2017/03/family-values-3/. Accessed June 11, 2019.

GHEX. 2012a. "Berlin Declaration." *Website of Global Home Education Exchange*. https://ghex.world/wp-content/uploads/2018/05/Berlin-Declaration-English.pdf. Accessed April 16, 2019.

———. 2012b. "Board Resolution." *Website of Global Home Education Exchange*. https://ghex.world/wp-content/uploads/2018/05/GHEC-Board-Resolution.pdf. Accessed February 20, 2020.

———. 2016. "Rio Principles, Declared in Rio de Janeiro, March 2016." *Website of Global Home Education Exchange*. https://ghex.world/advocacy/declarations /rio-principles/. Accessed April 16, 2019.

———. 2018. "Global Home Education Conference 2018: St. Petersburg & Moscow, Russia." *Website of Global Home Education Exchange*. https://ghex .world/conferences/ghec-2018/. Accessed April 16, 2019.

———. 2019. "About the African Home Education Indaba." *Website of Global Home Education Exchange*. https://ghex.africa/. Accessed February 28, 2020.

Glanzer, Perry L. 2002. *The Quest for Russia's Soul: Evangelicals and Moral Education in Post-Communist Russia*. Waco, Tex.: Baylor University Press.

Graham, Billy. 1965. *World Aflame*. 1st ed. Garden City, N.Y.: Doubleday.

Graham, Franklin. 2016. "Earlier this year I announced . . ." *Facebook*, August 2, 2016. https://www.facebook.com/FranklinGraham/posts /1212590925463753:0. Accessed February 25, 2020.

Greenhouse, Linda, and Reva Siegel. 2016. "The Difference a Whole Woman Makes: Protection for the Abortion Right after Whole Woman's Health." *Yale Law Journal Forum* 126. https://www.yalelawjournal.org/forum/the -difference-a-whole-woman-makes. Accessed July 31, 2020.

Grzymała-Busse, Anna Maria. 2015. *Nations under God: How Churches Use Moral Authority to Influence Policy*. Princeton, N.J.: Princeton University Press, 2015.

Habermas, Jürgen. 2005. "Religion in der Öffentlichkeit: Kognitive Voraussetzungen für den 'öffentlichen Vernunftgebrauch' religiöser und säkularer Bürger." In *Zwischen Naturalismus und Religion*, 119–54. Frankfurt am Main: Suhrkamp.

———. 2006. "Religion in the Public Sphere." *European Journal of Philosophy* 14 (1):1–25.

Habermas, Jurgen, and Josef Ratzinger. 2006. *The Dialectics of Secularization: On Reason and Religion*. San Francisco: Ignatius.

Hartman, Andrew. 2015. *A War for the Soul of America: A History of the Culture Wars*. Chicago and London: University of Chicago Press.

Hatewatch Staff. 2018. "How the World Congress of Families Serves Russian Orthodox Political Interests." *Southern Poverty Law Center*, May 16, 2018. https://www.splcenter.org/hatewatch/2018/05/16/how-world-congress -families-serves-russian-orthodox-political-interests. Accessed June 4, 2019.

Haynes, Jeffrey. 2013. "Faith-Based Organisations at the United Nations." EUI Working Paper. *RSCAS ReligioWest* (70).

Henderson, Jane. 2018. "Russia's Recent Dealings with the Council of Europe and European Court of Human Rights." *European Public Law* 24 (3):393–402.

Herman, Didi. 2001. "Globalism's Siren Song: The United Nations in Christian Right Thought and Prophecy." *Sociological Review* 49:56–77.

Hillery, George A. Jr., Susan V. Meas, and Robert G. Turner Jr. 1996. "An Empirical Assessment of Sorokin's Theory of Change." In *Sorokin & Civilization: A Centennial Assessment*, edited by Joseph B. Ford, Michel P. Richard, and Palmer Talbutt, 171–86. New Brunswick, N.J.: Transaction.

Himmelfarb, Gertrude. 2006. "Comment. The Other Culture War." In *Is There a Culture War? A Dialogue on Values and American Public Life*, edited by James Davison Hunter and Alan Wolfe, 74–82. Washington, D.C.: Pew Research Center, Brookings Institution Press.

Höjdestrand, Tova. 2016. "Social Welfare or Moral Warfare?: Popular Resistance against Children's Rights and Juvenile Justice in Contemporary Russia." *International Journal of Children's Rights* 24 (4):826–50.

———. 2017. "Nationalism and Civicness in Russia: Grassroots Mobilization in Defence of 'Family Values.'" In *Rebellious Parents: Parental Movements in Central-Eastern Europe and Russia*, edited by Katalin Fabian and Elzbieta Korolczuk, 31–60. Lund: Indiana University Press.

Holt, John, and Pat Farenga. 2003. *Teach Your Own: The John Holt Book of Homeschooling*. New York: Perseus.

Holzhacker, Ronald. 2013. "State-Sponsored Homophobia and the Denial of the Right of Assembly in Central and Eastern Europe: The "Boomerang" and the "Ricochet" between European Organizations and Civil Society to Uphold Human Rights." *Law & Policy* 35 (1–2):1–28.

Horsfjord, Vebjørn L. 2017. "Negotiating Traditional Values: The Russian Orthodox Church at the United Nations Human Rights Council (UNHCR)." In *Religion, State and the United Nations*, edited by Anne Stensvold, 62–78. London and New York: Routledge.

Horvath, Robert. 2016. "The Reinvention of 'Traditional Values': Nataliya Narochnitskaya and Russia's Assult on Universal Human Rights." *Europe-Asia Studies* 68 (5):868–92.

Hovorun, Cyril. 2014. "The Church in the Bloodlands." *First Things*, October 1, 2014. http://www.firstthings.com/article/2014/10/the-church-in-the -bloodlands. Accessed November 11, 2015.

HSLDA. 2017. "Why Homeschooling Is Gaining Respect in Russia." [Video]. *Website of the Home School Legal Defense Association*, April 4, 2017. https:// youtu.be/jVpJfmnuL6Q. Accessed February 28, 2020.

———. 2018. "Recordsetting Event Promotes Homeschooling in Russia and the World." *Website of the Home School Legal Defense Association*, May 30, 2018. https://hslda.org/content/hs/international/20180530-recordsetting-event-promotes -homeschooling-in-russia-and-the-world.aspx. Accessed December 4, 2018.

———. 2020. "Russia." *Website of the Home School Legal Defense Association*. https://hslda.org/content/hs/international/Russia/default.asp. Accessed February 20, 2020.

Hug, Simon, and Richard Lukács. 2014. "Preferences or Blocs? Voting in the United Nations Human Rights Council." *Review of International Organizations* 9:83–106. http://doi.org/10.1007/s11558-013-9172-2.

Human Rights Doctrine. 2008. "The Russian Orthodox Church's Basic Teaching on Human Dignity, Freedom and Rights (official translation)." *Official Website of the Department for External Church Relations of the Moscow Patriarchate.* http://www.mospat.ru/en/documents/dignity-freedom -rights/.

Hunter, James Davison. 1991. *Culture Wars: The Struggle to Define America.* New York: Basic Books.

———. 1994. *Before the Shooting Begins: Searching for Democracy in America's Culture War.* New York and Toronto: Maxwell Macmillan International.

Hunter, James Davison, and Alan Wolfe. 2006. *Is There a Culture War? A Dialogue on Values and American Public Life.* Washington, D.C: Pew Research Center, Brookings Institution Press.

Huntington, Samuel. 1993. "The Clash of Civilizations." *Foreign Affairs* 72 (3):22–50.

Inazu, John D. 2016. *Confident Pluralism.* Chicago: University of Chicago Press.

Inglehart, Ronald F. 2021. *Religion's Sudden Decline: What's Causing It, and What Comes Next?* Oxford: Oxford University Press.

Interfax. 2020. "V Konstitutsiiu predlozhili vnesti polozhenie o sem'e kak soiuze muzhchiny i zhenshchiny." *Interfax*, January 30, 2020. https://www .interfax.ru/russia/693381. Accessed August 24, 2020.

Interreligious Council. 2017. "6 yanvarya 2017 goda glavy i predstaviteli traditsionnykh religiy Rossii prinyali uchastiye v V Rozhdestvenskikh Parlamentskikh vstrechakh" [On January 26, 2017, Heads and Representatives of Traditional Religions of Russia Took Part in the V Christmas Parliamentary Meetings]. *Website of the Interreligious Council of Russia and other CIS countries*, January 26, 2017. http://interreligious.ru/news /news-religious-communities/26-yanvarya-2017-goda-glavy-i-predstaviteli -traditsionnyh-religiy-rossii-prinyali-uchastie-v-v-rozhdestvenskih -parlamentskih-vstrechah.html. Accessed February 25, 2020.

IOF Mission. 2020. "Mission." *Website of the International Organization for the Family.* https://www.profam.org/mission/. Accessed February 27, 2020.

Irvine, Jill A. 2012. "Exporting the Culture Wars: Concerned Women for America in the Global Arena." In *Women of the Right: Comparisons and Interplay across Borders*, edited by Kathleen M. Blee and Sandra McGee Deutsch, 36–51. University Park: Pennsylvania State University Press.

Ivanov, D. V. [Dmitrij]. 2011. "Tsennye predskazaniya Pitirima Sorokina: sotsial'naia i kul'turnaia dinamika v XXI veke" [Valuable Predictions of

Pitirim Sorokin: Social and Cultural Dynamics in the Twenty-First Century]. *Nasledie* 1:171–77.

————. 2017. "Litsenziya na abort—novyj kamen' pretknoveniya na puti otechestvennogo zdravookhraneniya." [Licence for Abortion—A New Stumbling Block for National Healthcare]. *Information Portal www.pravo-med.ru*, February 15, 2017. http://pravo-med.ru/articles/13405/. Last accessed April 11, 2017.

Janik, Ralph. 2019. "Konservative aller Welt, vereinigt: Die US-russische Achse beim 'World Congress of Families.'" *Addendum*, April 4, 2019. https://www.addendum.org/news/world-congress-of-families/. Accessed February 4, 2020.

Jeffries, Vincent. 2002. "Integralism: The Promising Legacy of Pitirim Sorokin." In *Lost Sociologists Rediscovered*, edited by M. A. Robinson, 99–135. New York: Mellon.

————. 2009. *Handbook of Public Sociology.* Lanham, Md.: Rowman & Littlefield.

Jenkins, Jack. 2018. "When Franklin Graham Met Putin." *Religion News Service*, August 7, 2018. https://religionnews.com/2018/08/07/the-russian-connection-when-franklin-graham-met-putin/. Accessed May 7, 2019.

Jenkins, Philip. 2002. *The Next Christendom: The Coming of Global Christianity.* New York: Oxford University Press.

————. 2006. *Decade of Nightmares: The End of the Sixties and the Making of Eighties America.* New York: Oxford University Press.

Johnston, Barry V. 1995. *Pitirim A. Sorokin: An Intellectual Biography.* Lawrence: University Press of Kansas.

————. 1996. "Sorokin's Life and Work." In *Sorokin & Civilization: A Centennial Assessment*, edited by Joseph B. Ford, Michel P. Richard, and Palmer Talbutt Jr., 3–14. New Brunswick, N.J.: Transaction.

Jordan, Pamela A. 2003. "Russia's Accession to the Council of Europe and Compliance with European Human Rights Norms." *Democratizatsiya* 11 (2):281–96.

Kaleda, Gleb. 1998. *Domashnyaya tserkov'.* Moscow: Izd. Zachat'evskij Monastyr'.

Kane, Gillian. 2009/2010. "Commentary: Exporting 'Traditional Values': The World Congress of Families." *Public Eye*, Winter/Spring. http://www.publiceye.org/magazine/v24n4/exporting-traditional-talues.html. Last access November 3, 2016.

Kaoma, Kapya. 2014. *American Culture Warriors in Africa: A Guide to the Exporters of Homophobia and Sexism.* Somerville, Mass.: Political Research Associates.

Karpov, Vyacheslav, and Kimmo Kääriäinen. 2005. "'Abortion Culture' in Russia: Its Origins, Scope, and Challenge to Social Development." *Sociological Practice* 7 (2):13–33.

Kaufmann, Eric. 2011. *Shall the Religious Inherit the Earth?* London: Profile.

Kayaoglu, Turan. 2014. "Giving an Inch Only to Lose a Mile: Muslim States, Liberalism and Human Rights in the United Nations." *Human Rights Quarterly* 36:61–89.

Keating, Joshua. 2014. "Russia Gets Religion." *Slate*, November 11, 2014. http://www.slate.com/articles/news_and_politics/foreigners/2014/11/russia _orthodox_church_will_vladimir_putin_eradicate_all_boundaries_between .single.html. Last accessed March 16, 2015.

Keck, Margaret E., and Kathryn Sikkink. 1998. *Activists beyond Borders: Advocacy Networks in International Politics.* Ithaca, N.Y.: Cornell University Press.

Khalturina, D. A., and A. V. Korotaev. 2006. *Russkij krest: Faktory, mekhanizmy i puti preodoleniya demograficheskogo krizisa v Rossii* [The Russian Cross: Factors, Mechanisms and the Ways of Overcoming Demographic Crisis in Russia. Moscow: URSS Publishing Group.

Klassicheskie Besedy. 2020a. "Istoriya [History]." *Website of the Russian Classical Conversations.* https://classical-conversations.ru/kb-history-in-russia/. Accessed February 24, 2020.

———. 2020b. "O programme" [About the Program]. *Website of the Russian Classical Conversations.* https://classical-conversations.ru/o_kb_general/. Accessed February 24, 2020.

Knorre, Boris. 2018. "Die anti-ökumenische Rhetorik orthodoxer Fundamentalisten." *Religion und Gesellschaft in Ost und West* 10:11–13.

Knox, Zoe. 2003. "The Symphonic Ideal: The Moscow Patriarchate's Post-Soviet Leadership." *Europe-Asia Studies* 55 (4):575–96.

———. 2004. *Russian Society and the Orthodox Church: Religion in Russia after Communism.* New York and London: RoutledgeCurzon.

Kon, Igor. 1995. *The Sexual Revolution in Russia: From the Age of the Czars to Today.* Translated by James Riordan. New York: Free Press.

———. 1999. "Sexuality and Politics in Russia, 1700–2000." In *Sexual Cultures in Europe: National Histories*, edited by F. H. Eder, L. Hall, and G Hekma. New York: Manchester University Press.

Kostjuk, Konstantin. 2000. "Pravoslavnyj fundamentalism" [Orthodox Fundamentalism]. *Polis* 5 (58):133–54.

———. 2013. *Istoriya sotsial'no-eticheskoi mysli v Russkoi pravoslavnoi tserkvi* [History of Social-Ethical Thought of the Russian Orthodox Church]. Saint Petersburg: Aleteia.

Kravchenko, Sergey A., and Nikita E. Pokrovsky, eds. 2001. *Return of Pitirim Sorokin.* Moscow: International Kondratieff Foudation.

Kuby, Gabriele. 2012. *Die globale sexuelle Revolution.* Kissleg: Fe-medienverlag.

Laruelle, Marlene. 2017. "Putin's Regime and the Ideological Market: A Difficult Balancing Game." *Carnegie Endowment for International Peace*,

March 16, 2017. https://carnegieendowment.org/2017/03/16/putin-s-regime
-and-ideological-market-difficult-balancing-game-pub-68250. Accessed
July 27, 2020.

———. 2018. "Russian Soft Power in France: Assessing Moscow's Cultural and
Business Para-diplomacy." *Carnegie Council for Ethics in International
Affairs*, January 8, 2018. https://www.carnegiecouncil.org/publications
/articles_papers_reports/russian-soft-power-in-france. Accessed June 1, 2021.

———. 2020. "Making Sense of Russia's Illiberalism." *Journal of Democracy* 31
(3):115–29.

Lega Salvini Premier. 2013. "Congresso Federale Lega Nord
2013—Ambasciatore Russo Nazioni Unite Alexey Komov." [Video].
YouTube, December 18, 2013. https://www.youtube.com/watch?v
=DsgJtcNZZwQ. Accessed October 21, 2019.

Lehmann, Karsten. 2013. "Shifting Boundaries between the Religious and the
Secular: Religious Organizations in Global Public Space." *Journal of Religion
in Europe* 6:1–28.

———. 2016. *Religious NGOs in International Relations: The Construction of
"the Religious" and "the Secular."* London and New York: Routledge.

Lenzerini, Federico. 2014. *The Culturalization of Human Rights.* Oxford:
Oxford University Press.

Levada Center. 2015. "'Invisible Minority': The Problem of Homophobia in
Russia" ["Nevidimoe men'shinstvo": K probleme gomofobii v Rossii]. *Levada
Center*, May 5, 2015. https://www.levada.ru/2015/05/05/nevidimoe
-menshinstvo-k-probleme-gomofobii-v-rossii/. Accessed September 9, 2020.

———. 2018. "'Number of People Who Condemn Abortions Increases"
[Osuzhdaiushchikh aborty stalo bol'she]. *Levada Center*, January 11, 2018.
https://www.levada.ru/2018/01/11/osuzhdayushhih-aborty-stalo-bolshe/.
Accessed September 9, 2020.

Levintova, Hannah. 2014. "How US Evangelicals Helped Create Russia's
Anti-Gay Movement." *Motherjones*, February 21, 2014. www.motherjones
.com/politics/2014/02/world-congress-families-russia-gay-rights. Accessed
October 9, 2018.

Lewis, R. Andrew. 2017. *The Rights Turn in Conservative Christian Politics: How
Abortion Transformed the Culture Wars.* Cambridge: Cambridge University Press.

Lipka, Michael, and Neha Sahgal. 2017. "9 Key Findings about Religion and
Politics in Central and Eastern Europe." *Pew Research Center*, May 10, 2017.
https://www.pewresearch.org/fact-tank/2017/05/10/9-key-findings-about
-religion-and-politics-in-central-and-eastern-europe/. Accessed
December 25, 2019.

Lipman, Maria, and Victoria I. Sakevich. 2019. "Abortion in Russia: How Has
the Situation Changed since the Soviet Era?" *PONARS Eurasia, George*

Washington University, February 12, 2019. https://www.ponarseurasia.org
/abortion-in-russia-how-has-the-situation-changed-since-the-soviet-era/.
Accessed June 2, 2021.

Ludwig, Heiner. 2004. "Die Sozialverkündigung der orthodoxen Kirche und
der Westkirchen—Spannungsfelder." In *Beginn einer neuen Ära? Die
Sozialdoktrin der Russisch-Orthodoxen Kirche vom August 2000 im
interkulturellen Dialog*, edited by Rudolf Uertz and Lars Peter Schmidt,
97–111. Moscow: Konrad Adenauer Stiftung e.V.

Luehrmann, Sonja. 2017a. "'God Values Intentions': Abortion, Expiation, and
Moments of Sincerity in Russian Orthodox Pilgrimage." *HAU: Journal of
Ethnographic Theory* 7 (1):163–84.

———. 2017b. "Innocence and Demographic Crisis: Transposing Post-
Abortion Syndrome into a Russian Orthodox Key." In *A Fragmented
Landscape: Abortion Governance and Protest Logics in Europe*, edited by S. De
Zordo, J. Mishtal, and L. Anton, 103–22. New York: Berghahn.

Mace, David R. 1963. "Sorokin's Theories on Sex and Society." In *Sorokin in
Review*, edited by Philip J. Allen, 140–59. Durham, N.C.: Duke University Press.

Maddock, James W., M. Janice Hogan, Anatoly I. Antonov, and Mikhail S.
Matskovsky. 1994. *Families before and after Perestroika: Russian and U.S.
Perspectives*. New York and London: Guilford.

Magister, Sandro. 2010. "A Holy Alliance between Rome and Moscow Is Born."
Chiesa Espresso, May 24, 2010. http://chiesa.espresso.repubblica.it/articolo
/1343399bdc4.html?eng=y. Accessed February 25, 2020.

Makrides, Vasilios. 2013. "Why Does the Orthodox Church Lack Systematic
Social Teaching?" *Skepsis: A Journal for Philosophy and Interdisciplinary
Research* 23:281–312.

Malinova, Olga. 2020. "Framing the Collective Memory of the 1990s as a
Legitimation Tool for Putin's Regime." *Problems of Post-Communism* 1–13.
http://doi.org/10.1080/10758216.2020.1752732.

Mälksoo, Lauri, and Wolfgang Benedek, eds. 2017. *Russia and the European
Court of Human Rights: The Strasbourg Effect, European Inter-University
Centre for Human Rights and Democratisation*. Cambridge: Cambridge
University Press.

Mancini, Susanna, and Kristina Stoeckl. 2018. "Transatlantic Conversations:
The Emergence of Society-Protective Anti-Abortion Arguments in the
United States, Europe and Russia." In *The Conscience Wars: Rethinking the
Balance between Religion and Equality*, edited by Susanna Mancini and
Michel Rosenfeld, 220–57. Cambridge: Cambridge University Press.

Manhattan Declaration. 2009. "Manhattan Declaration: A Call of Christian
Conscience." *manhattandeclaration.org*, November 20, 2009. https://www
.manhattandeclaration.org/. Accessed February 25, 2020.

Maquet, Jacques J. 1951. *The Sociology of Knowledge: Its Structure and Its Relation to the Philosophy of Knowledge; A Critical Analysis of the Systems of Karl Mannheim and Pitirim A. Sorokin*. Boston: Beacon.

Marsden, Lee. 2008. *For God's Sake: The Christian Right and US Foreign Policy*. London and New York: Zed.

Marshall, Katherine. 2017. "Religious Voices at the United Nations: American Faith Perspectives as an Example." In *Religion, State and the United Nations*, edited by Anne Stensvold, 127–36. London and New York: Routledge.

Marshall, Paul. 2011. "Exporting Blasphemy Restrictions: The Organization of the Islamic Conference and the United Nations." *Review of Faith & International Affairs* 9 (2):57–63.

Matveev, V. 1983. "Krizis morali i moral' krizisa" [Crisis of Morality and Morality of Crisis]. *Izvestiya* 241.

McCrudden, Christopher. 2014. "Human Rights, Southern Voices, and 'Traditional Values' at the United Nations." *University of Michigan Public Law Research Paper* 419. http://ssrn.com/abstract=2474241. Last accessed October 27, 2015.

———. 2015. "Transnational Culture Wars." *University of Michigan Public Law Research Paper* 447. https://papers.ssrn.com/sol3/papers.cfm?abstract_id =2589542. Last accessed October 27, 2015.

McGuckin, John. 2016. "The Mystery of Marriage: An Orthodox Perspective." In *Love, Marriage and Family in Eastern Orthodox Perspective*, edited by Theodore Grey Dedon and Sergey Tostyanskiy, xi–xiv. Berlin: DeGruyter.

McIntosch, C. Alison, and Jason L. Finkle. 1995. "The Cairo Conference on Population and Development: A New Paradigm?" *Population and Development Review* 21 (2):223–60.

Meduza. 2019a. "'I try not to exaggerate my own significance': Ex-lawmaker and former pro-Kremlin youth activist Robert Schlegel explains why he left Russia to raise his kids in Germany." *Meduza News Portal*, December 3, 2019. https://meduza.io/en/feature/2019/12/03/i-try-not-to-exaggerate-my -own-significance. Accessed July 27, 2020.

———. 2019b. "'We Don't Trust Feminists with Laws about Our Families': Conservatives Assembled in Moscow over the Weekend to Protest the Re-criminalization of Domestic Violence. Here's What They Said from the Stage and the Stands." *Meduza News Portal*, November 25, 2019. https:// meduza.io/en/feature/2019/11/25/we-don-t-trust-feminists-with-laws-about -our-families. Accessed January 8, 2020.

Metropolitan Kirill, of Smolensk and Kaliningrad. 2000a. "Norma very kak norma zhizni I." [The Norms of Faith as Norms of Life, Part I]. *Nezavisimaya Gazeta*. February 16, 2000. http://www.ng.ru/ideas/2000-02 -16/8_norma.html.

———. 2000b. "Norma very kak norma zhizni II." [The Norms of Faith as Norms of Life, Part II]. *Nezavisimaya Gazeta*, February 17, 2000. http://www.ng.ru/ideas/2000-02-17/8_norma2.html.

———. 2006. "The Experience of Viewing the Problems of Human Rights and their Moral Foundations in European Religious Communities. Presentation at the Conference 'Evolution of Moral Values and Human Rights in Multicultural Society,' Strasbourg, 30 October 2006." *Europaica Bulletin*, November 6, 2006, 108. http://orthodoxeurope.org/page/14/108.aspx#1.

Michel, Casey. 2017. "How Russia Became the Leader of the Global Christian Right." *Politico Magazine*, February 9, 2017. https://www.politico.com/magazine/story/2017/02/how-russia-became-a-leader-of-the-worldwide-christian-right-214755. Accessed June 18, 2019.

———. 2019a. "How Russia Infiltrated the World of American Religious-Right Filmmaking." *ThinkProgress*, February 8, 2019. https://thinkprogress.org/how-russia-infiltrated-the-world-of-american-religious-right-film-making-movieguide-ted-baehr-alexey-komov/. Accessed February 28, 2020.

———. 2019b. "Russians and the American Right Started Plotting in 1995. We Have the Notes from the First Meeting." *ThinkProgress*, June 19, 2018. https://thinkprogress.org/history-of-christian-fundamentalists-in-russia-and-the-us-a6bdd326841d/. Accessed February 28, 2020.

MID. 2003. "Ob itogakh zasedaniya rabochey gruppy po vzaimodeystviyu Russkoy Pravoslavnoy Tserkvi i Ministersvta Inostrannykh del Rossii" [On the Results of the Meeting of the Working Group on the Cooperation between the Russian Orthodox Church and the Ministry of Foreign Affairs of Russia]. *Website of Ministry of Foreign Affairs of the Russian Federation*, November 10, 2003. https://www.mid.ru/rossia-v-sisteme-mezkonfessional-nyh-otnosenij/-/asset_publisher/Z02tOD8Nkusz/content/id/497930. Accessed March 3, 2020.

Mikhailovsky, Alexander. 2015. "The Pressure Valve: Russian Nationalism in Late Soviet Society." *Eurozine* December 9, 2015. http://www.eurozine.com/articles/2015-12-09-mikhailovsky-en.html. Last accessed February 1, 2016.

Mohler, Albert. 2004. "The Case against Homosexual Marriage." *Webpage of Albert Mohler*, January 15, 2004. http://www.albertmohler.com/2004/01/15/the-case-against-homosexual-marriage/. Accessed May 16, 2017.

———. 2005. "The Age of Polymorphous Perversity, Part Four." *Webpage of Albert Mohler*, September 22, 2005. http://www.albertmohler.com/2005/09/22/the-age-of-polymorphous-perversity-part-four/. Accessed May 16, 2017.

———. 2015. *We Cannot Be Silent: Speaking Truth to a Culture Redefining Sex, Marriage, and the Very Meaning of Right and Wrong*. Nashville, Tenn.: Thomas Nelson.

Moslener, Sara. 2015. *Virgin Nation: Sexual Purity and American Adolescence*. New York: Oxford University Press.

Moss, Kevin. 2017. "Russia as the Savior of European Civilization: Gender and the Geopolitics of Traditional Values." In *Anti-Gender Campaigns in Europe: Mobilizing against Equality*, edited by Roman Kuhar and David Paternotte, 195–214. Lanham, Md.: Rowman and Littlefield.

Mourão Permoser, Julia. 2019. "What Are Morality Policies? The Politics of Values in a Post-Secular World." *Political Studies Review* 17 (3):310–25. http://doi.org/10.1177/1478929918816538.

Mourão Permoser, Julia, and Kristina Stoeckl. 2020. "Advocating Illiberal Human Rights: The Global Network of Moral Conservative Homeschooling Activists." *Global Networks: A Journal of Transnational Affairs*. Early View. http://doi/org/10.1111/glob.12299.

Movsesian, Mark. 2017. "Evangelicals and Orthodox Together." *First Things*, November 20, 2017. https://www.firstthings.com/web-exclusives/2017/11/evangelicals-and-orthodox-together. Accessed May 14, 2019.

Moynihan, Robert 2009. "Letter #47, from Moscow, Hilarion." *Inside the Vatican*, November 11, 2009. https://insidethevatican.com/news/newsflash/letter-47-from-moscow-hilarion/. Accessed February 25, 2020.

———. 2010. "Rome-Moscow Relations Begin New Era." *Zenit*, December 14, 2009. https://zenit.org/articles/rome-moscow-relations-begin-new-era/. Accessed February 25, 2020.

———. 2013. "Letter #3: A New Foundation." *Inside the Vatican*, January 17, 2013. https://insidethevatican.com/news/newsflash/letter-3-a-new-foundation/. Accessed February 25, 2020.

Myers, Steven Lee. 2003. "After Decades, Russia Narrows Grounds for Abortions." *New York Times*, August 24, 2003. http://www.nytimes.com/2003/08/24/world/after-decades-russia-narrows-grounds-for-abortions.html. Accessed April 7, 2013.

Nash, Kate. 2009. *The Cultural Politics of Human Rights*. Cambridge: Cambridge University Press.

———. 2016. "Politicising Human Rights in Europe: Challenges to Legal Constitutionalism from the Left and the Right." *International Journal of Human Rights* 20 (8):1,295–1,308.

NG. 1991. "Doktor Dobson kak nel'zia kstati" [Doctor Dobson Could Not Come at a Better Time]. *Nezavisimaya gazeta*, August 15, 1991.

Nichols, Lawrence T. 2001. "Sorokin's Integralism and Catholic Social Science: Concordance and Ambivalence." *Catholic Social Science Review* 6:11–24.

———. 2005. "Integralism and Positive Psychology: A Comparison of Sorokin and Seligman." *Catholic Social Science Review* 10:21–40.

———. 2009. "Burawoy's Holistic Sociology and Sorokin's Integralism: A Conversation of Ideas." In *Handbook of Public Sociology*, edited by Vincent Jeffries, 27–46. Landham, Md.: Rowman & Littlefield.

———. 2012. "Sorokin as Lifelong Russian Intellectual: The Enactment of an Historically Rooted Sensibility." *American Sociologist* 43:374–405.

Nieli, Robert A. 2006. "Critic of the Sensate Culture: Rediscovering the Genius of Pitirim Sorokin." *Political Science Reviewer* 35 (1).

Nisbet, Robert A. 1953. *The Quest for Community: A Study in the Ethics of Order and Freedom.* New York: Oxford University Press.

Østbø, Jardar. 2017. "Securitizing 'Spiritual-Moral Values' in Russia." *Post-Soviet Affairs* 33 (3):200–16.

PACE. 2012. "Motion for a Recommendation Tabled by Mr. Robert Shlegel and Other Members of the Assembly: Coordinated Strategies for Effective Internet Governance." *Parliamentary Assembly of the Council of Europe*, Doc. 13280. July 8, 2013.

———. 2014. "Activities of the Assembly's Bureau and Standing Committee (5 October 2013–26 January 2014)." *Parliamentary Assembly of the Council of Europe*, Doc. 13374, January 24, 2014. http://assembly.coe.int/nw/xml/XRef /Xref-XML2HTML-en.asp?fileid=20346&lang=en. Accessed July 27, 2020.

———. 2019a. "Internet Governance and Human Rights." *Parliamentary Assembly of the Council of Europe*, Doc. 14789, January 4, 2019. http:// assembly.coe.int/nw/xml/XRef/Xref-XML2HTML-en.asp?fileid =25227&lang=en. Accessed July 27, 2020.

———. 2019b. "Resolution Nr. 2256. "Internet Governance and Human Rights.'" *Parliamentary Assembly of the Council of Europe*, January 23, 2019. http://assembly.coe.int/nw/xml/XRef/Xref-XML2HTML-en.asp?fileid =25407&lang=en. Accessed July 27, 2020.

Papkova, Irina. 2011. *The Orthodox Church and Russian Politics.* New York and Washington, D.C.: Oxford University Press and Woodrow Wilson Center Press.

Parke, Cole. 2015. "Natural Deception: Conned by the World Congress of Families." *Political Research Associates.* http://www.politicalresearch.org/2015 /01/21/natural-deception-conned-by-the-world-congress-of-families/#sthash .sABt36MU.dpbs. Last access November 3, 2016.

Patriarchal Commission for Family Affairs. 2019a. "Ob otnoshenii Patriarshei Komissii po voprosam sem'i, zashchity materinstva i detstva k semeinomu obrazovaniiu i programme 'Klassicheskie besedy'" [Statement of the Patriarchal Commission for the Family, Motherhood and Childhood to the Homeschooling and the Program "Classical Conversations"]. *Official site of the Patriarchal Commission for Family Affairs*, December 4, 2019. http://pk -semya.ru/novosti/item/7671-ob-otnoshenii-patriarshej-komissii-po -voprosam-semi-zashchity-materinstva-i-detstva-k-semejnomu-obrazovaniyu -i-programme-klassicheskie-besedy.html. Accessed February 24, 2020.

———. 2019b. "Zayavlenie Patriarshej komissii po voprosam sem'i, zashchity materinstva i detstva v svyazi s obsuzhdeniem proekta Federal'nogo zakona

'O profilaktike semejno-bytovogo nasiliya v Rossijskoj Federatsii." [Statement of the Patriarchal Commission for the Family, Protection of Motherhood and Childhood Regarding the Discussion of the Draft Federal Law "On the Prevention of the Family and Domestic Population in the Russian Federation"]. *Website of the Patriarchal Commission for Family, Defence of Motherhood and Childhood*, December 3, 2019. http://pk-semya.ru/novosti/item/7669-o -profilaktike-semejno-bytovogo-nasiliya-v-rossijskoj-federatsii.html. Accessed February 4, 2020.

Patriarchia. 2018. "Predstaviteli Patriarshey komissii po voprosam sem'i, zashchity materinstva i detstva prinyali uchastiye v XII Vsemirnom Kongresse Semey." [The Representative of the Patriarchal Commission for the Family, Protection of Motherhood and Childhood Takes Part in the 12th World Congress of Families]. *Official Website of the Moscow Patriarchate*, September 18, 2018. http://www.patriarchia.ru/db/text/5269978.html. Accessed December 4, 2018.

———. 2019. "Projekt dokumenta 'O neprikosnovennosti zhizni cheloveka s momenta zachatiya.'" [Project Document "On the Inviolability of Human Life from the Moment of Conception"]. *Official Website of the Moscow Patriarchate*, June 24, 2019. http://www.patriarchia.ru/db/text/5459449.html ?fbclid=IwAR11uVB7SXMLV0JD-W8rP8AXlsIOwu2EWEdTWTqU5rPQ c5MhYQxCYyFF8_k. Accessed August 2, 2020.

———. 2022. "Patriarshaya propoved' v Nedelyu syropustnuyu posle Liturgii v Khrame Khrista Spasitelya." [The Sermon of the Patriarch after the Liturgy in Christ Savior Cathedral]. Offical Website of the Moscow Patriarchate, March 6, 2022. http://www.patriarchia.ru/db/text/5906442.html. Accessed March 8, 2022.

Pence, Mike. 2006. "Rep. Pence Calls for Marriage Protection Amendment." *VoteSmart*, July 18, 2006. https://votesmart.org/public-statement/194152/rep -pence-calls-for-marriage-protection-amendment#.WRtEtdykJhH. Accessed May 16, 2017.

Perversion. 1965. *Perversion for Profit* [Video]. YouTube. https://www.youtube .com/watch?v=pciD9gd3my0&t=252s.

Pew Research Center. 2014. "Russians Return to Religion, but Not to Church." *Pew Research Center*, February 10, 2014. http://www.pewforum.org/2014/02 /10/russians-return-to-religion-but-not-to-church/. Last accessed November 18, 2015.

———. 2017. "Religious Belief and National Belonging in Central and Eastern Europe." *Pew Research Center*, May 10, 2017. https://www.pewforum.org /2017/05/10/religious-belief-and-national-belonging-in-central-and-eastern -europe/. Accessed December 25, 2019.

———. 2020. "The Global Divide on Homosexuality Persists." *Pew Research Center*, June 25, 2020. https://www.pewresearch.org/global/2020/06/25 /global-divide-on-homosexuality-persists/. Accessed September 9, 2020.

Pickel, Susanne. 2002. "Pitirim Sorokin im Internet—Schwerpunkte der Darstellung im World Wide Web." In *Pitirim A. Sorokin: Leben, Werk und Wirkung*, edited by Bálint Balla, Ilija Srubar, and Martin Albrecht, 203–22. Hamburg: Krämer.

Polyakova, Alina, Marlene Laruelle, Stefan Meister, and Neil Barnett. 2016. "The Kremlin's Trojan Horses." *Atlantic Council*, November 15, 2016. https://www.atlanticcouncil.org/in-depth-research-reports/report/kremlin-trojan-horses/. Accessed July 27, 2020.

Pomerantsev, Peter. 2012. "Putin's God Squad: The Orthodox Church and Russian Politics." *Newsweek*, October 9, 2012. http://www.newsweek.com/putins-god-squad-orthodox-church-and-russian-politics-64649. Accessed November 8, 2015.

———. 2013. "Russia: A Postmodern Dictatorship?" *Legatum Institute: Transitions Lecture Series*, October 2013. https://li.com/wp-content/uploads/2019/03/pomeransevl_russia_imr_web_final.pdf. Accessed July 27, 2020.

Ponkin, Igor V., V. V. Yeremyan, M. N. Kouznetsov, and Alexandra A. Ponkina. 2014. "On the Legal Bases for Legal Recognition of the Value of Life, Human Dignity, and the Right to Life of a Child at the Stage of Prenatal Development." Published on the Website *www.orthodoxrights.org*, run by the Representation of the Russian Orthodox Church in Strasbourg on July 1, 2014. http://orthodoxrights.org/analytics/the-report-of-russian-jurists-on-the-legal-recognition-of-the-value-of-life-and-human-dignity-of-a-child-at-the-stage-of-prenatal-development. Last accessed April 11, 2017.

Ponomariov, Alexander 2017. *The Visible Religion: The Russian Orthodox Church and Her Relations with State and Society in Post-Soviet Canon Law (1992–2015)*. Frankfurt am Main: Peter Lang.

Potikha, Vladimir V. 2017. "Iz istorii prenatal'nogo infantitsida: vekhi i daty proshedshego stoletiya." [The History of Prenatal Infanticide]. [Video]. YouTube. *Festival Za Zhizn'*, March 2, 2017. Registered January 27, 2017, in the context of the XXV Christmas Readings, Hotel Salyut, Moscow. https://www.youtube.com/watch?v=8UoE_NvV8So. Accessed April 20, 2017.

Pravoslavie. 2018a. "Domashnee obrazovanie detei: Preimushchestva i problemy. Beseda s Alekseem Komovym" [Homeschooling for Children: Advantages and Problems]. *Pravoslavie.ru*, January 22, 2018. https://pravoslavie.ru/109930.html. Accessed February 24, 2020.

———. 2018b. "Kratkaya programma XXVI mezhdunarodnykh rozhdestvenskikh obrazovatel'nykh chtenij." [Program of the 27th International Christmas Readings]. *Pravoslavie.ru*, January 24, 2018. https://pravoslavie.ru/109064.html. Accessed December 4, 2018.

Press Release. 2016. "Herkel Will Take Over the Report of Russia's PACE Member." *Riigikogu Press Service*, June 22, 2016. https://m.riigikogu.ee/en/press-releases/others/herkel-will-take-report-russias-pace-member/. Accessed July 27, 2020.

Pro Vita. 2015. "Pro Vita e Komov: Un ciclo di conferenze per la famiglia in Europa." *Notizie Pro Vita*, February 16, 2015. http://www.notizieprovita.it /eventi-provita/pro-vita-e-komov-un-ciclo-di-conferenze-per-la-famiglia-in -europa/. Last accessed March 16, 2015.

Public Opinion Foundation. 2019. "Attitude to Sexual Minorities: On Sexual Minorities and Gay Parades" [Otnoshenie k seksmen'shinstvam. O seksmen'shinstvakh i gei-paradakh]. *Public Opinion Foundation*, June 13, 2019. https://fom.ru/Obraz-zhizni/14220. Accessed September 9, 2020.

Putin, Vladimir. 2012. "Poslanie Prezidenta Federal'nomu Sobraniiu." [Message of the President to the Federal Assembly]. *Official website of the Kremlin*, December 12, 2012. http://www.kremlin.ru/events/president/news/17118. Accessed August 24, 2020.

———. 2013. "Poslanie Prezidenta Federal'nomu Sobraniiu." [Message of the President to the Federal Assembly]. *Official Website of the Kremlin*, December 12, 2013. http://kremlin.ru/events/president/news/19825. Accessed August 24, 2020.

Püttmann, Andreas. 2014. "Putins nützliche Idioten." *Zeit Online*, November 22, 2014. http://www.zeit.de/politik/ausland/2014-09/russland -kirche-putin. Last accessed March 16, 2015.

Regnum. 2011. "Programma 'Razgovor s Vladimirom Putinym': Polnyi tekst" [TV Program "Conversations with Vladimir Putin": Full Text]. *Regnum.ru*, December 15, 2011. https://regnum.ru/news/polit/1479908.html. Accessed January 22, 2020.

———. 2016. "PATsE poruchila estontsu zavershit' rossijskij raport ob opasnostyakh interneta." [PACE Instructs Estonian to Complete "Russian report on the dangers of the Internet"] *Regnum.ru*, June 27, 2016. https:// regnum.ru/news/polit/2149813.html. Accessed July 27, 2020.

Reno, R. R. 2017. "The Party Theorist." *First Things*, March 2017. https://www .firstthings.com/article/2017/03/the-party-theorist. Accessed February 26, 2020.

———. 2020. "'This Is Not the Traditional Culture Wars': Interview with R. R. Reno." In *Postsecular Conflicts: Debates from Russia and the United States*, edited by Kristina Stoeckl and Dmitry Uzlaner, 53–56. Innsbruck: Innsbruck University Press.

Ria Novosti. 2020. "V RPTs podderzhali ideiu o popravke v Konstitutsiiu po zashchite sem'i." [The Russian Orthodox Church Supports the Idea of an Amendment to the Constitution to Protect the Family]. *Ria Novosti*, February 14, 2020. https://ria.ru/20200214/1564802300.html. Accessed August 24, 2020.

Riccardi-Swartz, Sarah. 2019. "American Conversions to Russian Orthodoxy Amid the Global Culture Wars." *Berkley Center Blog "The Culture Wars*

Today," December 18, 2019. https://berkleycenter.georgetown.edu/responses /american-conversions-to-russian-orthodoxy-amid-the-global-culture-wars. Accessed January 9, 2020.

Richters, Katja. 2013. *The Post-Soviet Russian Orthodox Church: Politics, Culture and Greater Russia.* London and New York: Routledge.

Rimashevskaya, Natalia, and Natalia Markova. 2006. "'Amerikanskaia seksual'naia revolutsiya' P. A. Sorokina v Rossii" [The "American Sexual Revolution" of P. A. Sorokin in Russia]. In *Amerikanskaia seksual'naia revolutsiya* [The American Sexual Revolution], by Pitirim A. Sorokin, 5–9. Moscow: Institut P. Sorokina—N. Kondrat'eva.

Rimestad, Sebastian. 2015. "The Interaction between the Moscow Patriarchate and the European Court of Human Rights." *Review of Central and East European Law* 40:31–55.

Risse, Thomas, and Kathryn Sikkink, eds. 1999. *The Power of Human Rights: International Norms and Domestic Change.* Cambridge: Cambridge University Press.

Rivkin-Fish, Michele. 2010. "Pronatalism, Gender Politics, and the Renewal of Family uspport in Russia: Towards a Feminist Anthropology of 'Maternity Capital.'" *Slavic Review* 69 (3):701–24.

———. 2013. "Conceptualizing Feminist Strategies for Russian Reproductive Politics: Abortion, Surrogate Motherhood, and Family Support after Socialism." *Signs* 38 (3):569–93.

Robinson, Neli. 2017. "Russian Neo-Patrimonialism and Putin's 'Cultural Turn.'" *Europe-Asia Studies* 69 (2):348–66.

Robinson, Paul. 2019. *Russian Conservatism.* DeKalb: Northern Illinois University Press.

ROC. 2010a. "Postoyannij predstavitel' Rossijskoj Federatsii pri otdelenii Organizatsii Ob''edinennykh Natsii i drugikh mezhdunardonykh organizatsiyakh v Zheneve udosten vysokoj tserkovnoj nagrady." [The Permanent Representative of the Russian Federation to the United Nations and Other International Organizations Receives High Church Honor]. *Press Release of the Department of External Relations of the Moscow Patriarchate,* October 5, 2010. http://www .mospat.ru/ru/2010/10/05/news27332/.

———. 2010b. "Sostoyalos' XV zasedaniye Rabochey gruppy po vzaimodeystviyu MID Rossii i Russkoy Pravoslavnoy Tserkvi" [The XV Meeting of the Working Group on Cooperation between the Ministry of Foreign Affairs of Russia and the Russian Orthodox Church]. *Press Release on the Official Website of the Moscow Patriarchate,* June 9, 2010. http://www.patriarchia.ru /db/text/4113658.html. Accessed March 13, 2020.

———. 2010c. "Vystuplenie mitropolita Volokolamskogo Ilariona na prezentatsii pol'skogo izdaniya knigi Svyatejshego Patriarkha Moskovskogo i Vseya Rusi

Kirilla 'Svoboda i otvestvennost': V poiskakh garmonii. Prava cheloveka i dostoinstvo lichnosti.'" [Presentation by Metropolitan Hilarion: The Search for Harmony; Human Rights and Dignity of the Person]. *Offical Website of the Moscow Patriarchate*, June 24, 2010. http://www.patriarchia.ru/db/text/1186072.html.

———. 2015. "B Moskve sostoyalos' sobranie pravoslavnoj obshchestvennosti, vystupayushchej protiv abortov." [A Meeting of the Orthodox Community Opposing Abortion Was Held in Moscow]. *Offical Website of the Moscow Patriarchate*, June 29, 2015. http://www.patriarchia.ru/db/text/4138346.html. Last accessed April 10, 2017.

———. 2016. "Sostoyalos' XXI zasedaniye Rabochey gruppy po vzaimodeystviyu MID Rossii i Russkoy Pravoslavnoy Tserkvi" [The XXI Meeting of the Working Group on Cooperation between the Ministry of Foreign Affairs of Russia and the Russian Orthodox Church]. *Press Release on the Official Website of the Moscow Patriarchate*, October 11, 2016. http://www.patriarchia.ru/db/text/4636412.html. Accessed March 13, 2020.

Rousselet, Kathy. 2020. "'Dukhovnost' in Russia's Politics." *Religion, State and Society* 48 (1):38–55. http://doi.org/10.1080/09637494.2019.1705086.

Roy, Olivier. 2009. *Holy Ignorance: When Religion and Culture Diverge*. New York: Columbia University Press.

Ryabykh, Igumen Filip. 2010. "V Sovete OON po pravam cheloveka proshel seminar posvyashchennyj pravam cheloveka i traditsionnym tsennostyam." [The UN Human Rights Council Hosted a Seminar on Human Rights and Traditional Values]. *Website of the Representation of the Russian Orthodox Church in Strasbourg*, October 8, 2010. http://www.strasbourg-reor.org/?topicid=649.

Safronov, Evgenii, and Elizaveta Antonova. 2014. "Sotsfak MGU bez dekana i filosofa" [The Sociological Department of Moscow State University without Its Dean and Philosopher]. *Gazeta.ru*. June 26, 2014. https://www.gazeta.ru/social/2014/06/27/6089569.shtml. Accessed May 24, 2017.

Sakevich, Victoria I., and Boris P. Denisov. 2014. "Birth Control in Russia: Overcoming the State System Resistance." *National Research University Higher School of Economics Working Paper Series: Sociology* 42 (SOC):25.

Sakwa, Richard. 2017. *Russia against the Rest: The Post-Cold War Crisis of World Order*. Cambridge: Cambridge University Press.

Shamolina, Irina, and Natalia Geda. 2018. "O klassicheskom i ne klassicheskom obrazovanii" [On Classical and Non-Classical Education]. *Website of the Russian Classical Conversations*, February 17, 2018. https://classical-conversations.ru/classical-nonclassical/. Accessed February 24, 2020.

Sharafutdinova, Gulnaz. 2014. "The Pussy Riot Affair and Putin's Démarche from Sovereign Democracy to Sovereign Morality." *Nationalities Papers* 42 (4):615–21.

Shekhovtsov, Anton. 2014. "A Rose by Any Other Name: The World Congress of Families in Moscow." *Anton Shekhovtsov's Blog*, September 15, 2014. http://anton-shekhovtsov.blogspot.co.at/2014/09/a-rose-by-any-other-name -world-congress.html. Last accessed March 16, 2015.

———. 2017. *Russia and the Western Far Right: Tango Noir*. London and New York: Routledge.

Sherwin, Emily. 2019. "Kremlin Aims to Unplug Russian Internet from World Wide Web." *Deutsche Welle*, February 12, 2019. https://www.dw.com/en /kremlin-aims-to-unplug-russian-internet-from-world-wide-web/a-47479169. Accessed July 27, 2020.

Shishkov, Andrey. 2017. "Two Ecumenisms: Conservative Christian Alliances as a New Form of Ecumenical Cooperation." *State, Religion and Church* 4 (2):58–87.

Shlapentokh, Vladimir. 1999. "Social Inequality in Post-Communist Russia: The Attitudes of the Political Elite and the Masses (1991–1998)." *Europe-Asia Studies* 51 (7):1,167–81.

Shlapentokh, Vladimir, Christopher Vanderpool, and Boris Doktorov, eds. 1999. *The New Elite in Post-Communist Eastern Europe*. College Station: Texas A&M University Press.

Shterin, Marat S. 1998. "Local Laws Restricting Religion in Russia: Precursors of Russia's New National Law." *Journal of Church and State* 40 (2):319–41.

Silk, Mark. 2019. "The Other Russian Collusion Story." *Religion News Service*, March 25, 2019. https://religionnews.com/2019/03/25/the-other-russian -collusion-story/. Accessed May 22, 2019.

Skorini, I. Heini, and Marie Juul Petersen. 2017. "Hate Speech and Holy Prophets: Tracing the OIC's Strategies to Protect Religion at the UN." In *Religion, State and the United Nations: Value Politics*, edited by Anna Stensvold, 44–61. London and New York: Routledge.

Smolkin, Victoria. 2018. *A Sacred Space Is Never Empty: A History of Soviet Atheism*. Princeton, N.J: Princeton University Press.

Social Doctrine. 2000. "The Bases of the Social Concept of the Russian Orthodox Church" (official translation). *Official Website of the Department for External Church Relations of the Moscow Patriarchate*. http://www.mospat.ru/en /documents/social-concepts/.

Sorokin, Pitirim A. 1948. *The Reconstruction of Humanity*. Boston: Beacon.

———. 1956. *The American Sex Revolution*. Boston: P. Sargent.

———. 1963a. *A Long Journey: The Autobiography of Pitirim A. Sorokin*. New Haven, Conn.: College and University Press.

———. 1963b. "Reply to My Critics." In *Sorokin in Review*, edited by Philip J. Allen, 371–496. Durham, N.C.: Duke University Press.

———. 2006. *Amerikanskaia seksual'naia revolutsiya* [The American Sexual Revolution]. Moscow: Institut P. Sorokina—N. Kondrat'eva.

————. 2010. *Social and Cultural Dynamics*. Revised and abridged in one volume. New Brunswick, N.J., and London: Transaction.

Sorokin, Pitirim A., and Carle C. Zimmerman. 1929. *Principles of Rural-Urban Sociology*. American Social Science series, under the editorship of H. W. Odum. New York: H. Holt.

Southern Poverty Law Center. 2015. "Everything You Need to Know about the Anti-LGBTQ World Congress of Families (WCF)." *Southern Poverty Law Center*. https://www.splcenter.org/news/2015/10/21/everything-you-need-know -about-anti-lgbtq-world-congress-families-wcf. Last access November 3, 2016.

————. 2018. "How the World Congress of Families Serves Russian Orthodox Political Interests." *Southern Poverty Law Center*. https://www.splcenter.org /hatewatch/2018/05/16/how-world-congress-families-serves-russian-orthodox -political-interests. Accessed October 4, 2018.

Spadaro, Antonio, and Marcelo Figueroa. 2017. "Evangelical Fundamentalism and Catholic Integralism: A Surprising Ecumenism." *La Civiltà Cattolica*, August 21, 2017. http://www.laciviltacattolica.it/articolo/evangelical -fundamentalism-and-catholic-integralism-in-the-usa-a-surprising-ecumenism /. Accessed May 28, 2019.

Sperling, Valerie. 2015. *Sex, Politics, and Putin: Political Legitimacy in Russia*. Oxford: Oxford University Press.

Stark, Werner. 1991. *The Sociology of Knowledge: Toward a Deeper Understanding of the History of Ideas*. New Brunswick, N.J.: Transaction.

Stella, Francesca, and Nadya Nartova. 2016. "Sexual Citienzship, Nationalism and Biopolitics in Putin's Russia." In *Sexuality, Citizenship and Belonging: Transnational and Intersectional Perspectives*, edited by Francesca Stella, Yvette Taylor, Tracey Reynolds, and Antoine Rogers, 17–36. New York: Routledge.

Stelletskij, Nicholas. 2011. *Opyt nravstvennogo pravoslavnogo bogosloviya v apologeticheskom osveshchenii* [The Experience of Moral Orthodox Theology in Apologetic Lighting]. Vols. 2–3. Moscow: FIV.

Stensvold, Anna. 2017a. "Concluding Remarks." In *Religion, State and the United Nations: Value Politics*, edited by Anna Stensvold, 185–90. London and New York: Routledge.

————. 2017b. "Religion, State and Symbol Politic: The Catholic Church at the UN." In *Religion, State and the United Nations: Value Politics*, edited by Anna Stensvold, 95–110. London and New York: Routledge.

————. 2017c. "Introduction." In *Religion, State and the United Nations*, edited by Anne Stensvold, 1–14. London and New York: Routledge.

Stepanova, Elena. 2015. "'The Spiritual and Moral Foundations of Civilization in Every Nation for Thousands of Years': The Traditional Values Discourse in Russia." *Politics, Religion and Ideology* 16 (2–3):119–36.

———. 2019. "Competing Moral Discourses in Russia: Soviet Legacy and Post-Soviet Controversies." *Politics, Religion & Ideology* 20 (3):340–60.

Stoeckl, Kristina. 2014. *The Russian Orthodox Church and Human Rights.* London and New York: Routledge.

———. 2015. "Vladimir Bibihin: His Biographical Notes and the Moscow Circle of Religious Intellectuals." *Stasis* 1:392–99.

———. 2016. "The Russian Orthodox Church as Moral Norm Entrepreneur." *Religion, State & Society* 44 (2):131–51.

———. 2017. "Political Liberalism and Religious Claims: Four Blind Spots." *Philosophy & Social Criticism* 43: 34–50.

———. 2018a. "Aktivisty vne konfessional'nykh granits: Konservativnyj ekumenizm Vsemirnogo kongressa semej." [Activists Beyond Confessional Borders: The Conservative Ecumenism of the World Congress of Families]. *Gosudarstvo, Religiya i Cerkov v Rossii i za rubezhom* 4 (36):58–86.

———. 2018b. "Transnational Norm Mobilization: The World Congress of Families in Georgia and Moldova." In *The Rise of Illiberal Civil Society in the Former Soviet Union*, edited by Adam Hug. London: Foreign Policy Think Tank. https://fpc.org.uk/wp-content/uploads/2018/07/The-rise-of-illiberal-civil-society-in-the-former-Soviet-Union.pdf. Accessed October 15, 2018.

———. 2020a. "The Rise of the Russian Christian Right: The Case of the World Congress of Families." *Religion, State & Society* 48 (4):223–38.

———. 2020b. "Russian Orthodoxy and Secularism." *Religion and Politics* 1 (2):1–75.

———. 2020c. "Three Models of Church-State Relations in Contemporary Russia." In *Constitutions and Religion*, edited by Susanna Mancini. Camberley, Surrey: Edward Elgar.

Stoeckl, Kristina, and Kseniya Medvedeva. 2018. "Double Bind at the UN: Western Actors, Russia, and the Traditionalist Agenda." *Global Constitutionalism* 7 (3):383–421.

Stoeckl, Kristina, and Dmitry Uzlaner, eds. 2020. *Postsecular Conflicts: Debating Tradition in Russia and the United States.* Innsbruck: Innsbruck University Press.

Strategiya natsional'noi besopasnosti. 2015. "Ukaz Prezidenta Rossiiskoi Federatsii ot 31.12.2015g No. 683 'O Strategii Natsional'noi Bezopasnosti Rossiiskoi Federatsii.'" [The Russian National Security Strategy]. *Official Website of the Kremlin*, December 31, 2015. http://kremlin.ru/acts/bank/40391. Accessed September 7, 2020.

Strategiya razvitiya vospitaniya. 2015. "Strategiya razvitiya vospitaniya v Rossiiskoi Federatsii na period do 2025 goda." [Russian Educational Development Strategy until 2025]. *Rossiiskaia Gazeta*, June 8, 2015. https://rg.ru/2015/06/08/vospitanie-dok.html. Accessed August 24, 2020.

Stroop, Christopher. 2014. "The Russian Origins of the So-Called Post-Secular Moment: Some Preliminary Observations." *State, Religion and Church* 1 (1):59–82.

———. 2016. "A Right-Wing International? Russian Social Conservatism, the World Congress of Families, and the Global Culture Wars in Historical Context." *Public Eye*, Winter: 4–10.

Sullivan, Winnifred F., Elizabeth Shakman Hurd, Saba Mahmood, and Peter G. Danchin, eds. 2015. *Politics of Religious Freedom*. Princeton, N.J.: Princeton University Press.

Suslov, Mikhail, and Dmitry Uzlaner, eds. 2019. *Contemporary Russian Conservatism: Problems, Paradoxes and Perspectives*. Leiden: Brill.

Talbutt, Palmer Jr. 1998. *Rough Dialectics: Sorokin's Philosophy of Value*. Amsterdam and Atlanta: Rodopi.

TASS. 2018. "Putin sravnil kommunisticheskuiu ideologiiu s khristianstvom" [Putin Compared Communist Ideology with Christianity]. *Tass.ru*, January 14, 2018. https://tass.ru/obschestvo/4872596. Accessed January 20, 2020.

Templeton. 2020a. "April 2016–December 2018: New Generation of Leaders for the Russian Orthodox Church." *John Templeton Foundation*. https://www.templeton.org/grant/new-generation-of-leaders-for-the-russian-orthodox-church. Accessed February 25, 2020.

———. 2020b. "Public Engagement: Expanding Scientific Training for Religious Leaders." *John Templeton Foundation*. https://www.templeton.org/discoveries/expanding-scientific-training-for-religious-leaders. Accessed February 25, 2020.

Tiryakian, Edward A., ed. 1963. *Sociological Theory, Values, and Sociocultural Change: Essays in Honor of Pitirim A. Sorokin*. New York: Free Press of Glencoe.

———. 1996. "Sorokin Remembered." In *Sorokin & Civilization: A Centennial Assessment*, edited by Joseph B. Ford, Michel P. Richard, and Palmer Talbutt Jr., 15–20. New Brunswick, N.J.: Transaction.

Trepanier, Lee. 2002. "Nationalism and Religion in Russian Civil Society: An Inquiry into the 1997 Law 'On Freedom of Conscience.'" In *Civil Society and the Search for Justice in Russia*, edited by Christopher Marsh and Nikolas K. Gvosdev, 57–75. Lanham, Md.: Lexington.

Tsygankov, Andrei. 2016. "Crafting the State-Civilization: Vladimir Putin's Turn to Distinct Values." *Problems of Post-Communism* 63 (3):146–58.

UDHR. 1948. "Universal Declaration of Human Rights." *United Nations Homepage*. http://www.un.org/en/documents/udhr/.

Uertz, Rudolf, and Lars Peter Schmidt, eds. 2004. *Beginn einer neuen Ära? Die Sozialdoktrin der Russisch-Orthodoxen Kirche vom August 2000 im interkulturellen Dialog*. Moscow: Konrad Adenauer Stiftung e.V.

UNHRC. 2009. "Follow-up to and Implementation of the Vienna Declaration and Programme of Action: Promoting Human Rights and Fundamental Freedoms through a Better Understanding of Traditional Values of Humankind." *United Nations Human Rights Council* A/HRC/RES/12/21, October 12, 2009.

———. 2011. "Resolution Adopted by the Human Rights Council: Promoting Human Rights and Fundamental Freedoms through a Better Understanding of Traditional Values of Humankind." *United Nations Human Rights Council* A/HRC/RES/16/3, April 8, 2011.

———. 2012a. "Preliminary Study on Promoting Human Rights and Fundamental Freedoms through a Better Understanding of Traditional Values of Humankind. Prepared by the Drafting Group of the Advisory Committee." *United Nations Human Rights Council* A/HRC/AC/9/2, June 1, 2012.

———. 2012b. "Study of the Human Rights Council Advisory Committee on Promoting Human Rights and Fundamental Freedoms through a Better Understanding of Traditional Values of Humankind." *United Nations Human Rights Council* A/HRC/RES/22/71, December 6, 2012.

———. 2014a. "Resolution 26/11 adopted by the Human Rights Council: Protection of the Family." *United Nations Human Rights Council* A/HRC/RES/26/11.

———. 2014b. "Summary of the Human Rights Council Panel Discussion on the Protection of the Family." *United Nations Human Rights Council* A/HRC/RES/28/40.

United Families International & World Congress of Families. 2017. *UN Negotiation Guide*. United Families International. P.O. Box 2620. Gilbert, Ariz. 85299. USA.

Uzlaner, Dmitry. 2014. "The Pussy Riot Case and the Peculiarities of Russian Post-Secularism." *State, Religion and Church* 1 (1):23–58.

———. 2017. "Perverse Conservatism: A Lacanian Interpretation of Russia's Turn to Traditional Values." *Psychoanalysis, Culture & Society* 22 (2):173–92.

———. 2019. "The Logic of Scapegoating in Contemporary Russian Moral Conservatism." In *Contemporary Russian Conservatism: Problems, Paradoxes and Perspectives*, edited by Mikhail Suslov and Dmitry Uzlaner, 103–27. Leiden: Brill.

Uzlaner, Dmitry, and Kristina Stoeckl. 2017. "The Legacy of Pitirim Sorokin in the Transnational Alliances of Moral Conservatives." *Journal of Classical Sociology* 18 (2):133–53.

———. 2019. "From Pussy Riot's 'Punk Prayer' to Matilda: Orthodox Believers, Critique, and Religious Freedom in Russia." *Journal of Contemporary Religion* 34 (3):427–45.

Vaïsse, Justin. 2011. *Neoconservatism: The Biography of a Movement*. Cambridge, Mass.: Harvard University Press.

Van Engen, Abram C. 2020. *City on a Hill: A History of American Exceptionalism*. New Haven: Yale University Press.

Vatican. 2016. "Words of Patriarch Kirill after the signing of the Joint Declaration with Pope Francis." *Official Website of the Vatican*, February 12, 2016. http://www.vatican.va/content/francesco/en/speeches/2016/february /documents/papa-francesco_20160212_dichiarazione-comune-kirill.html. Accessed July 26, 2020.

Vodolazkin, Eugene. 2017. "The Age of Concentration." *First Things*, June 2017. https://www.firstthings.com/article/2017/06/the-age-of-concentration. Accessed May 28, 2019.

VRNS. 1993. "Ustav." *Website of the World Russian People's Council*. http://vrns .ru/o_sobore/ustav.php. Accessed January 22, 2013.

VTsIOM. 2016. *Rossiya udivlyaet 2015: Nastroeniya, sluzheniya, tsennosti*. [Russia Surprises 2015: Moods, Services, Values]. Moscow: EKSMO.

Waaldijk, Kees. 2000. "Civil Developments: Patterns of Reform in the Legal Position of Same-Sex Partners in Europe." *Canadian Journal of Family Law* 17 (1):62–88.

Wagner, Peter. 1994. *A Sociology of Modernity: Liberty and Discipline*. London and New York: Routledge.

———. 2012. *Modernity: Understanding the Present*. Cambridge: Polity.

War Is Boring. 2014. "The Kremlin Builds an Unholy Alliance with America's Christian Right." *Medium.com*, July 13, 2014. https://medium.com/war-is -boring/the-kremlin-builds-an-unholy-alliance-with-americas-christian-right -5de35250066b. Accessed July 16, 2014.

WCF. 1997. "A Declaration from the World Congress of Families to the Governments of the Globe Adopted by the Delegates to the World Congress of Families Prague, the Czech Republic," March 22, 1997. http://www .worldcongress.pl/docs/en/pdf/prague_declaration_1997.pdf. Last accessed October 15, 2018.

Weigel, George. 2017. "Meeting with Moscow, Rome Must Refuse to Bend to the Putin Storyline." *National Review*, February 8, 2017. https://www .nationalreview.com/2017/02/catholic-church-russian-orthodox-church -ukrainian-greek-catholic-church-fribourg-meeting/. Accessed June 18, 2019.

Wilcox, Clyde, and Carin Robinson. 2011. *Onward Christian Soldiers?: The Religious Right in American Politics*. New York: Routledge.

Williams, Daniel K. 2010. *God's Own Party: The Making of the Christian Right*. Oxford: Oxford University Press.

Wuthnow, Robert. 1990. *The Restructuring of American Religion: Society and Faith Since World War II*. Princeton, N.J.: Princeton University Press.

Yakovets, Yuriy. 2006. "Volny seksual'noi revoliutsii i demograficheskoe budushchee Rossii" [Waves of Sexual Revolution and the Demographic Future of Russia].

In *Amerikanskaia seksual'naia revolutsiya* [The American Sexual Revolution], edited by Pitirim A. Sorokin, 10–16. Moscow: Institut P. Sorokina— N. Kondrat'eva.

Zhuikova, K. V., S. V. Lialikova, and V. M. Karpova. 2018. *Semeino-domashnee obuchenie kak model' obrazovaniya budushchego: Analiticheskii otchet po rezul'tatam sotsiologicheskogo issledovaniya* [Family and Home Education as a Model for Education of the Future: Analytical Report after a Sociological Research]. Edited by Anatoly Antonov. Moscow: MAKS.

Zimmerman, Carle C. 1947. *Family and Civilization*. Harper's Social Science Series. New York: Harper.

———. 1968. *Sorokin, the World's Greatest Sociologist: His Life and Ideas on Social Time and Change*. Sorokin lectures. Saskatoon: Distributed by the University of Saskatchewan Bookstore.

———. 2008. *Family and Civilization: With an Introduction by Allan C. Carlson*. Wilmington, Del.: Intercollegiate Studies Institute.

Zimmerman, Carle C., and Thottaman Kantan Kesavan Narayanan Unnithan. 1973. *Sociological Theories of Pitirim A. Sorokin*. Contributions to Sociological Analysis. Bombay: Thacker.

INDEX

Kristina Stoeckl is Professor of Sociology at the University of Innsbruck, Austria. The most recent of her books are *The Russian Orthodox Church and Human Rights* (Routledge, 2014) and *Russian Orthodoxy and Secularism* (Brill, 2020).

Dmitry Uzlaner is research fellow at the Moscow School of Social and Economic Sciences, Russia. The most recent of his books are *The Postsecular Turn: How to Think about Religion in the Twenty-First Century* (in Russian, Izdatel'stvo instituta gaiidara, 2020), *The End of Religion? A History of the Theory of Secularization* (in Russian, Higher School of Economics Press, 2019), and *Contemporary Russian Conservatism: Problems, Paradoxes, and Perspectives* (Brill, 2019, co-edited with Mikhail Suslov).

ORTHODOX CHRISTIANITY AND CONTEMPORARY THOUGHT

SERIES EDITORS
Aristotle Papanikolaou and Ashley M. Purpura

Christina M. Gschwandtner, *Welcoming Finitude: Toward a Phenomenology of Orthodox Liturgy*

Pia Sophia Chaudhari, *Dynamis of Healing: Patristic Theology and the Psyche*

Brian A. Butcher, *Liturgical Theology after Schmemann: An Orthodox Reading of Paul Ricoeur.* Foreword by Andrew Louth.

Ashley M. Purpura, *God, Hierarchy, and Power: Orthodox Theologies of Authority from Byzantium.*

George E. Demacopoulos, *Colonizing Christianity: Greek and Latin Religious Identity in the Era of the Fourth Crusade.*

George E. Demacopoulos and Aristotle Papanikolaou (eds.), *Orthodox Constructions of the West.*

John Chryssavgis and Bruce V. Foltz (eds.), *Toward an Ecology of Transfiguration: Orthodox Christian Perspectives on Environment, Nature, and Creation.* Foreword by Bill McKibben. Prefatory Letter by Ecumenical Patriarch Bartholomew.

Aristotle Papanikolaou and George E. Demacopoulos (eds.), *Orthodox Readings of Augustine* [available 2020]

Lucian N. Leustean (ed.), *Orthodox Christianity and Nationalism in Nineteenth-Century Southeastern Europe.*

John Chryssavgis (ed.), *Dialogue of Love: Breaking the Silence of Centuries.* Contributions by Brian E. Daley, S.J., and Georges Florovsky.

George E. Demacopoulos and Aristotle Papanikolaou (eds.), *Christianity, Democracy, and the Shadow of Constantine.*

Aristotle Papanikolaou and George E. Demacopoulos (eds.), *Fundamentalism or Tradition: Christianity after Secularism*

Georgia Frank, Susan R. Holman, and Andrew S. Jacobs (eds.), *The Garb of Being: Embodiment and the Pursuit of Holiness in Late Ancient Christianity*

Ecumenical Patriarch Bartholomew, *In the World, Yet Not of the World: Social and Global Initiatives of Ecumenical Patriarch Bartholomew.* Edited by John Chryssavgis. Foreword by Jose Manuel Barroso.

Ecumenical Patriarch Bartholomew, *Speaking the Truth in Love: Theological and Spiritual Exhortations of Ecumenical Patriarch Bartholomew.* Edited by John Chryssavgis. Foreword by Dr. Rowan Williams, Archbishop of Canterbury.

Ecumenical Patriarch Bartholomew, *On Earth as in Heaven: Ecological Vision and Initiatives of Ecumenical Patriarch Bartholomew.* Edited by John Chryssavgis. Foreword by His Royal Highness, the Duke of Edinburgh.

Davor Džalto, *Anarchy and the Kingdom of God: From Eschatology to Orthodox Political Theology and Back.*

Ina Merdjanova (ed.), *Women and Religiosity in Orthodox Christianity.*

Sarah Riccardi-Swartz, *Between Heaven and Russia: Religious Conversion and Political Apostasy in Appalachia.*

Kristina Stoeckl and Dmitry Uzlaner, *The Moralist International: Russia in the Global Culture Wars.*

CPSIA information can be obtained
at www.ICGtesting.com
Printed in the USA
JSHW021723251022
32142JS00001B/38